Six Nations Diplomat

ALSO BY DONNA TESIERO
AND FROM MCFARLAND

*A Revolutionary Woman: Elizabeth Freeman
and the Abolition of Slavery in the North* (2024)

Six Nations Diplomat

*Molly Brant
and the American Revolution*

Donna Tesiero

McFarland & Company, Inc., Publishers
Jefferson, North Carolina

LIBRARY OF CONGRESS CATALOGING-IN-PUBLICATION DATA

Names: Tesiero, Donna, 1954– author
Title: Six Nations diplomat : Molly Brant and the American Revolution / Donna Tesiero.
Description: Jefferson, North Carolina : McFarland & Company, Inc., Publishers, 2025 | Includes bibliographical references and index.
Identifiers: LCCN 2025017325 | ISBN 9781476694542 paperback ∞
    ISBN 9781476655550 ebook
Subjects: LCSH: Brant, Molly, 1736–1796 | Iroquois Indians—Biography | Iroquois Indians—History—18th century | Iroquois Indians—Government relations—History—18th century | United States—History—Revolution, 1775–1783 | BISAC: HISTORY / United States / Colonial Period (1600-1775) | HISTORY / Women | LCGFT: Biographies
Classification: LCC E99.I7 T487 2025
LC record available at https://lccn.loc.gov/2025017325

ISBN (print) 978-1-4766-9454-2
ISBN (ebook) 978-1-4766-5555-0

© 2025 Donna Tesiero. All rights reserved

No part of this book may be reproduced or transmitted in any form or by any means, electronic or mechanical, including photocopying or recording, or by any information storage and retrieval system, without permission in writing from the publisher.

Front cover images: Molly Brant bust (courtesy of the Kingston Historical Society). *Background* Map of the Country of the Five Nations, 1747 (Huntington Free Library, Division of Rare and Manuscript Collections, Cornell University Library)

Printed in the United States of America

McFarland & Company, Inc., Publishers
  Box 611, Jefferson, North Carolina 28640
    www.mcfarlandpub.com

For my children, their spouses,
and my grandchildren,
and in memory of my parents,
Donald and Janet Tesiero

Acknowledgments

There are many people who helped bring this book to fruition. I am grateful to my talented editor, Elizabeth Foxwell, who believed in the book, and the rest of the staff at McFarland who have assisted me throughout the publication process.

I'd also like to express my appreciation for the assistance rendered throughout the book's research phase by the reference staffs of the Boston Public Library, the Library and Archives of Canada, and the library of the University of New Brunswick as well as the docents at Old Fort Johnson, Fort Johnson, New York, and at the Johnson Hall State Historic Site, Johnstown, New York.

I am grateful to my father, Donald Tesiero, who first introduced me as a child to the lives of Molly and Joseph Brant and Sir William Johnson, and to my teachers at Cornell University who honed my critical thinking and research skills and deepened my fascination with American history and women's history. Finally, a loving thank-you to my children Maria, Donnie, Lisa, and Tom, who have given me their love and enthusiastic support throughout the research and writing of this book.

Table of Contents

Acknowledgments vi
Preface 1
Introduction 3

1. Early Days 7
2. A Man of Many Talents 15
3. The French and Indian War and a Frontier Romance 25
4. Motherhood and a New Home 37
5. A Diplomat's Partner 49
6. Providing for the Future 63
7. Gathering Clouds 78
8. The Worst of Times 91
9. The Lonely and the Brave 105
10. The Land of Their Fathers 118
11. Exile 133
12. Guerrillas and Refugees 142
13. Winners and Losers 158
14. A Home in Canada 169

Epilogue 185
Chapter Notes 187
Bibliography 206
Index 209

Preface

Molly Brant was able to read and write in her native Mohawk language, and she spoke excellent English. Unfortunately, only a few of her letters survive, and those few are either a translation of the originals into English by a family member or a dictation to an English scribe. In order to learn the story of this brave and talented woman, I often found it necessary to look to the words of those close to her, in particular her life partner, Sir William Johnson, but also her brother Joseph Brant and Sir William's sons-in-law, Daniel Claus and Guy Johnson. In Molly's later years, Sir Frederick Haldimand, military governor of the British Canadian colonies during much of the American Revolution, and Elizabeth Simcoe, wife of a later British governor of Canada, also provided important information about Molly's life and character.

The print edition of *The Papers of Sir William Johnson* (13 volumes), available at the Boston Public Library, and the digital collection, which includes the 14th volume, available at HathiTrust (hathitrust.org), were extremely important in establishing the timeline of Molly's life during her 15-year domestic partnership with Sir William as well as the critical significance that Sir William's roles as colonel of the Six Nations and Britain's superintendent of Indian affairs for the northern colonies played in the life he and Molly shared.

Sir William was often elliptical in his references to Molly, so it was the period after his death in 1774, when Molly was required to become an independent public actor, that makes it possible to obtain unmistakable evidence of her strong personality and accomplishments as a diplomat and negotiator. *The Sir Frederick Haldimand Unpublished Papers* and *The Diary of Mrs. John Simcoe*, available at the Boston Public Library, and the Loyalist Collection, Claus Family Papers, at the Library and Archives of Canada, with copies available at the University of New Brunswick, were very important resources for this period of her life. Critical digital resources for this period include the *Daniel Claus Papers, Eighteenth Century Selection of Documents Relating to Indian Affairs* and *Documents Relative to the Colonial History of the State of New York*.

Joseph Brant's voice comes alive in the *American Loyalist Claims, Series I and II*, as he describes his sister's heroism on behalf of the British cause and advocates for the fair treatment of her and her children by the British government after its defeat.

For the Patriots' view of a woman they regarded as a dangerous adversary, *Mohawk Valley in the Revolution: Committee of Public Safety Papers & Genealogy Compendium Tryon County Committee of Safety* by Maryly Penrose was of great importance, as was *The Revolutionary Journal of Joseph Bloomfield* and the *Memoir of Lieu. Col. Tench Tilghman, Secretary and Aide to Washington*.

Although all of the above sources helped me paint the picture of Molly Brant's life, it was the resources I encountered that explained the culture and history of her people, the Haudenosaunee, that were critical in understanding who she really was. Barbara J. Sivertsen's *Turtles, Wolves, and Bears: A Mohawk Family History* was vital to understanding Molly's ancestry, early years, and religious background. A deeper understanding of Haudenosaunee culture and history came from *Iroquoian Women: The Gantowisas* by Mary Alice Mann; *The Texture of Contact: European and Indian Settler Communities and the Frontiers of Iroquoia, 1667–1783* by Daniel L. Preston; *The Ordeal of the Longhouse: The Peoples of the Iroquois League in the Era of European Colonization* by Daniel K. Richter; and *The Iroquois in the American Revolution* by Barbara Graymont. A comprehensive description of the strengths, challenges, and pivotal role of Native Americans in the history of America during Molly's lifetime was provided by Ned Blackstone's *The Rediscovery of America*. Two biographies of Molly Brant written during the 1990s, *The Three Faces of Molly Brant* by Earle Thomas and *Molly Brant: A Legacy of Her Own* by Lois M. Huey and Bonnie Pulis, also provided important information to complete the picture of Molly's life and relationships.

Visits to the scenes of Molly's life, including the Johnson Hall State Historic Site in Johnstown, New York, and Old Fort Johnson in Fort Johnson, New York, as well as discussions with their knowledgeable docents have also enriched this book, as did visits to the Smithsonian Institution's National Museum of the American Indian in New York City and Washington, D.C.

Finally, a word about terminology. The Haudenosaunee were known to the French as the Iroquois and to the British as the Six Nations. Since "Six Nations" is the term that both Sir William Johnson and Molly Brant would have used in their diplomatic interactions with English speakers, I have elected to use that term when referring to the Haudenosaunee confederacy in this book.

Introduction

Molly Brant's people, the Haudenosaunee or People of the Longhouse, were a confederation of six tribes consisting of the Mohawks, Oneidas, Onondagas, Cayugas, Senecas, and—after 1710—the Tuscaroras. The Haudenosaunee were known to the French as the Iroquois, while the British called them the Six Nations. Their home territory was the beautiful Mohawk River valley and the Finger Lakes region of upstate New York. Their hunting grounds extended to Canada in the north, the Susquehanna River valley in the south, and the Ohio River valley in the west. More than a century before their first contact with the French and the Dutch in about 1609–1610, the original five tribes formed the Great League of Peace and Power. The five tribes agreed to cease fighting among themselves and to resolve all disputes at the great council established at Onondaga. To tribes outside the league, they became a formidable enemy. The Mohawks, Molly's tribe, were the Keepers of the Eastern Door of the metaphorical longhouse. They occupied three to four towns on the south side of the Mohawk River in the area between present-day Amsterdam and Canajoharie, New York, and controlled the lands as far east as the junction of the Mohawk and Hudson Rivers about 30 miles east of Amsterdam. Immediately to their west were the Oneidas, who occupied the territory around Oneida Creek. In about 1710 the Oneidas allowed the Tuscaroras, a tribe pushed out of North Carolina by the English, to settle in a portion of their territory. In the center of the Six Nations' Longhouse were the Onondagas, Keepers of the Council Fire. They occupied the territory around present-day Syracuse. Farther west were the Cayugas, who controlled the area between Owasco and Cayuga Lakes near present-day Ithaca. The Keepers of the Western Door, the Senecas, had two towns and two smaller settlements, all east of the Genesee River and north of the Finger Lakes. At the time of European contact, the 10 towns and related villages of the original Five Nations had a population of between 20,000 and 30,000 people.[1]

The Five Nations' control of the Mohawk River and the Finger Lakes meant that they controlled access to fur trade routes that stretched north to the St. Lawrence River in Canada and west to the Great Lakes. For most of the 17th century, the Five Nations dominated the fur trade with the Europeans and intimidated most of the tribes that bordered their territories.[2]

Despite this seemingly enviable position, within a decade or two of European contact the Five Nations' way of life and even their very existence were at great risk. The Mohawks, whose territory was closest to the encroaching European powers, were the first to be dramatically affected.

In 1633, the Mohawks suffered a devastating smallpox epidemic. In succeeding years, they were attacked by measles and influenza. These blights spread westward, and by 1640 even the westernmost Senecas were feeling the scourge of the European diseases. Lacking the immunity built up over centuries by the Europeans, the Five Nations' death rate was horrific. Demographers estimate that by the 1640s, the population of the Five Nations had declined to 10,000, and the easternmost Mohawks had suffered a 75 percent death rate.[3]

At the same time this tragedy was unfolding, the supply of beavers in the Five Nations' home territory was exhausted due to overhunting for the fur trade. This forced the Five Nations to wage almost continual warfare against their neighbors in order to supply European demand and to obtain in exchange the metal and cloth trade goods upon which the Five Nations had come to depend. Perhaps even more important, because of the catastrophic death rates they were suffering from the epidemics, they needed constant warfare to obtain captives who could be adopted and replace dead members of the tribe. Since, however, the tribes attacked by the Five Nations were also reeling from the European diseases and captives possessed no more immunity than Native Americans of the confederacy, this tactic did not ultimately solve the Five Nations' demographic problem, and their numbers continued to decline.[4]

The introduction of Christianity further reduced Mohawk numbers. As part of a peace treaty with New France in the mid–1660s, the Five Nations agreed to the presence of Jesuit missionaries in all of the Five Nations.[5] This was a particularly bitter pill for some of the Mohawks, whose forays into the St. Lawrence River valley for furs and captives had often brought them into conflict with the French. Nevertheless, within a few years the missionaries had gained some adherents in the Mohawk towns, and together with adopted Huron captives, who were often Catholic, a significant Catholic political bloc developed among the Mohawks.[6]

Seventeenth- and 18th-century missionaries, whether Catholic or Protestant, believed in the complete superiority of European cultural practices. For them, to be a Christian was to organize one's life on the European model because European cultural practices were ordained by God.

Introduction 5

When a Mohawk became a Christian, it became very difficult for him or her to remain a functioning member of Mohawk society. Participation in the ceremonial feasts, which reaffirmed community ties and redistributed wealth, was forbidden. Reliance on healing rituals, or belief in the importance of dreams (the Europeans had not yet met Dr. Sigmund Freud), was the work of the devil. Divorce and remarriage by consenting adults was hedonism.[7]

Politics within the tribe and within the Five Nations was based on consensus. After full discussion, a minority view was expected to give way to the majority. Missionaries often saw such compromises between their converts and the village traditionalists as a deal with the devil and made it clear to the converts that such compromises imperiled their souls. Not surprisingly, it became difficult for Catholic Mohawks and traditionalist Mohawks to live together. During the mid–1670s and early 1680s, several hundred Catholic Mohawks left the three Mohawk towns along the Mohawk River and established several settlements in the St. Lawrence River valley, the largest centered around a Catholic mission near Montreal, which was renamed Caughnawaga after one of the Mohawk valley towns its inhabitants had left.[8]

By the end of the 17th century, the Five Nations also found themselves embroiled in the conflict known as King William's War. This was the first of four wars for control of North America fought between 1689 and 1763 by England (after 1707 Great Britain) and France, the two dominant colonial powers. Allied with the English because of recent French incursions into Seneca territory, the Mohawks suffered a devastating night raid by the French and their Canadian Indian allies (some of them recent immigrants from the Mohawk towns) in January 1693. About 20 Mohawk men of military age were killed, a significant number of captives were taken, and all three Mohawk towns were burned to the ground. By the conclusion of the war in 1700 (which resulted in an unstable peace between the French and the English), the Five Nations had lost almost a quarter of the 2,150 men of military age they possessed in 1689, and their total population was reduced to about 6,600.[9]

1

Early Days

At the dawn of the American Revolution, Mary Brant, a Mohawk Indian known to posterity as Molly Brant, was the 39-year-old widowed partner of the legendary Sir William Johnson and the mother of their eight young children. Molly was still recovering from the agonizing pain of Sir William's death shortly before the outbreak of war, and her personal identity and her family's property rights were defined by her deceased partner's loyalty to the king of Great Britain. Now she was about to face the risk of becoming a homeless refugee as well as constant anxiety for the safety of her soldier son and her only brother. Despite these challenges, it would be her task to carve out a decent though much altered future for her children and her people.

* * *

Molly was probably born at the Mohawks' upper castle at Canajoharie, New York, in the Mohawk River valley in 1736. Her baptism records do not survive, but in 1783 she listed her age as 47 on a British military document that entitled her to draw rations from the king's stores.[1] Molly's Mohawk name was Konwatsitsiaienni or Gonwatsijayenni, meaning "someone lends her a flower."[2] Her mother was Margaret, a member of the Wolf Clan. Mohawk baptism and marriage records indicate that Margaret was probably the daughter of Onagsakearet, a Cayuga, and Maria, the daughter of Brant Saquainguaragton, one of the four sachems known to history as the "Four Kings" who visited London in 1710. Although there is a legend that Molly was a granddaughter of King Hendrick, a more famous member of the Four Kings, this is not borne out by the baptism records. Her brother Joseph's statement while visiting London in the 1770s that his grandfather had also visited London (the word for grandfather and great-grandfather are the same in the Mohawk language) was probably a reference to Brant Saquainguaragton.[3]

It is likely that Molly's father was Peter Tehonwaghkwangeraghkwa, who was baptized on November 9, 1707. He is listed as the husband in a

Molly Brant's great-grandfather, Sagayenkwaraton (baptized Brant), named Sa Ga Yeath Qua Pieth Tow, King of the Maquas (Mohawk), 1710. Library and Archives of Canada, Accession no. 1977-35-2, John Petre Collection. Reference R14181, Volume no. 2, box number OP-0127/x2-OP-0127/x3. Digital image C092418k, item 1 of 6.

marriage ceremony performed by Reverend Henry Barclay on July 6, 1735. Unfortunately, Reverend Barclay forgot to list the name of the wife.[4]

Despite this gap in the records, Peter Tehonwaghkwangeraghkwa and his wife Margaret are listed as the parents of Jacob, baptized on July 18, 1741, and Christina, baptized on February 6, 1742, both by Reverend Henry Barclay. These children died in infancy. Like Molly, the baptism records of her only surviving sibling, Joseph Brant, born in 1743, do not survive, but Joseph Brant later told his children that Tehonwaghkwangeraghkwa was his father.[5] Peter and Margaret's marriage would have been forbidden in earlier times, for Peter, like Margaret, was a member of the Wolf Clan. Traditionally, each should have sought a mate from either the Turtle Clan or the Bear Clan, the other two Mohawk clans, but more than a century of population decline caused by epidemics and war had apparently loosened this prohibition. None of the five baptism sponsors listed for Jacob and Christina were prominent members of the tribe, perhaps indicating some tribal disapproval of the union.[6]

* * *

The first quarter of the 18th century was relatively peaceful for the Five Nations because they remained neutral with respect to disputes between Britain and France. Nevertheless, by the time of Molly's birth in 1736, the Mohawks were becoming increasingly hemmed in and outnumbered by British and German settlers in the lower Mohawk valley. The loss of hunting grounds is probably what caused Molly's parents to go on an extended hunting expedition in the spring of 1742 or 1743 to the headwaters of the Ohio River in northwestern Pennsylvania. This was traditionally an area where members of the Six Nations hunted, but larger numbers were making the trip for longer periods under the pressure of growing European settlement in upper New York.[7]

It was a long journey, and on the way Molly's family stopped in one of the Cayuga towns, where they received the hospitality of relatives of Margaret's Cayuga father.[8] Decades later, Molly and Margaret would again require the succor of their Cayuga relatives as they fled from the ire of the American Patriots and their Oneida allies.

Although it was probably not the reason for the move, the family's extended stay in the Ohio River valley removed them from the Mohawk valley during all or most of King George's War (1744–1748), known in Europe as the War of the Austrian Succession.[9] Had they stayed, Peter would probably have joined other Mohawks in the defense of the area against the French in alliance with the most significant British military leader in the Mohawk valley, William Johnson, then about 30 years old.

As it was, Molly and her family remained in northwestern Pennsylvania for several years until her father, Peter, died. Growing up, Joseph Brant was told that his father was a "great warrior," so it is possible that Peter died during a raid against the Cherokees whose territory was to the south of the Six Nations and Mingo settlements. An elderly descendant of William Johnson, however, told a historian in 1879 that Molly and Joseph's father died in an epidemic. Regardless of the cause of Peter's death, in the late 1840s Margaret, now a widow, made her way back to Canajoharie with her two surviving children, Molly and Joseph. She certainly traveled in a group. She may have made the journey with other survivors of the epidemic.[10]

Molly, now about 12 or 13 years old, would have been of significant help to her mother on the arduous journey. Molly would have been expected to gather nuts and berries, help the other women dress any meat the men were able to kill, do some fishing, and keep an eye on her little brother, Joseph, then five or six years old. Due to the matrilineal structure of Six Nations' society, elder sisters were deeply respected. The bond between sister and brother would remain strong throughout Molly and Joseph's lives.

Possibly on the trip back, but more likely in Canajoharie, Margaret married a war chief named Lykas. During their short marriage Margaret gave birth to two daughters, Jacomine and Lea. Both children died in infancy. In the spring of 1750, Lykas went on a raid to Catawba country and was killed by fighting men of the southern tribes.[11]

Again a widow and now probably in her mid-30s, Margaret relied on the agricultural traditions of the Mohawks to feed her children. Although by the mid-18th century the Mohawks were beginning to adopt the European model of nuclear family homes, communal farming was still practiced by the women of Canajoharie. Margaret and Molly worked with the other women in the fields surrounding the village and received their share of corn, beans, squash, and wheat.[12]

During the spring of 1752 when the women were not engaged in agriculture and the men were not hunting, virtually everyone was in the woods gathering ginseng. Due to its alleged aphrodisiac properties, there was a great demand for the herb in China. When British merchants became aware of its existence in the Mohawk River valley, they were prepared to buy as much of the herb as the Mohawks could harvest. It became a significant cash crop for the Mohawks in the period 1752–1754.[13]

It may have been in the woods searching for ginseng that spring when Margaret met Brant Kanagaradunkwa, a sachem of the Turtle Clan. Brant Kanagaradunkwa lived in the Mohawk's lower castle of Tiononderoge at Fort Hunter, about 40 miles east of Canajoharie. He was in his mid-50s and was very recently widowed by the death of his second wife, Christina, a senior matron of the Bear Clan at Tiononderoge. He was also a close friend of William Johnson.[14]

1. Early Days

Christina was alive in June of 1751 when Daniel Claus came to board with her and Brant in order to learn the Mohawk language. Claus, a talented linguist and recent German immigrant, then 23 years old, hoped to become an Indian agent for the province of Pennsylvania. Instead, Claus would accept employment as William Johnson's deputy and later become his son-in-law.[15] Claus would also become an important source of information for posterity about Molly Brant's life.

But all this was very far in the future that day in 1752 when Brant and Margaret met. The attraction between the two soon led to a pregnancy. On March 4, 1753, Reverend John Ogilvie, Reverend Barclay's replacement at Fort Hunter, christened a baby boy named Jacob, who was described in the baptism register as "Jacob Son of Marg. the widow of Lykas by Brandt of Canajoharie."[16] Ogilvie married Margaret and Brant six months later on September 9, 1753.[17]

The marriage was not popular among Christina's relatives at Tiononderoge. Brant and Margaret had definitely conceived the baby well within the one-year mourning period that was expected of a Mohawk spouse. It is even possible that the conception occurred while Christina was still alive. The delay between the baptism and the marriage may have been a futile effort to conceal from people in Tiononderoge the identity of Jacob's father, or it may have been an attempt to soothe the sensibilities of Christina's family. If a Mohawk couple had young children, it was expected that the widowed husband would marry his dead wife's sister to preserve continuity of care. This was not applicable to the middle-aged Brant and Christina, but one of her sisters may have felt insulted by Brant's hasty choice of Margaret, and Brant may have thought it was necessary to give Christina's family time to adjust to the situation before he took marriage vows with Margaret. In the end, the bad feelings were enough that Brant moved out of his two-story house in Tiononderoge and established a new home with Margaret and the children at Canajoharie.[18]

Reverend Ogilvie, probably uncertain as to the precise date of Jacob's out-of-wedlock conception and probably having heard an earful from Christina's angry relations, decided that Margaret (but not Brant) should receive public censure. Although Ogilvie performed the marriage ceremony, he informed Margaret that she would not be allowed to receive communion again until she stood up in church and publicly asked forgiveness for having committed adultery. At first Margaret balked, but she was sufficiently religious that this sanction outweighed the public humiliation that Ogilvie was inflicting. On February 17, 1754, Margaret came to the front of the church and told the congregation that she was sorry for having sexual relations with her son's father.[19] Molly, then about 17, may have witnessed this embarrassing event. She was certainly well aware that it had taken place. It may have played an important role in her own decision to delay sexual relations with a man.

The marriage between Margaret and Brant Kanagaradunkwa was a happy one. Although baby Jacob died in infancy, Brant proved to be a good stepfather to Molly and Joseph. Brant built a fine house in Canajoharie, similar to the one he and Christina had shared at Tiononderoge, and the children began using his surname.[20]

With the family now materially secure, there was time for 10-year-old Joseph to go to school. Paulus Peters, the son of Mohawk sachem Hendrick Theyanoguin, ran a school at Canajoharie. There, Joseph learned to read and write the Mohawk language.[21] Peters may also have taught him a bit of English, but Joseph's first introduction to spoken English apparently came from Brant and from the children of European settlers who rented farmland from the Canajoharie Mohawks.[22]

There is evidence that Molly could also read and write the Mohawk language, but probably not the English language. Years later when Joseph attended Eleazar Wheelock's Indian school in Lebanon, Connecticut, Wheelock mentioned in a letter to William Johnson that Joseph had received a letter from Molly that Wheelock had not inspected because he assumed it was in Mohawk.[23] In the early 1770s when Molly's son, Peter Johnson, was in Philadelphia, Peter mentioned in a letter written in English to his father that he was planning to write a letter to his mother that day. It is known that Peter was bilingual. The letters between mother and son are lost, but in the same letter to his father Peter asked him to send him "an Indian book" so he would not lose his knowledge of the Mohawk language for lack of practice.[24] During the American Revolution, Daniel Claus received several letters from Molly. A copy of a letter dated April 12, 1781, sent from Carleton Island, states that it is a translation of a letter from Molly to Daniel Claus.[25] Also during the war years, her stepson, Sir John Johnson, obtained from her a receipt that she signed "wari," the Mohawk way of spelling "Mary," with the words "Mary Brant her mark" inscribed adjacent to the signature.[26]

A Mohawk named Daniel Asharego served as a schoolmaster at Canajoharie in the early 1740s.[27] It is possible that Molly learned to read and write Mohawk from him at the age of five or six before her family's departure to the Ohio valley, although retaining this skill for several years without additional practice would have been difficult. It is more likely that Molly attended Paulus Peters's school for a year or two as a teen after her return from the Ohio valley, or that young Joseph taught his sister what he had learned at Peters's school.

* * *

1. Early Days

In the fall of 1754, Brant Kanagaradunkwa was part of a delegation of Mohawks who journeyed to Philadelphia to discuss the validity of a deed to land in the Susquehanna valley with officials of the government of the province of Pennsylvania. Margaret and her children accompanied him, and Daniel Claus came along as the group's interpreter.[28] It was an exciting experience for 18-year-old Molly: the first time she visited a large Anglo-American city or laid eyes on the Atlantic Ocean. The trip was also the first time she received the attentions of a prominent Englishman. On the way back to the Mohawk valley the group stopped at Albany, arriving on February 8, 1755. Captain Staats Morris, the 27-year-old nephew of the governor of Pennsylvania, was stationed there. Yet another friend of William Johnson, Morris was attracted to the lovely young Molly. Daniel Claus would later write that "Capt. St M fell in love with Ms. Mary Brant who was then pretty likely not having had the smallpox."[29]

Traditionally, Mohawk boys and girls had been allowed freedom to engage in premarital sex. If a young couple liked each other and the young woman's elder female relatives approved, the young man moved into the longhouse of the young woman's matrilineage, a home run by the girl's mother, the mother's sisters, and the girl's maternal grandmother and great aunts if they were still alive. If after a period of time the couple continued to get along and the girl's mother and aunts were satisfied that he was a good hunter, capable of doing his share to provide the family with meat, a marriage feast was held, and thenceforth fidelity was expected. If the trial arrangement didn't work out, the young man gathered up his hunting weapons and was given back any gifts he had given the young woman, and he returned to his mother's longhouse, with no opprobrium attached to either party.[30]

While this way of life was still alive and well in the western tribes of the Six Nations, by 1755 the majority of Mohawks were Christians, and Christian teaching forbade premarital sex. Although it was not uncommon for a Mohawk couple to present themselves to one of the several European ministers in the region with the woman visibly pregnant, some ministers felt the need to show disapproval. Within the previous year, Molly's own mother had been subjected to public humiliation for infringing on Christian rules about sex, and this probably made Molly cautious, since she understood that Morris's interest in her did not involve marriage. It is also possible that by now she had developed a crush on her stepfather's friend, William Johnson. In any event, she did not succumb to Morris's blandishments.

Molly would see Staats Morris again. A few months later in the summer of 1755, there was a regimental muster in Albany. Johnson was there. Molly's family was also there, probably to receive the annual distribution of presents from the province of New York that was a symbol of the friendship between New York and the Six Nations. There is a story in the Johnson family that Molly accepted a ride on the back of a horse from an officer and that all eyes were on the two as they took a quick gallop around the parade ground.[31] The observer, who thought she cut quite a figure and that all eyes were upon her, was probably William Johnson. Once again, however, Molly apparently limited her interaction with Morris to flirting. She brought no children to her relationship with William Johnson, although she proved her ample fertility by presenting Sir William with eight children in 15 years.

Perhaps Molly was just having some fun when she took her ride with Morris. Perhaps she was trying to get William Johnson's attention. Whichever it was, Staats Morris would soon be on his way to Britain to claim an aristocratic bride, but it would be another three and a half years before Molly and William became lovers.[32]

2

A Man of Many Talents

Forty-year-old William Johnson was a very busy man in the summer of 1755, and he did not lack for romantic partners. William was born in 1715 in County Meath, Ireland. His father, Christopher Johnson, was the second-largest tenant of Michael Warren, a member of the local landed gentry and the son-in-law of an Irish baronet. Both the Warrens and the Johnsons were Catholics.[1] Michael Warren had fought for King James II against King James's Protestant daughter and son-in-law, William and Mary in 1688, but had chosen the loyalty oath over exile when William and Mary proved victorious. Although Michael Warren kept his lands, they were encumbered with mortgages to pay the heavy fines levied on King James's former supporters. Warren no longer had the ability to provide his daughter Anne with the kind of dowry that would allow her to marry a social equal. Instead, she married Christopher Johnson, and as part of her dowry they received rent concessions, and Christopher was appointed the Warren family's land agent. His duties included collecting rent from the other tenants.[2]

Anne Warren Johnson's younger brother, Peter, also faced reduced prospects, and his future also needed to be dealt with creatively. Catholics could not join the England's navy or army, nor could they enter the professions. It was decided when Peter was 13 that he would convert to the Church of England and join the Royal Navy. There was a precedent for this in the Warren extended family. Peter and Anne's maternal uncle, Mathew Aylmer, had joined the Royal Navy after converting in 1674 and had risen to become admiral of the fleet and an Irish peer.[3] Like Aylmer, young Peter Warren would go on to an illustrious naval career.

As he grew to young manhood, William Johnson could not fail to understand two important things: no matter how talented he was, a man could not rise unless he was a member of the Church of England, and in a harsh world, what a woman brought to the marriage was critical to a family's prospects.

Meanwhile, in the early 1730s, the Royal Navy's prize system of

15

dealing with captured ships was making William Johnson's uncle, Peter Warren, then stationed in New York City, a wealthy man. This had also allowed him to marry into the politically well-connected De Lancey family. As a result of the marriage, even more opportunities came Peter Warren's way. In the mid-1730s he was able to purchase from the widow of the recently deceased governor of New York, William Cosby, a 14,000-acre tract of land on the south side of the Mohawk River near its junction with Schoharie Creek.[4]

But how was the busy navy captain to manage his new estate? Why not form a relationship with his sister Anne Johnson's son, William, similar to the one Peter Warren's elder brother had with Anne's husband?

Part of the understanding was that William would convert to the Church of England. Otherwise, he would be an embarrassment to his up-and-coming uncle. William's father, and his mother if she was still alive, probably feared for his soul and were saddened by the thought that they would probably never see him again, but for William the choice was clear.[5] In 1738 at age 23, William Johnson left Ireland forever. Six feet tall with dark hair and hazel eyes, he was "of a most comely aspect and in every way well formed for the most manly exercises."[6] William possessed an outgoing and friendly nature. He had a keen intelligence, and for someone headed to the wilds of North America, he was a well-educated young man. Not only could he read and write both English and Latin, but he had also received practical lessons in estate management from his father.[7]

William brought with him 12 Irish Protestant families to a location 180 miles north of New York City and 21 miles west of Schenectady on the south side of the Mohawk River. These families, together with seven or eight German families already there, were to be the tenants of what his uncle had named Warrensburgh.[8]

The site was adjacent to Fort Hunter, a rectangular fortification with four blockhouses, a few cannons, and about 20 soldiers. The fort was commanded by Walter Butler, whose son and grandson would share the Johnson family's fate when decades later the American Revolution demanded that hard choices be made. The fort's small chapel was supervised by a Church of England missionary, Reverend Henry Barclay, who oversaw a mostly Mohawk flock. At the time of William Johnson's arrival, there were about 580 Mohawks living in upper New York in two main settlements of about 250 souls each: Tiononderoge, in the shadow of Fort Hunter, and Canajoharie, about 40 miles west, also on the banks of the Mohawk. There was a much smaller settlement on Schoharie Creek, and a few other Mohawks lived at a predominantly Oneida village at Oquaga in the Susquehanna valley.[9]

* * *

2. A Man of Many Talents

In addition to managing his uncle's estate, William began trading for his own account. His uncle envisioned this, but had no idea how successful William would become. William soon established friendly business relations with the Mohawks at Tiononderoge and Canajoharie and paid a trading visit to the Oneidas and Mohawks at Oquaga. The Indians sold him furs in exchange for metal and cloth goods.[10]

William also traded with German settlers who had established settlements at Stone Arabia, a farming community between Warrensburgh and Canajoharie on the north side of the Mohawk River, and at German Flatts, almost directly across the river from Canajoharie. The Germans had fled to London from a war in Palatine two decades before. Within a few years when Queen Anne found them becoming too numerous, they were shipped to the wilderness of upper New York.[11]

It was not long before William's store was a great success. Its presence at Fort Hunter meant that neither the German farm families nor the Six Nations fur traders had to travel farther down the Mohawk to Schenectady or Albany for their supplies. In addition to its favorable location, the store succeeded because William was friendly and fair. This meant a great deal to the Mohawks and other members of the Six Nations as well as the German farmers, since both groups were often cheated by the Dutch traders at Schenectady and Albany.[12]

Only a year after his arrival, William was able to buy land on the north side of the Mohawk across from Warrensburgh. Initially, the plot was a quarter of a mile long and a mile deep. He built himself a house he called Mount Johnson, and he established his store and a sawmill there.[13]

As he built his new life in the wilderness of upper New York, William yearned for female company. The kind of young ladies of quality whom William would consider marrying resided in New York City. The idea of one of them joining him on the frontier was absurd. There were the daughters of wealthy Dutch traders in Albany and Schenectady, but his store was heavily cutting into the Albany and Schenectady traders' profits, and they all loathed him for it.[14]

This meant that female companionship could come from the daughters of modest German or Irish farmers or from young women of the Six Nations. At about the same time that William left Ireland, a young woman named Catherine Weissenburg, then about 15 years old, paid for her passage to America by becoming the indentured servant of Richard Langden, a ship's captain. Catherine was apparently trying to reach relatives among the Palatine Germans settled in the Mohawk valley. At some point Catherine's mother also made the journey and would end up living in William Johnson's home until her death in 1766.[15]

Langden lived in New York City, far from the Mohawk valley.

Catherine may not have understood this when she signed the indenture. It is also possible that she sincerely intended to serve out the term, but Langden proved to be an abusive master. In any event, she ran away in January 1739. Langden's advertisement, offering 20 shillings for her return, describes her as "about 17 years of Age, middle stature, Slender, black-ey'd, brown complexion, speaks good English, tho' a Palatine born."[16]

When William met Catherine a few months later, she was working as a domestic servant for Alexander and Hamilton Philips, neighbors who lived a few miles from Warrensburgh. Explaining his need for a housekeeper, William paid the Hamilton brothers a sum of money and brought Catherine back to Mount Johnson. Although indentures could be bought and sold without a servant's consent, she apparently went willingly.[17]

The three children William and Catherine had together would grow up thinking that their parents were married, but they were not. Catherine wore a gold ring until she died. When William died many years later, one of their children placed this ring in their father's coffin. It was found when William's body was disinterred for reburial in 1862. The ring was inscribed "June 1739, 16." One of William Johnson's recent biographers has suggested that the ring was a gift from William Johnson to Catherine on her 16th birthday, and was meant as a way of acknowledging that she was carrying his child and of providing a salve to her pride without actually marrying her.[18]

Their oldest child, Anne, named for William's mother, was baptized by Reverend Barclay at Fort Hunter on June 8, 1740. She was listed in the baptismal records as the child of Catherine Wysenberg. When their son John was baptized in February 1742, he was listed as the son of Catherine Wysen Bergh, and their daughter Mary, who was baptized in 1744, was listed as the daughter of Catherine Wysenberk.[19]

It was certainly no secret at Mount Johnson that Catherine was more than a housekeeper to William. Michael Tyrell, a cousin of William who had come over from Ireland with him and had lived at Warrensburgh for about two years before joining the Royal Navy, told William to give her his regards in the spring of 1741: "Remember to all frinds and Best Respects to Doctor Barclay Mr. and Mrs. [] Dillon to Catty and all that Inquire for me."[20]

* * *

As William and Catherine's family grew, so did William's relationship with the Mohawks. His closest friend among them was his trading partner, Brant Kanagaradunkwa. In addition to the business relationship, they enjoyed hunting together, and William was a frequent guest at Tiononderoge, soaking up the language and coming to respect Mohawk customs. In about 1742, he was adopted into the Mohawk tribe. He was given the name Warraghiyagey, meaning "he who does much business."[21]

2. A Man of Many Talents

Perhaps because he wanted to make it clear to himself or to Catherine that they were not married and probably because his growing closeness to Brant Kanagaradunkwa's family presented him the opportunity, not long after little Anne's birth, William began a relationship with Elizabeth, a maternal niece of Brant's wife Christina.[22]

Catherine's second child, John, was baptized by Reverend Barclay in February 1742. A child named Brant, listed in the baptism register as the son of Brant Kanagaradunkwa and his wife Christina, was baptized on June 13, 1742. This child who would later be known as Brant Keghneghtaga and sometimes as Brant Johnson was actually the son of William Johnson and Elizabeth. William would acknowledge this boy throughout his childhood and leave him a substantial bequest in his will.[23]

Maybe because the rules were harsher for Native Americans or maybe because Reverend Barclay would have been shocked by William simultaneously having two illicit families, Brant Kanagaradunckwa and his wife, who was then about 48 years old, were to be little Brant Johnson's parents in the eyes of the Church of England. The ruse was carried out again when a baby named Thomas was christened on May 27, 1744, this time within months of the birth of Mary, Catherine Weisenberg's third child. On June 23, 1745, when William and Elizabeth's third child, Christian, was baptized, Reverend Barclay refused to play the fool and accept that 51-year-old Christina was the mother. The child was listed in the baptism records as "adopted son of Brant."[24]

Little Thomas and Christian died in infancy. There is a record of William paying for mourning clothing for Brant's family when Christian died. Their mother, Elizabeth, lived past 1765, long enough to raise Brant Johnson to manhood.[25] According to Mohawk custom, a child belonged to his or her mother's clan and continued to live with the mother in the event of divorce.[26] This suited William's lifestyle well. At some point not long after Christian's death, William and Elizabeth broke off their relationship. Perhaps Elizabeth finally understood who Catherine Weisenberg's children were or found out about another liaison that William may have begun with another Mohawk woman. The disintegration of the relationship could also have been due to the stress of losing two babies in rapid succession. In keeping with the Mohawks' liberal view of divorce, the breakup did not affect William's warm relationship with Brant.

* * *

In 1745, danger came to the Mohawk valley in the form of King George's War. William Johnson stood to lose everything he had built up over the past seven years should the French seize the Mohawk valley. He was determined to resist.

Peter Warren, William's uncle, was one of the early heroes for the British side. In June 1745 when William Pepperell seized the French fortress of Louisbourg in Nova Scotia, the naval forces that supported him were commanded by Warren. Warren would be promoted to rear admiral and receive 20,000 pounds in prize money as a reward for his role in the victory.[27]

To William Johnson's chagrin, the war soon moved south. In November 1745 a force of 400 French soldiers and 220 of their Canadian Native American allies attacked Saratoga, a settlement only about 25 miles to the northeast of Mount Johnson, killing or capturing 100 people. At about the same time, the French put a bounty on William's head because of his family relationship with Warren.[28]

The attack on Saratoga was a wake-up call for William. He concluded that Mount Johnson was not a safe place for Catherine and their three small children. He sent them to New York, accompanied by Catherine's mother. They would live there and later in Albany for the next several years.[29] At this point, it became necessary to decide what his children's last name was. He decided that it was Johnson. Catherine, with her gold ring, cannot be blamed for failing to correct those who called her Mrs. Johnson.

With his European family out of harm's way, William threw himself into the war effort. Peter Warren sent him a brass cannon with swivels, which he set up at Mount Johnson. William's brother, Warren Johnson, a captain in the British Army, arrived from Ireland to raise a militia company for a possible attack on Canada, and William actively recruited among his tenants to help fill his brother's company. Forty to 50 men answered his call.[30]

New York governor George Clinton viewed William as the leading man of the Mohawk valley and looked to him to help hold it. William understood that the Six Nations were a crucial element in the balance of power in northern New York, and he had a profound respect for their prowess as woodland fighters. He told his brother that 300 Native Americans could defeat 1,000 regulars in wooded terrain.[31]

Governor Clinton invited the Six Nations to a conference at Albany in the summer of 1746 in the hope of persuading them out of the neutral stance the confederation was maintaining toward the warring European powers. William knew that the only hope of bringing the Six Nations into the conflict on the side of the British was to make the Mohawks strong advocates for war within the confederacy.[32]

A few days before the Albany conference with Governor Clinton, William held a feast at Tiononderoge featuring a large bull and plenty of rum. William hosted the feast not as William Johnson but as Warraghiyagey. As the adopted brother of the Mohawks, he intended to convince them that the French and their Canadian Native American allies were a threat to not only the European settlers of the Mohawk valley but also Mohawk fur trading routes and Mohawk settlements. Completely abandoning his European identity, William wore a kilt of deer skins and a skull cap with a great eagle feather. His arms and torso were painted with designs, his wrists and knees were adorned with rattles of dried deer hooves, and he rose and performed the war dance, chanting in fluent Mohawk about King George's greatness and the power of his army, which would help the Six Nations drive their enemies into the sea. Men who agreed with William got up and sang solos as well.[33]

Alliances were extremely personal things to the Mohawks. Over the past eight years, William had proved himself to be someone who could be trusted. He was an honest store owner who didn't cheat them; was a neighbor who helped in times of trouble; and later was a brother who spoke their language, hunted with them, feasted with them, and was the father of Mohawk children. Although some of the very young men were excited simply by the prospect of warfare, more mature men decided that they would rather cast their lot with him than with the Dutch traders in Albany, who opposed the war because it interfered with the northern fur trade route dominated by Canadian Native American tribes.[34]

Days later, William, dressed in war paint and breech cloth, led the Mohawks, also wearing war paint and breech cloths, down the northern side of the Mohawk River to meet the governor at Albany. Representatives of the other tribes of the Six Nations, still maintaining their neutral stance, traveled down the south side of the river for the parley wearing everyday clothing.[35]

It is fair to say that Governor Clinton and every other European who beheld it were amazed by William's entry into the city. Clinton excitedly ordered his cannoneers to return the Mohawks' rifle salutes. Over the course of four days, the rest of the Six Nations were convinced to enter the war as Great Britain's allies. Clinton named William "Colonel of the forces to be raised out of the Six Nations." William's orders were to enlist both Native Americans and European Americans for a campaign against the French and their Native American allies.[36]

Despite William's success in convincing the Six Nations to ally themselves with the British, the New York Assembly's failure to provide funding meant that no organized attack on Canada ever took place.[37] William spent the remainder of the war directing the defense of the Mohawk valley and sending out Native American raiders and European American militia rangers to attack French and Canadian Native American settlements. In June 1748, the governor appointed him colonel of the militias operating in the Mohawk valley in addition to his responsibilities as colonel of the Six Nations.[38]

* * *

During Catherine's long absence, William conducted an affair with Angelique Vitry, one of a number of French prisoners of Indigenous allies whose freedom he obtained by paying their bounties. Prior to Angelique's residence at Mount Johnson, William also conducted a liaison with Mary McGrah, the wife of Sgt. Christopher McGrah, an Irish American militiaman who was missing in action. Apparently believing her husband to be dead, Mrs. McGrah conceived a child by William. To William's credit, when he learned that Sergeant McGrah was a prisoner of war, he sent much-needed money to him at Quebec. William later recommended McGrah for a military pension. Upon his return, McGrah elected to overlook the indiscretion. When William Johnson died, he left the child, a girl also named Mary, 200 acres of land.[39]

Despite William's busy military career and active sex life, it was during this period that he began to complain of a chronic bowel disorder that may have resulted from a parasite infection. The condition would trouble him for the rest of his life, sometimes leaving him bedridden for weeks at a time.[40]

During the period 1748–1750, Catherine and the children continued to live primarily in Albany and New York but did visit Mount Johnson periodically. William loved the three children, looked forward to seeing them, and gave the household staff at Mount Johnson explicit instructions to have the house in perfect readiness for each family visit. When the family was not present, the household operated much like a college fraternity house. When the day's work was done, the several Irishmen who helped him run Mount Johnson joined William for lengthy dinners irrigated by generous amounts of rum and Madeira. After dinner, there was musical entertainment supplied by bagpipes, a flute, and a violin.[41]

During this period, William also had a relationship with another unidentified Mohawk woman that resulted in the birth of a child named William Tagawirunta, who would later be known as William of Canajoharie. Records from 1750 indicate that "little Will" was sometimes at Mount Johnson.[42] His mother may have died when he was quite young. Although he was raised primarily by relatives at Canajoharie, he would later spend significant periods at Fort Johnson when Molly lived there, and she would come to refer to him as her son.[43]

In late 1748, William began construction of a larger home located about a mile from the first Mount Johnson. It was ready for occupancy in early 1750. During the French and Indian War the house was fortified and came to be known as Fort Johnson. The new home was 60 feet by 32 feet and made of stone. The basement contained a large kitchen and storage areas. Above were two main living floors and an attic where house servants slept. The surrounding compound contained a sawmill, houses for skilled

2. A Man of Many Talents

Sir William Johnson House, State Routes 5 & 67, Fort Johnson, Montgomery County, New York. Library of Congress, Prints & Photographs Division, HABS NY, 29-FORJO, 1-control no. ny0312. Historic American Buildings Survey, creator. Thomas T. Waterman et al., photographers. Documentation compiled after 1933.

laborers such as the miller and the cooper, dormitories for servants and enslaved people, barns, stables, and a bakehouse. There was also a council house, and there were cabins for prominent visiting Native Americans.[44]

William's status as a slaveholder was not unusual in colonial New York. Prior to the American Revolution, New York had the highest population of Black slaves in the northern colonies. The census for 1749 counted 10,592 Black residents (the vast majority enslaved people) in a total population of 74,348, making enslaved people about 14 percent of the population of the colony. Those numbers would increase in the decades leading up to the American Revolution.[45] Peter Warren owned a number of slaves, some seized from foreign vessels he had taken as prizes of war. Warren sent these enslaved people up to Warrensburgh to work the fields that were not rented to tenants.[46] Over time, William Johnson bought Black slaves from merchants who engaged in the trade in New York City and Philadelphia. Through the same merchants, he also contracted with European indentured servants. These two groups provided the manual and semiskilled labor required for his own growing estate.[47] During his occupancy of Fort Johnson, he owned 10 to 12 slaves. In the last decade of his life when he occupied Johnson Hall in Johnstown, he owned between 30 and 40 slaves, making him one of the largest slaveholders in the colony. There is no evidence that he had any moral compunction about exploiting the labor of enslaved persons.[48]

By the early 1750s, when Peter Warren died, William, now in his late 30s, owned well over 20,000 acres of land in the Mohawk valley, purchased from both Native Americans and European patent holders. These acquisitions made him the largest European landowner in the valley. His father Christopher, still alive in Ireland, must have continued to miss him badly and worry about his salvation, but probably found some comfort in knowing that his son had become a great man.[49]

3

The French and Indian War and a Frontier Romance

In the summer of 1755 when Molly took her horseback ride around the militia drill field with Captain Staats Morris, war was once again brewing in the Mohawk valley. The previous year young George Washington, commander of a small force of militiamen, had been forced to surrender Fort Necessity in the Monongahela River valley, a tributary of the Ohio River, to French forces sent from nearby Fort Duquesne. Both the British and French claimed rights to the Ohio valley and surrounding areas. This dispute was only one of several between Britain and France that would boil over into what was known as the Seven Years' War in Europe and the French and Indian War in America.[1]

William Johnson was to play a prominent role in this conflict. In April 1755, he was summoned to Virginia to meet with General Edward Braddock, commander in chief of His Majesty's forces. Braddock gave Johnson the mission of capturing the French fortress at Crown Point.[2]

This was a big assignment and would bring together militia forces from the colonies of New York, Massachusetts, New Hampshire, Vermont, Connecticut, and Rhode Island. William was to report directly to Braddock and would receive funding from the British Crown.[3]

Crown Point lay in a heavily forested wilderness on the edge of Lake Champlain in northeastern New York. In order to reach Crown Point, William would need to hack a road from the Great Carrying Place at the headwaters of the Hudson River, about 50 miles north of Albany, to the southern edge of Lake St. Sacrement, a distance of about 14 miles. His forces could then proceed by bateaux up Lake St. Sacrement to attack the lightly defended Fort Ticonderoga at the inlet to Lake Champlain. Having secured Fort Ticonderoga, they would then travel by bateaux 15 miles up Lake Champlain to Crown Point.[4]

William was keenly aware of the cultural differences between the New Yorkers and the New Englanders that would only make his arduous task more difficult. The Puritan New Englanders were more sternly religious than the Church of England and Dutch Reformed New Yorkers. The New Englanders did not countenance drinking, swearing, or dirty jokes, and their common soldiers were used to a much more democratic style of leadership than the New Yorkers. William was amazed at the lack of discipline among the New England units but recognized that he would have to accept it if his forces were not to disintegrate.[5]

William went on a charm offensive that proved highly successful. A Massachusetts surgeon wrote of him that "I must say he is a complete gentleman, and willing to oblige and please all men, familiar and free of access to the lowest sentinel, a gentleman of uncommon smart sense and even temper; never yet saw him ruffle or use any bad language."[6]

Matthew Pratt (Att.), *Sir William Johnson*, 1772. Canvas, oil paint, 30 inches high × 25 wide. New York State Office of Parks, Recreation, & Historic Preservation. Johnson Hall State Historic Site. JH.1971.309.

In hopes of raising Native American forces for the campaign, William called a conference of 11 nations to assemble at Fort Johnson. The conference began on June 21, 1755, and lasted for nine days. As was customary among the Six Nations and other Native American tribes, whole families attended the conference.[7] Brant Kanagaradunkwa was one of William's staunchest allies among the Mohawks. Molly, her mother Margaret, and her brother Joseph were certainly there.

Nineteen-year-old Molly would have watched William deliver the keynote address of the conference in fluent Mohawk. As was expected, he delivered his speech in a strong voice, punctuated by dramatic gestures:

If you treat me as your Brother, Go with me. My war kettle is on the Fire, my Canoe is ready to put in the water, my Gun is loaded, my sword by my side and my ax is sharpened. I desire and expect you will now take up the Hatchet and join Us your Brethren, against all our Enemies.[8]

On the night of June 29, Molly and hundreds of others watched William perform the war dance, his still athletic body undulating to the beat of the drums. He was the dynamic, almost spellbinding leader of his people and the deeply respected ally of her people. Her emotions as she watched her stepfather and other friends and neighbors take up the war belt must have been strong. In the coming weeks, about 250 Native Americans, many of them Mohawks, would join William's forces. Molly's family and her people were once again acknowledging their strong ties to William Johnson and binding their fate to his.[9]

During the first two weeks of August, 2,000 militiamen under William's command began carving out the road from the Great Carrying Place to Lake St. Sacrement, which William renamed Lake George. They also began construction of a fort at the Great Carrying Place to protect the army's supply line. Initially called Fort Lyman for William's second-in-command, it would later be renamed Fort Edward after one of the king's sons. Additional militia forces arrived, bringing William's army to between 3,100 and 3,200 militiamen and 250 Native Americans. William and Catherine's 14-year-old son, John Johnson, accompanied his father as a volunteer. Meanwhile, a French force of 2,300 regulars and militiamen and 600 Native American allies, commanded by Baron Ludwig Dieskau, initially encamped at Crown Point, was brought down to Ticonderoga. The two armies relied primarily on Native American scouts to search for each other in the vast wilderness.[10]

By August 29 William was able to establish a camp, which included some cannons, on the shore of Lake George. He immediately ordered a breastwork consisting of tree trunks, branches, and overturned wagons to be constructed around the camp's perimeter. Shortly after arriving at Lake George, William received intelligence that Dieskau was marching toward the Great Carrying Place and Fort Lyman. The messenger William sent to warn Fort Lyman was killed by Dieskau's Native American allies, alerting Dieskau that William's army was nearby. Dieskau decided to stage a surprise attack on William's forces.[11]

As Dieskau approached William's encampment on the morning of September 8, he encountered about 1,000 militia and 200 Native Americans whom William was sending to the relief of Fort Lyman. During the ensuing skirmish, known to history as the Bloody Scout, Hendrick Theyanoguin, chief sachem at Canajoharie, and Mathew Farrell, husband of William's sister Catherine, were both killed. Most of the militiamen and their Six Nations allies were able to make it back to the British camp about three miles away, but with the French in hot pursuit.[12]

Upon encountering William's breastwork, even though the French regulars immediately attempted to breach the camp's defenses, the French Canadian militia and Canadian Native Americans halted, giving William a chance to rally his forces within the camp. Over the course of four and a half hours and despite their allies' reluctance to join the assault, the French regulars took heavy losses as they attacked in waves. William was shot in the hip while moving up and down his lines organizing the camp's defense. It was a significant wound, but he returned to the fight as soon as it was dressed. As the extent of the French casualties became apparent, the militiamen and Six Nations fighting men jumped over the breastwork and drove the remaining French forces into the forest. As Dieskau's men retreated, they left behind their wounded commander.[13]

As was customary, the Six Nations warriors intended to kill the severely wounded Dieskau by burning him at the stake in revenge for the death of Hendrick Theyanoguin, but William intervened. Claiming Dieskau as his prisoner, he had him sent to his house in Albany, where William's newly widowed sister, Catherine Johnson Farrell, was asked to nurse him back to some semblance of health. Dieskau would remain grateful to William Johnson and Catherine Farrell for the rest of his life.[14]

The news of William's victory at Lake George was greeted with joy in both New York and London. It was an important antidote to the shocking news of Braddock's defeat and death in the Monongahela River valley earlier that summer.[15] The king and Parliament fell over themselves honoring William. Parliament voted William a gift of appreciation of 5,000 pounds. George II made him America's second baronet. Only William Pepperell, hero of King George's War a decade earlier, held a similar honor in the colonies. King George II's cabinet also granted William a commission as sole superintendent of Indian affairs for the northern colonies and colonel of the Six Nations. The position came with an annual stipend of 600 pounds sterling. William was to report directly to the Crown, thus freeing him from the authority of the New York provincial assembly.[16]

The honors and authority came with a cost. Surgeons were unable to remove the musket ball in William's hip. It would remain in his body for the rest of his life and, together with his chronic bowel complaint, permanently undermined his once robust health.[17]

* * *

The British victory at Lake George was followed by a series of French military successes. In 1756 the French captured Fort Oswego, located on the south side of Lake Ontario at the mouth of the Oswego River, laying

3. The French and Indian War and a Frontier Romance 29

open the Mohawk valley to French invasion from the west. The settlement at German Flatts and the Mohawks' upper castle across the Mohawk River at Canajoharie where Molly and her family lived, were now seriously exposed. William's newly fortified home 40 miles to the east was the outermost British defense.[18]

The newly minted baronet, known now always as Sir William, was again commander of the Mohawk valley militia, and he did his best to defend the valley and the surrounding region. In August 1757 he led 1,500 militiamen and 180 Native Americans to Fort Edward when he received word that Fort William Henry, the fort he constructed after the Battle of Lake George, just 14 miles from Fort Edward, was under attack. To Sir William's disgust, the commander of Fort Edward, British general Daniel Webb, refused to allow a relief expedition to William Henry, forcing the fort to surrender to General Louis-Joseph de Montcalm, who was unable to prevent a massacre of prisoners by his Canadian Native American allies.[19]

In the fall of 1757 the physical and mental stress caught up with Sir William, and he was bedridden with a near fatal attack of pleurisy. He wrote to Lord Loudon, Braddock's replacement as commander in chief: "My Lord I was greatly mortified at my not being able to wait on your Lordship while at Albany but my Disorder was so severe for 7 weeks that I could not turn in my Bed. I am far from being able to go abroad, the Pain still continuing in my Side tho not so severe."[20]

It was while Sir William was prostrate with pleurisy that the long-awaited attack on German Flatts finally came. Molly and her family watched with horror as smoke rose over the settlement across the river. Eight Palatine farmers were killed, and 114 men, women, and children were taken prisoner.[21]

As Molly and her family wondered if the French would directly attack Canajoharie, Sir William was beginning to wonder if he had much longer to live. During the winter, he gloomily wrote that even if he survived, he doubted he would ever again "be able to endure much fatigue."[22]

William's mood was further darkened by the growing understanding that Catherine Weisenberg was dying. By the mid-1750s, Catherine and their three children were living at Fort Johnson on a permanent basis.[23] The children had by then concluded the few years of formal education given to well-off young people in the mid-18th century, making their continued residence in Albany or New York unnecessary. Therefore, Catherine's declining health combined with Sir William's desire for the children's company made Fort Johnson the best place for the family to reside.

Catherine apparently had contracted tuberculosis.[24] She does not appear very often in the historical record during this period, but she was doing her best to perform her duties as mother of the family, hostess, and household administrator. In 1756 a Schenectady merchant, Daniel Campbell, billed Sir William two shillings nine pence for "one pair gloves for Mrs. Caty."[25] Daniel Claus, who by now was quietly courting Sir William and Catherine's 17-year-old daughter Anne (Nancy), subsequently referred to Nancy's "profound love and duty to her parents" in a letter to Sir William, implying that Catherine continued to be an important presence in her daughter's life.[26] After Catherine's death, a friend of William's, Peter Wraxall, wrote him a condolence note referencing a recent visit when Sir William and Catherine had hosted him together: "When I left you, I thought there appeared little hope of Miss Katy's life. I condole with you thereupon, and hope Miss Nancy's management of the house will supply the loss you have sustained."[27]

As it turned out, Miss Nancy would not need to manage the house. As Catherine's health declined in 1758, Sir William's health improved. During January 1759, William attended a conference at Canajoharie and stayed at Brant and Margaret's home. Based on the birth of their first child, Peter, in September 1759, this period at Canajoharie was probably the beginning of Sir William and Molly's sexual relationship.[28]

Now age 22 or 23 and possibly having been attracted to him since her teens, Molly decided to accept the only kind of union she could have with Sir William Johnson. Perhaps he promised her that the Fort Hunter pastor would not dare to try to humiliate the baronet's partner as he had humiliated her mother, Margaret. Perhaps it helped that the senior Mohawk matron, Catharine, head of the Turtle Clan and sister of Johannes Dekarihokenh, the senior Mohawk league sachem, had formerly been the unmarried partner of George Croghan, Sir William's subordinate in the Indian Department.[29] Sir William may also have told Molly that he had not made love to Catherine Weisenberg in many years. This was probably true, but in the small world of Canajoharie and Tiononderoge, Molly was certainly aware of Sir William's Mohawk children, Brant Keghneghtaga and William Tagawirunte. The relationships with Brant's and William's mothers were also now years in the past. What Molly knew of Sir William's more casual liaisons both recent and in the past we do not know. It is likely that war and illness were slowing him down, so Molly may not have been delusional to hope for a fairly monogamous relationship.

Catherine Weisenberg died in April 1759.[30] Peter Wraxall's comment that he hoped young Nancy could assume management of the house makes it clear that Molly was not a presence at Fort Johnson prior to Catherine's death. Moreover, Sir William had always shown some discretion in ensuring that the women in his life lived in separate locations. Thus, while he had one family at Mount Johnson and another family at Tiononderoge in the early 1740s, he sent Angelique Vitry back to Canada when he wanted Catherine Weisenberg and their children to return to Mount Johnson from Albany at the end of King George's War. In addition to whatever remaining feelings he had for Catherine, Sir William genuinely loved Anne, John, and Mary. Bringing his pregnant lover to their home while their mother gasped her last breaths would have been cruel, and he was not a cruel man.

Just as important, it was now necessary that Catherine's status be elevated. When George II granted Sir William the baronetcy in 1756, the letter patent stated that the title was to be passed down to Sir William's legitimate male heirs.[31] If it was known that Sir William had not been married to Catherine, then young John Johnson, then age 14, could not succeed him as baronet. The situation could not be cured by a subsequent marriage to Catherine. If William and Catherine were not married at the time of John's birth, he was not legitimate and could not inherit the baronetcy.

This presented a real quandary for Sir William. Although one old friend, who knew the true situation, was still urging him to marry and beget himself an heir as late as 1760, Sir William didn't want to do it.[32] He had three beloved teenage children who had grown up thinking their parents were married. Could he look into their eyes now and tell them they were bastards? Twenty years of hard work, intelligence, and determination in war and peace had made him a wealthy and titled man. He no longer needed the prosperous marriage alliance that his upbringing had told him was crucial, and at some point after the bestowal of his title, he decided to dispense with it. He began referring to the dying Catherine as his wife and counted on the fact that very few people knew for sure that she wasn't. If she ever asked in her last months to make it true, he told her that for young John's sake, there could be no record of a recent marriage. Her son was to be a baronet but only if they handled things carefully.

Thus, when Molly came to live at Fort Johnson in the months after Catherine's death, the arrangement suited Sir William's needs very well. At age 44 and in only middling health, he had reached a point where he wanted the stability of a monogamous live-in relationship. He also wanted John to inherit the baronetcy, so the relationship could not be with a woman who demanded marriage, since a wife's eldest son, not John, would be his legitimate male heir. What reason he gave Molly for this failure to offer a legal marriage we do not know. She was an intelligent young woman, and she well understood that the teachings of his church and hers required it. She of course had only to look around to see how few legal marriages existed between European American men and Native American women, and perhaps that was the answer—his people would not accept it. It is unlikely that he ever told her the secret of his elder children's illegitimacy.

What William offered Molly instead was his promise that she and their children would be well provided for both during his life and afterward. She would have the title "housekeeper," a well-known euphemism of the time for the unmarried partner of an aristocrat. They would openly share a bedroom at Fort Johnson, and her children would be acknowledged by him and bear his name. Although John, Anne, and Mary would be the primary heirs, as was the right of legitimate children, each of Molly's children would receive a handsome inheritance, deemed at the time to be the honorable way of providing for the natural children of aristocratic Englishmen. Sir William would keep this promise, and it would only be the vicissitudes of the American Revolutionary War that would strip away from Molly and her children the life that he had planned for them.

What Anne, John, and Mary thought of this arrangement is hard for modern minds to grasp. In the patriarchal and deferential society in which they grew up, the decisions of a father and the decisions of a great lord were rarely questioned. There was a sense that fathers and lords should be benevolent, but since they didn't have to be and often weren't, there was a feeling of deep gratitude when they actually did behave decently. Like many other powerful men of his time, Sir William failed to follow the rules of Christianity in his sexual relationships. But the reality is that few aristocrats of the time would have conceived a plan to pass off the bastard children of an indentured servant as legitimate heirs, given that by the late 1750s there were plenty of wealthy heiresses in New York City who would have been happy to marry a baronet and provide him with highborn legitimate heirs.

Although Anne, John, and Mary didn't know of their bastardy, they probably understood the vast social class difference between their parents and felt lucky that Sir William was a generous and loving father. Indeed, it may have been a relief to them that there would be no wealthy European American stepmother dominating their lives. There were well-known stories of fathers disinheriting elder children in favor of younger second families.

Anne, John, and Mary were certainly cordial to Molly during their father's life. After his death and under the severe stress of the Revolution, John Johnson, Anne's husband Daniel Claus, and Mary's husband Guy Johnson would all to varying degrees work with Molly and her brother, Joseph Brant, to keep the Six Nations loyal to the king and to win back the Mohawk valley, the beautiful and fertile land that they all believed had been stolen from them by traitors and thieves.

* * *

But that was all a long time in the future. In 1759, a very much alive Sir William Johnson was focused on the defense of the Mohawk valley and

3. The French and Indian War and a Frontier Romance 33

the destruction of French colonial power in North America. The Crown looked to him to bring the Six Nations decisively into the British camp. Sir William had prevailed on some Six Nations warriors, especially Mohawks, to participate in some of the earlier battles of the conflict, but the Six Nations confederacy was still officially neutral, and many Senecas, the powerful Keepers of the Western Door, leaned toward the French because of geographic proximity and trade patterns.[33]

Opinion within the Six Nations began to shift only when Colonel John Bradstreet, employing Six Nations scouts provided by Sir William, made a successful surprise attack on Fort Frontenac, located at present-day Kingston, Ontario, at the confluence of Lake Ontario and the St. Lawrence River. The British were able to seize irreplaceable supplies intended for Fort Duquesne in the Ohio valley and for the army that was preparing to assault the Mohawk valley. The entire French fleet on Lake Ontario was seized in the harbor, virtually guaranteeing that no assault from the west could threaten the Mohawk valley for at least a year.[34]

The ultimate carrot that decided the Six Nations in favor of the British was given in the fall of 1758, when the proprietors of Pennsylvania agreed to sell back to the Six Nations for the token sum of five shillings, all of their land claims beyond the Allegheny Mountains in the Ohio River valley system. The French had been telling the Senecas and other tribes that hunted in the Ohio region that they would seize the land from the British and give it back to them; now the Penn family had erased this incentive to ally with the French.[35]

Sir William held a conference with the Six Nations at Canajoharie in April 1759 to discuss a summer offensive. Molly, now three or four months pregnant, was there, as was her brother, 16-year-old Joseph, who intended to take part in the campaign.[36]

Sir William and the Senecas agreed that the French fortress at Niagara must be seized. From Sir William's perspective, seizure of the fort would cut off the French forts on the Great Lakes and the Ohio River from French Canada in the east. From the Senecas perspective, the capture of Fort Niagara would mean the end of the French monopoly as a market for their pelts and the reopening of an advantageous trade route east to the Anglo-American markets.[37]

Sir William needed to get the new British commander in chief, Jeffery Amherst, behind this idea and traveled to Albany to argue his case. Molly remained in Canajoharie. If Sir William was successful in convincing Amherst, he would soon be back to organize the campaign.[38]

Unfortunately, General Amherst had a visceral hatred of Native Americans and a thinly veiled contempt for the man who had spent a significant portion of his adult life learning their language and culture.

Amherst was sufficiently adroit to understand that he could not be openly rude to the man whom the king regarded as the hero of the Battle of Lake George, but the meeting was coldly formal, and Amherst gave no indication about which way he would decide. Unbeknownst to Sir William, his strategic arguments were bolstered by orders from London that mentioned Fort Niagara as an important secondary target so long as any attack did not diminish efforts to capture Quebec and Montreal.[39]

Amherst decided that the Niagara campaign would be led by Colonel John Prideaux, with a force of about 4,000 regulars and European American militia at his command. At the last moment, to preserve secrecy from the Native Americans, Amherst informed Sir William that he was to go too, bringing as many Native Americans as possible but not telling them where they were going. This was an impossible order, since the men of the Six Nations regarded themselves as independent allies and because not even a Six Nations sachem could command men of the confederacy to participate blindly in any military action. Sir William disobeyed the order and was able to gather a force of 600 fighting men.[40]

* * *

Sir William and Joseph said goodbye to Molly at Canajoharie. Although proud of them both, she could only be concerned about her young brother's lack of experience in war, and she must have been keenly aware of the musket ball in Sir William's hip and feared what any additional wound would do to him.

At Oswego, Prideaux left half of his force to construct a fort that would guard his supply line. The commander of the men left at Oswego was Colonel Frederick Haldimand, an officer who many years later would become a loyal friend and benefactor to Molly and her family during their Canadian exile.[41]

On June 30, 1759, Prideaux and Sir William left Oswego, with Prideaux's men traveling in whale boats and his cannons transported by bateaux. Sir William's Six Nations forces, among them Molly's brother Joseph, traveled in canoes. The entire expedition hugged the southern coast of Lake Ontario in the hope of avoiding detection. Throughout the six-day journey, Sir William must have prayed that none of his Native American allies, especially the Senecas, had betrayed the plan to Francophile friends or neighbors. The commander of Niagara had a large ship at his disposal that was capable of blowing them out of the water. Surprise was essential.[42]

To everyone's relief, the British and their Native American allies landed undetected at a point just four miles from Fort Niagara. They set up their camp in the woods without opposition and began digging a trench

3. The French and Indian War and a Frontier Romance   35

that would protect them from the fort's cannons as their own artillery fired on the fort with impunity.[43]

As the British trenches advanced toward the fort, Seneca sachems, some allied with the British and others allied with the French, openly moved back and forth between the British camp and the fort trying to convince each other to come over to the other side. Sir William was deeply involved in the negotiations at the British camp, laughing off claims of French strength, and promising his Seneca allies the right to pillage the fort.[44]

By July 14, the British trenches were close enough to put British cannons within range of the fort's walls. A blistering artillery barrage began. On July 20, Colonel Prideaux was killed when one of his own artillery shells exploded prematurely, not an uncommon occurrence.[45]

A messenger was sent to Fort Oswego to report Prideaux's death. Colonel Haldimand immediately set out from Oswego to assume command. Meanwhile, Sir William Johnson, colonel of the Six Nations, took command of the attack. Senecas who slipped out of the fort to join the British informed him that French Canadian reinforcements were coming from the upper lakes. While continuing to advance the trenches toward the fort, Sir William also set up an ambush to deal with the Canadian relief column.[46]

Positioning Anglo-American militiamen and Six Nations men skilled in woodland fighting in the forest on both sides of the portage road, and having erected a breastwork of tree trunks and branches at the end of the road, Sir William waited. As the French Canadian militiamen advanced down the road on the morning of July 25, the Anglo-American militiamen and Six Nations warriors in the woods greeted them with a heavy fusillade. The French forces frantically returned fire. Sir William, who was in the woods commanding the ambush, later told his brother that there were 14 musket balls in the tree where he was taking cover. The Canadians, finding themselves unable to scramble over the breastwork at the end of the road, finally turned and ran.[47]

Almost every French Canadian militiaman not cut down on the road was captured or killed by the Six Nations men who pursued them. Sir William immediately demanded that the fort surrender. When a French officer under a flag of truce returned to the fort and confirmed Sir William's claim that the members of the relief force were all dead or had been taken prisoner, the fort's commander surrendered at 2 o'clock that afternoon.[48]

Colonel Haldimand arrived on July 28 to find British forces in control of Fort Niagara and Sir William Johnson wildly popular among the men. Everything was in such good order, and the men were so loyal to Sir William that Colonel Haldimand thought it would be impolitic to strenuously

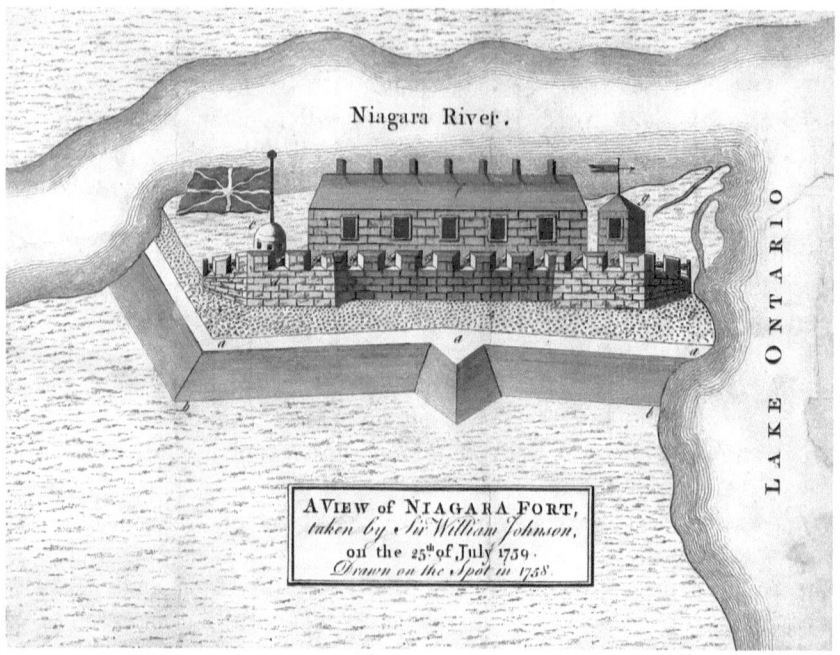

Fort Niagara, the site of one of Sir William Johnson's greatest military victories. "A view of Niagara Fort, taken by Sir William Johnson on the 25th of July 1759, drawn on the spot in 1758" (1759–1885). The Miriam and Ira D. Wallach Division of Art, Prints and Photographs: Print Collection, New York Public Library.

challenge William's claim that as colonel of the Six Nations, he actually outranked Colonel Haldimand.[49]

Sir William's victory at Niagara was even more important than his triumph at Lake George four years earlier. The only remaining French fort west of Niagara was Detroit, which was now completely isolated. The French had no hope of launching a campaign in the Ohio valley, leaving the British Fort Pitt as the only European military presence there. The king and Parliament were once again ecstatic. The toast in New York City was "Johnson forever!"[50]

4

Motherhood and a New Home

On August 4, 1759, Sir William, having left a garrison at Niagara, sailed for Oswego to confer with General Thomas Gage, the man Jeffery Amherst had sent to assume command there.¹ Meanwhile Molly, now almost eight months pregnant, had received the joyous news that both Sir William and Joseph were safe and that Sir William had achieved a momentous victory. Molly wanted to join her man despite any possible discomforts due to her condition. Oswego, in Onondaga country, was only about 95 miles from the Mohawk settlement at Canajoharie. Mohawks and Oneidas were constantly moving back and forth between the two points, which were about a two-day journey via the Mohawk River, Wood Creek, Oneida Lake, and the Oswego River. Molly would have to walk several miles on a trail between the last navigable point on the Mohawk River and Wood Creek, but she was eager to do so. She sent Sir William a letter asking if she could join him. One of the Canajoharie Mohawks would happily let her hitch a ride in his canoe.

Sir William would probably have loved to see her, and he must have been itching to tell her of his heroics at Niagara, but he was well aware of the diseases and other dangers rife in military camps. There were Onondaga women in the vicinity who could assist her with the birth, but wasn't she really better off in Canajoharie with her mother to attend her? Moreover, he was in discussions with General Gage about a possible attack on La Gallette, an island in the St. Lawrence River west of Montreal. Sir William might have to depart with the Six Nations men within days of her arrival.²

On Tuesday, August 21, 1759, Sir William made a terse entry in his journal: "Very stormy, and rained all night—continued stormy all day. I wrote a letter to my brother by Lieutenant Linnall of the Highland Regiment; another to Kelly, Corry, Date, Wallace, and my daughter Nancy. Sent another to Molly, by Hance Clermont, not to come here."³

The wording of this entry strongly implies that Nancy and Molly were in two different places, thus, the need to send the letters by different methods. Nancy was likely at Fort Johnson. Molly was probably at Canajoharie, where she gave birth to Peter surrounded by her mother and other female relations. Sir William's journal again references letters sent to Nancy and Molly on Monday, September 10.[4] By then, he may have received word of the birth of the child he would name after his famous uncle, Peter Warren, a child who would be a source of love and pride for the remainder of Sir William's life.

The choice of the name "Peter" was also a sign of respect for Molly's father, Peter Tehonwaghkwangeraghkwa, and that was probably how the Mohawks viewed it. Little Peter Warren Johnson had a name that would allow him to move comfortably in the culture of each of his parents, an important asset in the complicated society into which he was born. By midautumn 1759, Sir William returned to Fort Johnson. It was probably at this time that Molly and baby Peter moved there. When General Amherst met with Sir William at Fort Johnson not long after, Amherst was disgusted by Sir William's domestic arrangements: "Several Indians there living on him," he huffed in his journal. One of his staff officers recorded making a gift to "a little Indian boy," probably William of Canajoharie, then about nine years old.[5]

The house that Molly moved into that fall was very much part of a working fort. There were two blockhouses adjacent to the residence, with a third blockhouse located on the hill that overlooked the site. A small contingent of regulars was assigned to the fort, and there were a few small cannons. "A heavy swing gate well ironed" protected the compound at night.[6]

Fort Johnson was also a large working farm. Although Sir William had fine Madeira and specialty foods such as limes shipped to him from New York City, most of the food consumed at Fort Johnson was raised, hunted, or fished on the estate. Sir William owned cattle, pigs, and sheep, and his men hunted wild turkeys, which were plentiful in the area. William's fields produced wheat, corn, oats, barley, potatoes, and peas. His orchards produced apples. Wild strawberries and peaches were abundant. Trout, pike, and freshwater oysters were available in the Mohawk River, 40 yards from the main house, and sugar was extracted from maple trees, which were everywhere.[7]

Molly's household duties changed over time. At first, she probably did little more than care for her infant. Due to Catherine Weisenberg's long absences and terminal illness, Sir William had long been in the habit of purchasing household supplies and giving instructions to household servants. During the years before Catherine's death, he left detailed written instructions when he was absent.[8] However, not long after Molly came to Fort Johnson, although he still left instructions for fieldwork when he was

4. Motherhood and a New Home

A sketch of Fort Johnson by Guy Johnson when it was a working fort. "A north view of Fort Johnson drawn on the spot by Mr. Guy Johnson, Sir Wm. Johnson's son" (1760–1799). The Miriam and Ira D. Wallach Division of Art, Prints and Photographs: Print Collection, New York Public Library.

away, he began to trust Molly to keep the household running smoothly. Sir William continued to make large purchases of supplies throughout the 1760s and early 1770s, although there was a growing list of entries in the account books of local merchants recording purchases that Molly made for the family.[9] In the absence of a banking system, she was also free to withdraw cash from these merchants, which Sir William later repaid as part of his regular account payments.[10]

Throughout their 15-year domestic partnership, Molly probably always did more household work than would have been done by any wealthy New York City lady Sir William might have legally married. There is an account, for example, of her rising before dawn to prepare breakfast for house guests who needed to depart very early in the morning.[11] No De Lancey or Livingston would ever have done such a thing. Molly's experience was probably more akin to the experience of a prosperous middle-class housewife of the era. Like many such women, Molly was a fine seamstress. There are numerous instances of her purchasing cloth, thread, and buttons. She apparently made much of the clothing used by her eight children.[12] Also like many such women, she had at least two house slaves to do heavy household labor. Increasingly, they were supervised by her rather than by Sir William. These house slaves did much of the food preparation, but Molly did not hesitate to pitch in to provide Sir William's many guests with a pleasant experience. At the same time, she was a hostess. Although she normally wore Indian dress, she also owned several fine gowns that she probably wore when distinguished British and European American guests were present.[13]

As the years passed, Molly also had some influence on household staffing. In 1766 Sir William asked Robert Adems, a Johnstown merchant, to see if he could sell for him both a young male slave named Harry and "a healthy young Wench" named Jenny when he traveled to Philadelphia on business.[14] Jenny was the sister of Juba, a domestic slave in the Johnson household. Juba or Jenny apparently asked Molly to intervene, because Sir William changed his mind, and Jenny was soon assigned to Molly. When Sir William died, he bequeathed Jenny to Molly and bequeathed Juba to Molly's children. There is no evidence that Molly was troubled by these arrangements. Indigenous people sometimes held prisoners of war as slaves, and this may be how Molly viewed Jenny and Juba's fate. They, together with a male slave named Abraham, also bequeathed to Molly's children, would eventually accompany Molly and her family into their Canadian exile.[15]

* * *

Molly came to Fort Johnson in the midst of Britain's final push to drive the French out of Canada. Quebec had fallen to British forces under the command of General James Wolfe (who died during the battle) in the summer of 1759. With Sir William's victory at Niagara that fateful summer, Montreal was the last remaining stronghold in Canada. The British were determined to seize this final prize during the fighting season of 1760.[16]

Sir William spent much of the winter of 1759–1760 engaged in diplomatic efforts to bring the Canadian tribes over to the British side or at least convince them to remain neutral.[17] Amherst planned a three-pronged attack on Montreal. One force would proceed westward from Quebec, and a second would move northward from Crown Point on Lake Champlain. The third and largest force, led by Amherst himself, would cross Lake Ontario from Oswego and proceed eastward down the St. Lawrence River. Amherst's force would have to pass by the Oswegatchie and Caughnawaga settlements as well as the settlements of several other tribes before reaching Montreal.[18]

Sir William arrived in Oswego in midsummer 1760 with 1,368 Native Americans. About 600 of these people were men of military age. An additional 100 Native American fighting men joined him there. The rest were

4. Motherhood and a New Home   41

women and children. The women and children were to remain at Oswego while the men joined in the attack on Montreal.[19] It is not known whether Molly and little Peter were in this group. Molly very likely asked to go, but Sir William would have had much to consider in agreeing to her request. General Amherst had rendezvoused with Sir William at Fort Johnson, and they traveled to Oswego together. It was at this time, as a guest in Sir William's home, that Amherst came face-to-face with Sir William's family life, and Amherst's journal indicates that although he must have previously heard rumors, he was taken aback.[20] Sir William was well aware that having Molly accompany him would be an irritant to Amherst, and Sir William may have wondered if he himself could keep his temper if she was openly insulted.

Molly would certainly have enjoyed going. There would be many female friends and relations with whom she could visit. Her presence would also have reassured the hundreds of Native American women waiting at Oswego that their husbands and sons were fighting alongside a brother and a friend. In later years she would attend many conferences at Onondaga and Canajoharie, but she didn't need to go to this gathering in the way that many Six Nations women did. They relied on their husbands' hunting and fishing in the months before the harvest. Molly and Peter were well provided for at Fort Johnson. There was also the ever-present question of disease. Molly had not yet had smallpox, and that disease as well as many others stalked large military camps. So, although it is possible she was there, it is more likely that she was not, especially given the fact that her second child was not born until September 1761.

The expedition set off from Oswego on August 10, 1760. When Fort Levis on the island of La Gallette, a stone's throw from the Oswegatchie settlement, surrendered, Amherst refused to grant the Six Nations fighting men and their allies a respectable share of the booty, despite Sir William's emphatic pleas. Of Sir William's 691 Native American allies, 506 left La Gallette in disgust.[21]

Sir William and his remaining forces patrolled the riverbanks as the British armada shot the rapids between La Gallette and Montreal. It was a vulnerable place where the French could have attacked, but again because of Sir William's diplomacy, the Canadian tribes in the vicinity refused to aid them. As Amherst's force approached Montreal, 500 Caughnawaga men stood on the riverbank unarmed. Sir William saluted them as friends and invited five of them to row his whaleboat to the island of Montreal as evidence of his trust.[22]

Amherst's other two armies had already arrived. When it was clear the Caughnawagas had gone over to the British, the Canadian militia decided it was foolish to resist and did not respond to the call of French governor Pierre de Rigaud de Vaudreuil de Cavagnial to defend the city. He and his regulars had no choice but to surrender to Amherst.[23] France's long domination of Canada was over. Britain was the preeminent colonial power in North America.

Sir William received no credit from Amherst except for keeping his Native American allies "in humane bounds."[24] Sir William would later tell his brother Warren that Canada could not have been captured but for the neutrality of the Canadian Native American tribes.[25]

* * *

Sir William was barely back from Montreal when his brother arrived at Fort Johnson for an extended visit. Setting sail on July 23, Warren experienced a stormy six-week sea voyage from Cowes on the Isle of Wight to Philadelphia. After some sightseeing in Philadelphia, he proceeded by horseback to New York City, where he took a ship 150 miles up the Hudson River to Albany. He traveled the last 30 miles in a two-wheeled open carriage drawn by two horses on a road he described as "indifferent" that followed the northern bank of the Mohawk River.[26]

Warren arrived just in time. The Mohawk valley was about to experience one of the harshest winters in living memory. By November 16, parts of the Mohawk River had frozen over. On December 28, Warren reported in his journal that it was "soe cold as to freeze almost any thing even by the fire's side."[27]

Despite the weather, the inhabitants of Fort Johnson were not entirely cut off from the world. On January 8, they received word that George II had died suddenly in England on October 25, 1760. Perhaps just as shocking, Warren noted sadly on January 13, 1761, that a fine pipe of Madeira was frozen solid in the main house at Fort Johnson "in a Room with a good fire." For those more concerned about food, there was "bread soe frozen that there is noe eating it."[28]

If the cold was hard for Warren to bear, Molly must have been very worried about her ability to preserve the life and health of baby Peter, only about 15 months old at the beginning of the winter. There were numerous deaths at neighboring Tiononderoge from a complaint sounding much like influenza, with small children particularly at risk.[29] With room temperatures barely above freezing, little Peter would have slept between his parents for warmth. Nevertheless, Warren reported that "in Bed People are cold even with ten Blankets on."[30]

In mid–January, there were 28 inches of snow on the ground. By the end of February, the snow was four feet deep. On February 19, Warren wrote that "wolves & foxes came about 7 o'clock this Night into Sir William's yard to a Dead Cow."[31]

4. Motherhood and a New Home 43

Like many world travelers of the time, Warren apparently intended his journal for publication. Given the sensibilities of mid-18th-century Europeans, it would have been indelicate to mention his brother's domestic arrangements. Although he lived as Sir William and Molly's house guest for six months, Warren never mentions her directly in his journal. This is true even for a four-day period just before Christmas 1760 when he, Sir William, Molly, and little Peter were guests in her mother and stepfather's home at Canajoharie.[32]

From both Sir William and Molly's perspective, the Canajoharie visit was a very momentous one, well worth braving the frigid weather, for Sir William was to be given an enormous gift by Molly's people. The group set out from Fort Johnson on December 20, 1760, by sleigh, the method of travel favored by both European Americans and Native Americans during upper New York's long winters. Canajoharie, however, was on the south side of the Mohawk, while Fort Johnson was on the north side. Apparently the river was only partially frozen over at Canajoharie upon their arrival, so a canoe crossing was necessary. Warren Johnson noted that they arrived at Canajoharie that evening "but not without great Difficulty in crossing the Mohawk River—being full of Ice."[33] Molly carried baby Peter on her back wrapped in furs and tied to a wooden board "with a top over the child's face, on which hangs a curtain." Warren was fascinated by the device in which his nephew was carried but discreetly generalized in his journal that "mostly all" Indian women used it.[34]

The visit consisted of three days of meetings. On the second day, according to Warren, the Mohawks "unanimously gave Sir William a Gift of 100,000 Acres of Land or thereabouts that is 16 by 10 miles, & reckoned the very best in the Country."[35]

This was Kingsborough, a tract of land located between Fort Johnson and Canajoharie where Sir William would establish his county seat at Johnstown, and out of which he would later carve handsome bequests for both Catherine Weisenberg's and Molly's children as well as smaller ones for William of Canajoharie and Brant Johnson. Sir William feared that enemies in the legislature would deny him the license required to purchase this land. He overcame this impediment by asking the Mohawks to make him a gift of the land, and then, as was customary among the Six Nations, he gave them a reciprocal gift: 1,200 pounds in cash and presents for each family. Molly's brother, an unmarried young man, received 50 pounds as his gift.[36]

The Mohawks recognized that their lands were being steadily encroached upon by European settlers who had little regard for them or their way of life, which still prominently featured hunting. This grant was an insurance policy that much of the land between Tiononderoge, the

Lower Castle, and Canajoharie, the Upper Castle, would be occupied by their adopted brother and ally Sir William and his children, both European and Native American, and by tenants controlled by Sir William. As their own numbers dwindled, it was a far better option than selling the land piecemeal to the flood of European immigrants who were advancing on the Mohawk valley.

The transaction was also a way of protecting themselves from Ury Klock, sometimes known as George Klock, a local Palatine farmer who had recently adopted the practice of getting a few Canajoharie Mohawks drunk and then getting them to sign deeds for land in the vicinity of Canajoharie that the tribe as a whole had no intention of selling. In addition to the reciprocal gifts, Sir William agreed to commission a survey to make clear what the Mohawks' remaining lands were. Such a survey would benefit both him and the Mohawks.[37]

A few weeks after the trip to Canajoharie, Sir William wrote to Alexander Colden, surveyor general of the province of New York, requesting a survey "in the plainest & most intelligible manner you can, so as Everry Pattent or Tract between Albany & Fort Stanwix on both sides ye. Mohawk River Schohare Stoneraby & Cherry Valley with ye. Pattentees Names, ye quantity of Each & year pattented may be easily known. by which means, what is yet unpatented & belongs to the Indians may plainly appear."[38]

Although the Mohawks engaged in this transaction, not because of Sir William's relationship with Molly Brant, but because Sir William had been their ally and brother for more than 20 years, and also because they perceived it to be beneficial to them, Molly and Peter were nevertheless an important symbol of that continuing family relationship with Sir William that gave the Mohawks confidence that they were making the right decision. Molly's stepfather, Brant Kanagaradunkwa, Sir William's longtime friend and a leading sachem at Canajoharie, was certainly one of the most important advocates for the deal within the tribe's internal councils.

These factors made Kingsborough a kind of dowry for Molly, the sort of valuable contribution Sir William's upbringing told him a woman and her family were supposed to bring to a marriage. The staying power of Sir William and Molly's domestic partnership had several sources—a genuine affection and physical attraction, Sir William's advancing middle age and declining health, and his growing respect for Molly's intelligence, household management, and political skills—but Kingsborough probably helped fix in his mind that their partnership was as close to a marriage as his unconventional life would ever permit. All of this would come more clearly into focus for Sir William as the events of the next year unfolded. It was about this time that he and Molly conceived their second child.

4. Motherhood and a New Home

* * *

For Warren Johnson, the trip to Canajoharie and indeed his entire six months in the Mohawk valley were an encounter with a vastly different culture that he was only slowly able to digest. Initially he was disgusted by the Tiononderoge Mohawks he met shortly after his arrival at Fort Johnson, noting that the women threw the lice they picked from each other's hair into the broth cooking on the fire and that there was a high rate of alcoholism among the Lower Castle's inhabitants.[39] Putting the lice in the broth, of course, kept the little creatures from reinfesting the women and was also a source of additional protein when cooked. As to the alcoholism, Sir William informed Warren, "they were moderate untill we corrupted them & now love Rum Excessively."[40]

Warren's attendance at the Canajoharie conference also gave him a glimpse into the far more equal relations between the sexes enjoyed by the people of the Six Nations. In a sad commentary on the rights of mid-18th-century European American women, Warren noted with astonishment that although only designated male speakers orated at councils, what they said was decided in advance by both male and female leaders of the tribe. When he commented on this to Sir William, Warren was informed that senior matrons could often prevent men from going to war, and if these women approved a military action, it was a great disgrace for the men to return without prisoners and booty.[41] Having assumed that European patriarchy was the only way of organizing a society his whole life, Warren also reported with shock that "the Mothers have the intire disposal of their Daughters."[42]

By the time Warren left Fort Johnson on April 22, 1761, he had developed a grudging respect for the Mohawks. He admired the depth of their friendships, the keenness with which they mourned their dead, even finding the loss of one comrade in battle unacceptable, and the orderliness of their political councils.[43]

What Warren told his elderly father, Christopher Johnson, who was still alive in 1761, upon his return to Ireland we do not know. Whether Christopher went to his grave believing that his son William, the wealthy landowner, military hero, and baronet, was a widower with three adult children or whether Warren dared to tell him of his Native American grandchildren and of Molly Brant is a tantalizing secret of history. In either case, Sir William's life had certainly taken pathways that Christopher Johnson could scarcely have imagined when he bid him farewell in 1738.

* * *

About the time of Warren's departure from the Mohawk valley, it became clear that Sir William would again have to undertake a challenging and dangerous mission for his country. He had just fended off a proposal from an influential friend in London that he accept the vacant governorship of New York.[44] William viewed the proper execution of his role as superintendent of Indian affairs as far more important than the governorship, because it was crucial to Britain's ability to hold onto the gains that it had achieved by his hard-won victories at Niagara and Montreal. This was particularly true given Amherst's attitude toward Native Americans and the resulting harsh policies that emanated from Amherst's command.

Thus, when Sir William received intelligence from his Mohawk friends that a number of the tribes in the Ohio Country remained pro-French and that an alliance was coming together to force the British from Fort Pitt and Detroit, he knew that his direct intervention was required.[45]

Sir William decided to undertake a mission to Detroit to make a peace treaty with the western tribes. Molly must have been heartsick when she heard the news. The trip would be 500 miles in each direction. William had never traveled so far into the wilderness before. Mohawk friends and relatives warned him against doing it. He would be passing through the territories of several tribes who would be happy to see him dead. Even in Seneca country, the land of the Western Gatekeepers of the Six Nations, many were enraged by the continuing presence of the British at Fort Niagara and by crimes perpetrated against Native Americans by the garrisons and traders at all three western forts.[46]

Sir William was undeterred. In order to make it clear that he came in peace and in a sign of how much his Indian Department was also the family business, he decided that he would only be accompanied by his 19-year-old son, John, and by his nephew, 21-year-old Guy Johnson. Young John, Sir William's only European American son, had lived in close proximity to Native Americans most of his life. Guy, the son of Sir William's younger brother John, had come over from Ireland in 1756 and had spent the last five years as a militia ranger, living and fighting beside Sir William's Six Nations allies.[47]

The three of them set out from Fort Johnson on July 5, 1761. Molly, now about six months pregnant with their second child, must have wondered if she and Sir William would see each other again. She certainly knew that he would not be back from his dangerous journey before she again experienced the perils of childbirth.[48]

It was an arduous two-month trip on horseback and by boat, during which 46-year-old Sir William frequently slept on the ground exposed to the elements and during which time he continued to receive reports from Six Nations allies that his life was in danger. It must have been with some relief that Sir William and his young companions arrived at Detroit on September 3, 1761.[49]

4. Motherhood and a New Home 47

They spent more than a week at Detroit, holding a conference outside the walls with representatives of most of the significant western tribes, including the Hurons, Shawnees, Delawares, Wyandots, and Chippewas. Senecas were also present, some of whose friendship was equally in doubt. Sir William distributed presents and offered the western tribes the significant concession that they would each henceforth be recognized as independent nations. The western tribes viewed this as a very important enhancement of their bargaining position, and they accepted Sir William's offer of peace.[50]

Sir William's other mission while at Detroit was to make the French inhabitants of the town feel that the members of the British garrison were now their protectors and that they could continue to enjoy prosperity in a British-controlled North America. This would decrease the possibility that they would connive with the western tribes to undermine the British occupation. Two balls were given for the foremost French citizens during Sir William's stay, the first hosted by the commander of the British garrison, Captain Donald Campbell, and the second by Sir William himself. On both occasions, Sir William opened the ball with the daughter of Detroit's leading citizen, the wealthy fur trader, Antoine Cuillerier.[51]

Angelique Cuillerier was beautiful and well-educated despite her wilderness upbringing, and to Sir William's delight, she could speak several of the western Native American languages. At 26 years old, she was actively engaged with her father in Native American diplomacy, but unfortunately, with the departure of the officers of the French garrison, her hopes for a worthy marriage with a countryman had been dashed, and she was now facing the reality that by mid-18th-century standards, she was rather old to be a belle. Sir William represented her best and probably last remaining opportunity for an excellent marriage. Officially, of course, he was a widower.

She and Sir William flirted with each other and danced until dawn at both balls. Unlike most of the European women Sir William had met since his departure from Ireland 23 years before, she was a member of the gentry class and thus able to virtuously ask Sir William his intentions when their repartee became a tad too familiar. The somewhat startled Sir William, who clearly did regard her as a lady of quality, wrote in his journal the morning after the second ball that "all parted very much pleased and happy. Promised to write Mademoiselle Curie [sic] as soon as possible my sentiments; there never was so brilliant an assembly here before."[52]

The long journey back to Fort Johnson cleared Sir William's head of any fantasy of pursuing the matter further. As a baronet, he was certainly entitled to an attractive and wealthy lady of the European gentry as his wife, but was that what he wanted? Neither Angelique nor Molly could stand for the other's presence at Fort Johnson. He pictured the hurt in Molly's eyes as she packed up their promising little son Peter and the new baby, and had her brother Joseph escort them back to Canajoharie. And what of the reaction of his friends, the Canajoharie Mohawks, with whom he had so recently concluded the Kingsborough transaction and whose continuing cooperation might be needed as he pursued the patenting process with the British authorities? The Mohawks had a liberal view of divorce, but he wouldn't be leaving Molly for another Mohawk woman as he had done with other Mohawk women in his younger days. No, this would be for a European woman, and such an action might be deeply insulting to the Canajoharies.

There was also his son John to consider. A legitimate son by Angelique would be the true heir to the baronetcy. Sir William could continue with the lie that Catherine had been his wife, but there were a few old acquaintances who knew otherwise. Angelique was highly intelligent and 20 years younger than he was. If someone ever let the truth slip in front of her, she would be free to investigate the matter after his death. A review of the baptism records at Fort Hunter would show that John had been baptized as John Weisenberg, not John Johnson. In his middle years, his beloved son John could find his life turned upside down by Angelique and her son.

Angelique had been a pleasing diversion during his high-stress week of negotiations with the western tribes, but the people he already loved and the things he had worked so hard for by far outweighed any attraction he felt for her. There would never be any letter to Angelique about "his sentiments."

On Wednesday, October 21, 1761, now only days from Fort Johnson, Sir William was able to gratefully report in his journal: "Encamped about three miles above the Three Rivers. Captain Etherington told me Molly was delivered of a girl; that all were well at my house, where they stayed two days."[53]

5

A Diplomat's Partner

As Molly lay in their bed at Fort Johnson and nursed their newborn daughter, Elizabeth, she didn't know that she had just surmounted the greatest threat to her relationship with Sir William that would ever exist. Indeed, she would probably never hear Angelique's name. What Molly knew was that she had just given birth to a healthy firstborn daughter. For the matrilineal Mohawks, who passed their clan identities from mother to daughter, this was a highly consequential event. In Molly's case, it would also be this daughter, in her midteens at the beginning of the American Revolution, who would be Molly's greatest emotional support as Molly faced the harrowing challenges of bringing her fatherless family through the dangerous days to come.

As for Angelique Cuillerier, it took her some time to accept the finality of her situation. Eight months after Sir William's return home, she asked Captain Campbell about him. "She never neglects an opportunity of asking about the general.... 'What says she, is there no Indian councils to be held here this summer?'... She desired I would present you her best compliments."[1] The following year she tried again; sending her compliments through Detroit's new commander. Sir William responded gallantly but very much in the past tense: "I have not forgot the powerful effect of the charms of the lady who honors me with a place in her remembrance."

Angelique took the not too subtle hint. Now age 28, she entered into an unhappy and abusive marriage with a social inferior, James Sterling, an Irish fur trader, who told a friend he was marrying her for her dowry and so he would not have to pay an interpreter when he transacted business with the Indians.[2]

As for Molly, November 1761 brought not only Sir William's return but her brother Joseph's as well. The previous spring Sir William had received a letter from Reverend Eleazar Wheelock, the head of Moor's Indian Charity School in Lebanon, Connecticut. Wheelock's letter announced that the Society in Scotland for Propagating Christian Knowledge was subsidizing three scholarships for young men of the Six Nations "in order to their being fitted as Soon as may be for Interpreters or other publick usefulness among their Own Nations." Enclosed with the letter was a recommendation from Major General Phineas Lyman, Sir William's second-in-command during the Lake George campaign. Assured by Lyman that Wheelock was a good man and that the school was reputable, Sir William raised with Molly the possibility of 18-year-old Joseph becoming one of the three students.[3]

Molly must have been concerned about asking her mother, Margaret, to consent to this. Most Mohawk daughters lived either in the same dwelling with their mothers or no more than a stone's throw away. Molly lived 40 miles from her mother, and now her partner was suggesting that Margaret's only other living child leave Canajoharie for an extended period to be educated in Connecticut.

The ability to fluently speak, read, and write English could make an enormous difference in Joseph's prospects. Joseph wanted to go, and Sir William sweetened the deal by promising that Joseph could return home for a visit in a few months.[4] Joseph set off with two other young Mohawks of the Wolf Clan, Sander and Nickus, both of whom had accompanied Sir William on the Montreal campaign. They departed for Connecticut about the same time that Sir William left for Detroit. They were escorted by David Fowler, a Native American who had already lived at the school for two years.[5]

Now Joseph was back for the promised vacation, accompanied by a young European American missionary named Samuel Kirkland. Kirkland brought Sir William a letter from Reverend Wheelock giving a very good report of Molly's brother: "[Joseph] appears to be a considerate, Modest, and manly spirited youth. I am much pleasd with him."[6]

Joseph's success at the school was a tribute to his intelligence (both academic and social), his patience, and his desire to acquire British learning. Reverend Wheelock, though honest and well-intended, was very much a man of his time. A strict Calvinist with all the usual fire and brimstone beliefs that he propounded to his young charges at great length, he was also completely convinced of the superiority of British cultural mores and possessed a deep contempt for Joseph's native culture. Wheelock believed that through instruction in the Christian religion and British cultural practices, he could save a few Native Americans from the backward and heathen life from which they came. Joseph was, of course, a Christian when he came to the school, but the Congregationalist Wheelock would probably have preferred to work with a clean slate on that score rather than deal with the Church of England doctrines that Joseph had already imbibed from the pastors at the Fort Hunter chapel.

Sander and Nickus did not like the school. Both came home for good at the end of October 1761. Joseph would spend two years there, becoming proficient in English reading and writing. His positive experience at the school was doubtless helped by his greater knowledge of British customs observed on his visits to Molly and Sir William's household at Fort Johnson. It also mattered that Joseph already could speak some English and had arrived better dressed than Nickus and Sander, whom Wheelock described as "almost naked."⁷ Sir William had also apparently managed to convey to Wheelock that Joseph was special by letting the reverend know that Joseph was the brother of Sir William's housekeeper. Reverend Wheelock would have strongly disapproved had he understood the precise nature of Sir William and Molly's relationship. However, Sir William was by now so famous that Wheelock may have understood and chosen to ignore William and Molly's relationship, as many clergymen did when dealing with aristocratic benefactors. In any event, Wheelock did gain the impression that Joseph was "of a Family of Distinction," and Sir William was not shy about instructing the good reverend to let Joseph know that "his Sister & ca. are well and will be glad to hear often from him."⁸

The Moor School would play an important role in preparing Joseph Brant for a future unforeseen role on the international stage. Just as surprisingly, the young missionary sitting at Sir William and Molly's table in November 1761 would come to have a very serious impact on the lives of Molly Brant and her children. If he could have foreseen it, Sir William would have thrown Kirkland out of the house. Instead, after young Kirkland completed his theological studies, it was Sir William who influenced the Oneidas, the Six Nations tribe whose lands bordered the Mohawks, to accept Kirkland as their minister. Over the years Kirkland would become extremely influential with the Oneidas, and it would be Kirkland who would convince the Oneidas to break with the rest of the Six Nations and ally themselves with the Patriot cause. Fear of the Oneidas as much as fear of the Patriots would force Molly and her children to flee their Canajoharie home in the summer of 1777. Perhaps as she did so, she recalled the hospitality she had extended to her brother's friend so many years before. For the present, she fed the earnest young man and watched her brother instruct him in the Mohawk language.

* * *

In addition to Joseph, other members of Sir William and Molly's family circle were reaching adulthood in 1761, and that was soon to bring big changes for them all. In the spring of 1761 Daniel Claus, on assignment in Canada as Sir William's emissary to the Canadian Indians, had written Sir William a letter making two requests. Claus wanted a loan of 800 pounds so he could purchase a commission in the British Army, and he wanted to marry Sir William's elder daughter, Anne, now aged 21. Sir William had expected the first request. Claus had served him faithfully throughout the French and Indian War, and William had promised to help him get a start in life, which at age 34 was overdue. The second request was an utter shock. Although a fond and indulgent father, Sir William was frequently absent during the war, and he had apparently failed to notice that Nancy, as he called her, was now a young woman. When he expressed astonishment to Molly and his male Irish friends, he was met with knowing smirks. Had he really not noticed that Nancy and Daniel were sweet on each other?[9]

After pushing Claus off for months while Sir William undertook the mission to Detroit and Claus labored in Montreal, decision time finally arrived for Sir William. It was what Nancy wanted, and now that he was forced to think about it, didn't he really want her living close by him, married to a man he liked and respected?

When Claus returned to the Mohawk valley, Sir William gave his consent and asked Claus if rather than become an active-duty officer, he would instead become his deputy in charge of relations with the Canadian Indians. Claus sold his commission and accepted Sir William's offer. Anne Johnson and Daniel Claus were married on April 13, 1762, and moved into Sir William's original home, Mount Johnson, which they renamed Williamsburg in his honor. Each summer, Daniel Claus took a trip to Montreal to deal with the Canadian Indians on Sir William's behalf.[10]

Nancy and Daniel's nuptials broke the marital logjam in the Johnson family. Not too long afterward, Guy Johnson spoke to his uncle about his feelings for Mary (Polly) Johnson, Sir William's younger daughter, now about 19. This was easier for Sir William than Daniel Claus's proposal. William loved Guy almost like a son, and this union would mean that Polly too would live close by him. In a time when marriage between cousins was not unusual among the British gentry, Guy and Mary Johnson made their vows in late 1762 or early 1763 and soon moved into Guy Park, about two miles from Fort Johnson in present-day Amsterdam, New York.[11]

After a crusty start with poor Claus, Sir William now settled happily into his role as patriarch, writing to an old friend in February 1763 that "my Family is increased since you left us by Mrs Claus bringing forth a fine child of ye best or Female kind, and my youngest daughter marrying Lieut. Guy Johnson."[12]

That same month, Sir William had "thirty or forty sleds" bring up from New York City the materials for construction of what he would call "Johnson Hall." Located about 12 miles from Fort Johnson in present-day Johnstown, New York, it was larger and grander than Fort Johnson.[13] This would be the home that Sir William, Molly, and their children would occupy for the rest of Sir William's life. It was probably here that their third child was born, a daughter whom Molly named Magdalene.[14]

5. A Diplomat's Partner

Johnson Hall, Johnstown, Fulton County, New York. Library of Congress, Prints & Photographs Division, HABS NY-3107 Historic Buildings Survey, November 9, 1936. William Johnson and Thomas T. Waterman, creators. Nelson E. Baldwin, Stanley Mixon, and Thomas T. Waterman, photographers. Documentation compiled after 1933.

With Sir William's European American daughters now married women living in their own homes, Johnson Hall was probably where Molly felt herself finally and unquestionably to be the lady of the house. As her children's laughter rang through its spacious rooms and the household staff looked to her for instructions, it may have been easier to assure herself that despite the absence of a Christian marriage ceremony, Sir William would keep his promises.

* * *

Even as Molly and Sir William oversaw the changes in their family life and undertook the move to Johnson Hall, the outside world continued to claim much of Sir William's attention. Jeffery Amherst's Native American policies threatened to unravel not only the agreements Sir William had achieved at Detroit but also the entire legacy of his 20 years of Native American diplomacy.

Amherst had no respect for the spirit of reciprocity that underpinned Native American culture. No matter how much Sir William tried to explain the importance of the custom, Amherst viewed the gift giving that was expected at every Native American conference as bribery. Deeply distrustful of Native Americans, Amherst also issued the draconian order that they would no longer be allowed to trade for ammunition at British posts, and insisted that they should revert to the use of bows and arrows. Hundreds of Native Americans starved as husbands and fathers attempted to relearn the long lost skill.[15]

Over Sir William's strong objections, Amherst also seized control of the Niagara Carrying Place in Seneca country and built a blockhouse at the intersection of Lake Erie and the Sandusky River, enraging the Senecas and the western tribes.[16] The incursion of European American settlers into the Ohio Country was also a source of bitter resentment to Native Americans. Sir William argued to both Amherst and London that it should not be allowed. He also asked London to overrule Amherst's policy on ammunition and to grant Sir William money for presents and for staff for his Indian Department.[17]

By the spring of 1763, Sir William and everyone in his inner circle understood that the treaty with the western tribes was unlikely to hold and that the French Canadians, unhappy with the British domination of Canada, might stage surprise attacks in the Mohawk valley with the help of Canadian Native American allies.

In May, Molly sent Joseph, who was completing his second year at Reverend Wheelock's school, a letter written in Mohawk summoning him home. Wheelock was mystified as to the reason, but Joseph complied, arriving at Johnson Hall in mid–July. There he found Sir William sick in bed, exhausted from a trip to Albany to recruit militiamen for the defense of the frontier. Sick as he was, Sir William intended to travel to German Flatts to confer with his Six Nation allies. Meanwhile, he ordered that Johnson Hall be fortified by construction of a stockade, and he requested that Amherst send him some regulars to secure his home.[18]

At this dangerous time, Joseph's mother Margaret, Molly, and Sir William all wanted Joseph at home. On June 13 Johannes Tekarihoga, head sachem of the Mohawks, sent Sir William a message from Canajoharie that he had received war belts from the west. The rumors the Canajoharie Mohawks had been hearing were true. The conference at German Flatts must focus on diminishing the number of Senecas involved in the hostilities and preparing for the defense of the Mohawk valley.

The west was already ablaze. An Ottawa chieftain, Pontiac, encouraged by the Senecas, was leading a campaign, known as Pontiac's War, that would result in the death or capture of 2,000 settlers over the course of four months.[19]

Sir William rose from his sickbed and traveled to German Flatts. The conference began on July 18. In attendance were 340 Native Americans, with representatives from all of the Six Nations except the Senecas. Joseph Brant was there, and Molly very likely attended as well.[20] Every pro–British voice was needed to tamp down the resentments that Amherst's policies had caused. Although Molly would not have spoken at the council, she was undoubtedly active among the other Six Nations matrons, urging those with ties to the Senecas to bring them back into the fold and promising them that Sir William was laying their grievances before the king.

The Mohawks, Oneidas, Onondagas, Cayugas, and Tuscaroras did not let Sir William and Molly down. It was agreed that four representatives, including Little Abraham of the Mohawks, would go to the Senecas to inform them that the five eastern members of the confederacy would not go to war and urging that the Senecas too should refrain from participating in the conflict.[21]

Unable to get assistance from Amherst, Sir William reinforced Oswego with his own tenants. It was a tense summer as Sir William and Molly waited for events to play out at Johnson Hall. Two female slaves saw an unknown Native American man with a lance hiding in the woods. When they came running back to report it, Sir William "had all my people under arms the whole night."[22]

Joseph, home from Reverend Wheelock's school for good, acted as a messenger between Canajoharie and Sir William several times that summer. Finally, Joseph was able to bring word that the delegates had returned to Canajoharie. The news was somewhat encouraging. Two of the three Seneca castles had agreed to lay down their arms, and it was understood that the Senecas would not venture into the territory of the five eastern members of the confederacy to oppose the British.[23] Six Seneca representatives arrived at Johnson Hall in early September. It was Molly's role to provide hospitality and, by her presence and the presence of her children, to remind these wary men that Sir William was an ally.

Much of the energy was taken out of Pontiac's War when word came that the British and French had made peace in Europe. The Seven Years' War was over. As part of the deal, France ceded all of its territory east of the Mississippi River except New Orleans to Britain. There would be no help for the warring tribes from the French garrison at Fort Chartre in Illinois Country.[24]

Meanwhile, Sir William's advice was being heeded in London. Jeffery Amherst, who had once angrily told an aide he would like to give the Indians blankets contaminated with smallpox, was replaced as commander in chief by Thomas Gage. Gage had developed a deep respect for Sir William after Sir William's victory at Niagara. During the Montreal campaign, Gage had even allowed the distribution of some ammunition to Native Americans in contravention of Amherst's order because Sir William believed it was vitally important. After his promotion, one of Gage's first acts as commander in chief was to meet with Sir William at Albany.[25]

The British government also decided to accept Sir William's advice about western expansion. In the Proclamation of 1763, the border between the British colonies and Native American territory was set at the top of the Allegheny Mountains. European settlement west of the boundary was prohibited.[26] To deal with Native American complaints that they were being swindled by unscrupulous European Americans east of the boundary because such men often obtained deeds of land from one or two drunk Native Americans when the tribe had no intention of selling, the Crown decreed that future land purchases could only be undertaken by provincial governors at public councils attended by the entire tribe whose land was being purchased.[27]

Locally, in keeping with his agreement with the Canajoharie Mohawks, Sir William brought several justices of the peace to a meeting at Canajoharie attended by 33 women and 30 men of the tribe. The purpose was to make a formal complaint to the royal governor about George Klock's land claims. Molly's stepfather, Brant Kanagaradunkwa, was one of the speakers: "Brother[.] It is very hard we must be thus treated, there would have been mischief done long ago, had we not restrained our Warriors—We beg you will suppose it your own case, & reflect how you would act in case you had been wronged by us, as we have been wronged by Klock." Brant urgently requested a remedy: "As there are so many Justices now present, we hope they will consider what has passed, and that the whole proceedings may be Confirmed by them and faithfully transmitted to the Governor."[28]

Brant Kanagaradunkwa's speech in March 1763 is one of the last times he appears in the historical record. He died not long after. With the passing of this important ally, Sir William turned to Molly's brother, now about 20 years old, as one of the rising young men of the tribe. Although Joseph was not of aristocratic lineage, men of talent could rise among the Mohawks if they were successful war leaders or gifted orators. Sir William saw Joseph's potential in both of these capacities. Joseph's status in the tribe was enhanced by his family relationship with Sir William, and with Brant Kanagaradunkwa's passing, Sir William wanted and needed another intelligent ally among the Mohawks who deemed himself to be a member of Sir William's family.

* * *

During the fall of 1763, Sir William gave serious consideration to sending Joseph to New York City to study with Reverend Henry Barclay, the former pastor at Fort Hunter and now an influential Church of England minister, so that Barclay could prepare Joseph for admission to King's College (later Columbia University).[29] Although Sir William thought Joseph very capable academically, he was all too aware of the prejudices of the city folk Joseph would encounter. In the end, Sir William concluded that the chances of a constructive experience for Joseph were slight. Instead, Joseph continued his studies intermittently for another year or so with Cornelius Bennett, a British missionary at Canajoharie.[30]

Meanwhile, Joseph was continuing his apprenticeship as a warrior. The Six Nations' perennial enemies, the Shawnees and the Delawares, continued to raid European American settlements. In March 1764 Sir William sent Henry Montour, William Hare, and John Johnston (no relation) of the Indian Department with a war party of Mohawks and Oneidas that included Joseph Brant to retaliate against those two tribes. On their way south, the group stopped at Oquaga to recruit additional fighting men. The village, located on the east side of the Susquehanna River, contained 15 or 16 traditional longhouses. The village inhabitants were mainly Oneidas, with a few Mohawks and Tuscaroras also residing there.[31]

It was at Oquaga that Joseph met Neggen Aoghyatonghsera, a daughter of Oquaga's chief sachem, Isaac. Like Joseph, Isaac and his family were devout Christians. Sir William, who had known Isaac for many years, quoted Isaac as saying he was "determined to follow the Words of Jesus Christ as near as I can."[32]

Neggen was called Peggie, apparently because her baptismal name was Margaret. She was later described by Reverend Theophilus Chamberlain, a British missionary trained by Eleazar Wheelock, as "a handsome, Sober, discreet & a religious woman."[33]

Meanwhile, life continued at a busy pace at Johnson Hall. Molly, now firmly entrenched as the mother of a growing family there, was taking an active role in running the household. A letter survives from the period in which an Albany merchant apologizes to Sir William regarding "Mrs. Brant's complaint" for the poor performance of a stove that Sir William had purchased from him.[34]

Soon after Joseph's return from the Susquehanna valley, Sir William received congratulations from a friend on the birth of Polly and Guy Johnson's first child, a second granddaughter.[35] As he celebrated his newest descendant, Sir William also reflected on the lives of his ancestors. He had recently received word of his father's death in Ireland and decided to have a monument erected there in his memory. Tellingly, the inscription Sir William composed honored not only his parents, Christopher and Anne Johnson, but also Sir William's maternal grandfather and maternal uncle, Oliver and Peter Warren: "of a family Ancient in Descent, honorable in its Alliances, he married Anne Daughter of the aforesaid Sister to the before mentioned, Illustrious Commanders."[36]

As he contemplated his life, Sir William knew in his heart of hearts that much as he loved his father, without Anne Warren Johnson as his mother, he would have lived his life in County Meath as the Warren family's second-largest tenant. It was Peter Warren, difficult though he could be, who had given him a start in this new country, where a man of exceptional talent could rise far more easily than in Ireland, and it was the family relationship with this admiral and war hero that had made William acceptable to the snobbish aristocratic families of New York City who had the power to make a newcomer's path in the province difficult. It is no wonder that marriage on the frontier had always been such a fraught concept for Sir William. When he was young enough to undertake it, there was no woman willing to live in such primitive circumstances who could make Anne Warren Johnson's contribution to their children's future, and by the time he was a catch for such a woman, he was unwilling to sacrifice the children he loved, or his feelings for Molly Brant.

* * *

In the beginning of 1765, the price of receiving a constant flow of Native American delegations and numerous European and European American visitors at their home became clear when smallpox descended on Johnson Hall. On January 17 Sir William wrote to his Pennsylvania deputy, George Croghan: "The smallpox in my family will prevent my meeting the Six Nations as Soon as I intended."[37] On January 20 he sent a message to the Six Nations warning them to stay away from Johnson Hall because his family had smallpox.[38] On February 7 he wrote thanking the Six Nations sachems "for the concern expressed at my Family's Indisposition." Like many Europeans, he had apparently survived the disease in childhood, because in the same message he also announced his intention to travel to Canajoharie to conduct business. Given his concern about spreading the disease to the Six Nations, he would not have decided to visit Canajoharie unless he knew he was immune.[39]

Molly and their children all eventually recovered from the disease. Given the far higher death rates suffered by Native Americans, Molly, now about 29 years old, was lucky to survive, but her beauty suffered. Daniel Claus described her as having been "likely" prior to her bout with smallpox.[40] Although outsiders may have found her less attractive, the scars did not affect Sir William's attraction to her. The couple would have five more children in the remaining nine years of his life.

Molly and Sir William's three young children's chances of survival were probably improved by having a genetic makeup that was 50 percent European. The experience was sufficiently terrifying, however, that Sir William became a proponent of inoculation. Although first introduced to America in 1721, the procedure was only now becoming more widely

5. A Diplomat's Partner

available and was still considered to be both experimental and dangerous. Nevertheless, when smallpox returned to the Mohawk valley in 1769, Sir William insisted that Anne Claus and Mary Johnson's children be inoculated.[41] He also arranged for "Inoculating near 40 Indians" at Crown expense.[42] He would again have inoculations performed in 1772 for "54 Indian children at the request of their Nation"[43] and in 1773, "Innoculating near 100 Indians in their own Countrys."[44]

By the spring of 1765 the family had recovered, and Sir William and Molly were again hosting a stream of visitors at Johnson Hall. Sir William was also still going through the highly political process of getting his massive land grant from the Canajoharie Mohawks approved by the Crown. He was only too happy to receive a letter from Major Charles Lee, a regular British Army officer who had served with Sir William in the Niagara and Montreal campaigns (and would one day be a general in the Continental Army) regarding the embarrassment of a very prominent noble family. Lady Susan Strangway, a niece of a member of the king's council, had married a commoner. "Her father and uncle ... are desirous of providing for them, but not at home. They turned their eyes to America where they have thoughts of ... obtaining a grant of lands as an establishment for their family."[45]

Who better to consult about this awkward situation than Sir William Johnson, lord of the Mohawk valley? Sir William wrote gleefully to Cadwallader Colden, an ally in the New York provincial government: "I have had Lord Adam Gordon & Lady O Bryen & her Husband here, the Two latter Spoke to me a good deal on the Subject of their land. ... I have proposed to him ... [that] I should procure an Additional Tract to that of mine at Canajohare which I should divide with him, provided his Majesty would Grant the Whole." Lest Colden fail to connect the dots, Sir William added, "As I apprehend their Connections at home can verry easily procure this, I realy don't know a better Step to take than to interest them therein.... I can without much difficulty I think obtain a good addition to this Tract from the Oneidas."[46]

It was customary in the 18th-century British Empire for the government to financially reward war heroes for their services to king and country. Sir William's uncle, Admiral Peter Warren, had become a wealthy man through the prize system, which granted a naval commander the right to personally seize the cargoes of enemy ships he captured. Sir William, though granted a baronetcy and a cash gift of 5,000 pounds after the battle of Lake George, had actually found his service to the Crown to be expensive. He constantly had to spend his own money for gifts to the Six Nations and for expenses of the colonial militia. Reimbursement by the colonial legislature was slow and sometimes never came. He was completely convinced that the Crown had a moral obligation to "grant the only favour I have ever asked" by confirming the deal he had struck with the Canajoharie Mohawks via the required royal patent. Most great men of the empire would have agreed with him.[47]

The other personage mentioned in Sir William's letter to Colden was Lord Adam Gordon, the uncle of a duke and also interested in New York land investments. Gordon and Sir William hit it off immediately. They actually liked each other and also understood that they could be useful allies to one another. Upon hearing that Sir William was concerned that his son had never been to England, Lord Adam offered to be young John Johnson's host for an extended visit:

> "If ever it is in my Power—I am ready—& shall feel pleased in obeying Your Commands; particularly should they relate, to a Young Gentleman of worth, whose only misfortune, is not knowing more of Home—& the World, at Home." Gordon assured the fond father, "You may trust me—He'll return to America, more fit to serve it—& not less so, to serve himself."[48]

These words were written unashamedly by Lord Gordon, and they were music to Sir William's ears. This is how a young man of quality was educated in the 18th-century British Empire. He was expected both to serve his country and to provide for himself and his family, just as Sir William had done. In order to accomplish this, a young man's relatives and friends of his relatives saw to it that he was introduced to the right people, that he cultivated important relationships and developed an understanding of how personal and political goals were achieved. When Lord Gordon sailed for England in the fall, John Johnson, then about 23, accompanied him for what would be a visit of almost two years.[49]

Molly was an active presence during the visit of these three important guests. Lady Susan would later comment favorably on her bearing and good humor, describing her as a "well-bred and pleasant lady."[50] Lady Susan, of course, had cast convention aside to marry the man she wanted. She may have been something of a free spirit, willing to judge a person outside the constraints of class and race.

Lord Gordon, though a jolly fellow, apparently viewed Molly more conventionally, as one would expect of a British aristocrat. He was used to men of his class having mistresses, many of them of lower social rank than their lovers. One was, of course, polite to such a woman when an aristocratic lover chose to have her about, but she could never be considered a social equal. Thus, Lord Gordon's thank-you note to Sir William after his stay at Johnson Hall contained a sincere but limited apology: "I was so ashamed of our riotousness ... and of our friend Guy's Noise, after you were asleep—that I made off, before Sun Rise—wishing to avoid [if I con] a sight of Lady Susan.... When I see You again—we will not be hampered, with fine Ladies.—I suffered much for Mrs. Claus—and endeavoured, all in my power not to disturb Her—but Guy must answer for all."[51]

In Lord Gordon's world, Lady Susan and Sir William's daughter, Anne Claus, were ladies. Their comfort must be considered. Molly Brant, who slept (or attempted to sleep) beside Sir William while Lord Gordon and Guy Johnson partied on, was not worthy of such consideration. Obliviously, Lord Gordon added a postscript to his letter, which was sent from Canada: "The squaws here are but middling—My love to Molly & thanks for her good breakfast."[52]

Molly apparently rose before dawn after a sleepless night to give Lord Gordon breakfast before he departed. As far as Gordon was concerned, it was just another of her services. The fact that Sir William had three children with her did not raise her status in Lord Gordon's eyes, but Sir William was to be complimented for having better taste in woman flesh than the British officers in Canada. Whether or not Sir William winced when he read Gordon's postscript, Gordon's attitude confirmed his belief that in his complicated world, although Molly was his wife in the eyes of the Native American allies who had helped him attain his honored position in the British Empire, she could never be his wife in the eyes of his own people.

Sir William's determination on this point would be tested further that summer. On July 22, 1765, at Canajoharie, Reverend Theophilus Chamberlain married Joseph Brant and Peggie as well as Sir William's son Brant Keghneghtaga Johnson and Margaret Campbell, a young European American woman who had been held captive for much of her childhood by one of the western tribes but had been recently released as part of the peace treaty Sir William negotiated the previous year.[53]

The marriages were a big event. At the feast that followed the ceremony, a whole ox was roasted for the village, complemented by generous amounts of rum and wine, the Mohawk staple of boiled corn, and a variety of pies for dessert.[54] Molly attended the weddings, but Sir William did not, pleading illness. Sir William certainly did suffer chronic ill health, so it is possible that he was truly too sick to attend the weddings of his son and Molly's only sibling, but his health did not prevent him from entertaining guests at Johnson Hall only a few weeks before or from conducting business throughout the summer. What is more likely is that being forced to stand beside Molly and their three children while his son and her brother took the vows of holy matrimony with their fiancées was just too uncomfortable a situation for Sir William too bear.

Whether Molly used the occasion to reopen discussion of their own lack of the sacrament can only be surmised. Thomas Jones, a justice of the

Supreme Court of the province of New York, a friend of Sir William's and a visitor at Johnson Hall, described Molly as "handsome, sensible, judicious, and political." He also observed her and Sir William to have "all the intimacy of the most conjugal affection."[55] Molly certainly saw the contempt in Jeffery Amherst's eyes when he visited Fort Johnson. She was probably also discerning enough to notice the little ways in which Lord Gordon treated Lady Susan and Anne Claus differently and better than her at Johnson Hall. These things probably confirmed Sir William's argument that his people would not accept their marriage.

If a marriage ceremony was only a British legal detail in her mind, perhaps she would have remained silent. "She loved Sir William to adoration," according to Justice Jones,[56] and therefore probably believed he would provide for her and their children after his death, an event she didn't like to think about. But what about their souls? She was well aware from the time of her mother's humiliation at the Fort Hunter chapel when she was a teen that the Christian religion forbade sex outside of marriage. Like her brother Joseph, whom Reverend Chamberlain described as praying nightly, Molly was religious.[57] In later years she was known to own a Mohawk Bible, and she and her younger son, George, would be founding members of the Anglican Church at Kingston, Ontario, which she attended regularly.[58] How did Sir William respond when she worried that they were risking damnation?

It is clear that Sir William did believe in God. The motto he chose when he was made a baronet was "Deo regique debeo" (I owe God and the King).[59] It is also clear that he believed God expected him to treat both his tenants and his Native American allies as human beings, a concept foreign to many other Christian Europeans of the time, and that he was prepared to expend both effort and money to fulfill that obligation. His last advice to his son John contained in his will was "I do most earnestly recommend it to my Son to shew lenity to such of the Tenants as are poor and an upright conduct in all his dealing with mankind, which, will (upon reflection) afford more satisfaction & heart feeling pleasure to a noble & generous mind, than the greatest opulency."[60]

What Sir William told Molly when she tried to discuss their unmarried state with him is their secret. Perhaps he reminded her that God knew how much she wanted to be married, that she was much younger than he, and if after his death she wished to seek forgiveness from a minister, Sir William watching from the other side would understand. For himself, he would rely on God's mercy for a life in which, but for the glaring exception of slavery, which he did not acknowledge, Sir William had tried to treat others decently and to provide for everyone he loved.

6

Providing for the Future

As summer passed into fall, happy news arrived at Johnson Hall that Anne Claus was safely delivered of a second child, Sir William's first grandson, named William Johnson Claus, in his grandfather's honor.[1] Hard on the heels of the happy event came political news that was a harbinger of the challenging future awaiting Molly and the rest of Sir William's large and growing family. Word came from Boston of violent protests against the Stamp Act. Recently enacted by Parliament, the act was an attempt to finance the cost of frontier forts and garrisons required to enforce the terms of the peace treaty with France and to facilitate trade with the Native American tribes.[2]

Sir William saw the Stamp Act as a way to properly finance the Indian Department's efforts to prevent trade abuses against Native Americans. Under the reforms he had recommended, trade was only to occur at the forts, where a representative of the Indian Department and an interpreter would always be present. In addition, a much-desired blacksmith would be available at each of the forts to repair Native American weapons and implements.[3]

From Sir William's perspective it was obvious that these reforms were necessary if peace was to be maintained on the frontiers. Living far from Boston and New York City, Sir William dismissed the leaders of the Stamp Act protests as "a few pretended patriots" who "have propagated their republican principles amongst an ignorant people."[4] When Parliament gave way to the protests and repealed the Stamp Act only a year after it was enacted, Sir William wrote to London warning that the lack of funding would tie his hands and that Native American anger over continuing trade abuses could cause another Indian war.[5]

Shortly thereafter Henry Moore, the governor of New York, arrived at Johnson Hall. He was there to assist Sir William in his quest to finalize the Kingsland patent. Also present were 80 Oneidas, who were there to sell to the governor (as now required by law) two tracts of land near German Flatts. The governor could then legally convey this land to Sir

William and his partners. This was the land that Sir William had mentioned the previous year in his letter to Cadwallader Colden. Also present at Johnson Hall was a delegation of Canajoharie Mohawks who confirmed their 1760 gift to Sir William.[6] Sir William now had enough land to divide among those people, both in New York and in London, who were critical in pushing through the patenting of the vast Kingsland tract. The financial future of Sir William's children, both European and Native American, was now close to being ensured. As Molly walked among the assembled Oneidas and Mohawks seeing to the distribution of food and presents, she was keenly aware that this event was the capstone of seven years of effort. Although she probably understood that in the British way of doing things Sir William's eldest son, John, would benefit most, she also knew that her own children would live financially secure lives because of these transactions.

Sir William wrote triumphantly to General Gage, a partner in the deal: "I exerted my Interest so far as to obtain from the Oneidas a verry Valuable & extensive Tract of Land lying near the North side of the Mohawk River above the German Flatts. ... I cannot only affirm that no body else could have effected this purchase, but also that it is both with regard to Soil & Scituation the verry best and only Tract that could have been obtained. I have reserved to my self Just a fifth part."[7]

While all of this is shocking to present-day eyes and would be completely illegal today, none of the British men involved in the partnership thought they were doing anything wrong. The group of partners who had been assembled were distinguished individuals capable of getting the attention of the king and council to conclude a favorable business transaction. The Oneidas and the Canajoharie Mohawks were to receive some money for the land, and Sir William had agreed to help both the Oneidas and the Canajoharie Mohawks seek legal redress against George Klock, who was continuing his program of obtaining deeds of tribal lands from individual Native Americans under the influence of alcohol.[8] From the Oneidas' and Mohawks' perspective, if they could turn back the hands of time, they would certainly have preferred that all the European people in the Mohawk valley had never come there, but they were well aware of the many crimes and depredations being inflicted on Native American tribes in Pennsylvania, Virginia, and North Carolina by European settlers, and they preferred that the territory near their villages be settled by tenants of Sir William and his friends, a man who did not wish them dead and who kept his word.

There continued to be a few warning signs that the hierarchical society of Britain, where the government and the economy were dominated by a coterie of men privileged by birth and those talented and useful enough

6. Providing for the Future

to intermarry with them, was not taking such firm root in America. A few months after Sir William's successful real estate closing at Johnson Hall, some impertinent farmer from the Mohawk valley (very possibly George Klock) sent an anonymous open letter to the Sons of Liberty in Albany suggesting that Sir William Johnson should be chastised for his support of the Stamp Act.

News of the fate of Thomas Hutchinson's Boston mansion had by now reached upper New York, so this was no laughing matter, especially since the Dutch merchants of Albany had never been friends of Sir William. Sir William sent his son-in-law, Guy Johnson, to a lawyer in New York City to find out if he could obtain any redress in the courts. The lawyer was sympathetic, but not encouraging: "Tho I think it clear the Anonymous Author had Mischief in his Heart, yet I fear he is not liable to be punished for it is not a Libel, because if every Thing he alledges was true, it is not scandalous." Moreover, the writer had been careful to make no specific threat: "nor is it a threatening Letter to extort money ... nor is there any express Request or Desire that the Sons of Liberty should do any Mischief, tho' probably it was his Intent, to excite them to it."[9]

Despite this alarming incident, it was difficult for Sir William to understand the titanic shift in thinking that was occurring in America. He and friends such as Lord Adam Gordon and another frequent correspondent, James Rivington, the prominent New York City Tory newspaper editor and bookseller, believed that force might have to be used against the radicals who were rioting in Boston and New York City, but the idea that in less than a decade America would be engulfed in wholesale rebellion would have left them incredulous.[10] Sir William believed profoundly that the British Constitution was the best system of government ever created by man. He also believed that every man had an obligation to be honorable, be he a king, a baronet, or a tenant farmer. Important components of honor were fair treatment and charity by superiors to inferiors and respect and loyalty from inferiors to their superiors. When these moral imperatives were observed, it was a happy life for all. Through intelligence, hard work, courage, and, yes, a little help from Peter Warren, Sir William had made this system work for him. He had trouble understanding that in Boston, New York City, Philadelphia, and increasingly in rural areas such as the Mohawk valley, there were men of intelligence and talent who rejected these traditional reciprocal obligations as a restraint on their liberties.

* * *

Molly cared little about the Stamp Act repeal except as it affected Sir William's ability to ensure smooth relations between the European Americans and her people. Amid the constant flow of activity at Johnson Hall in

1766, there was little time to worry about it. She was probably more preoccupied with important departures from her family circle that occurred at this time. Joseph and Peggie accompanied Sir William to the peace treaty negotiations following Pontiac's War and remained at Oswego so Joseph could work as the Indian Department interpreter there. Sir William conferred upon Joseph a fine salary of 70 pounds sterling per year, more than either a minister or a schoolmaster could earn. Sir William also intervened when the fort's commander tried to assign Joseph to quarters in the barracks. Joseph and Peggie were instead given their own quarters. It is there that their first child, a son named Isaac Karaguantier, was born.[11]

The more wrenching parting for Molly that year was with her eldest child, Peter, now seven years old. There was still no school in the vicinity of Johnson Hall, so Sir William sent him to board with Reverend Thomas Brown in Albany.[12] Although sending male children of that age to boarding school was fairly common practice among well-off European Americans living in rural areas, it was a difficult transition for Molly. Male Six Nations teens went on extended hunting trips with fathers and uncles, but boys younger than 12 were rarely without their mothers. Molly apparently insisted on lengthy vacations. On January 30, 1767, Reverend Brown wrote to Sir William diplomatically "suggesting" that it was time for "Master Peter" to return to school.[13]

Probably responding to Molly, Peter, and his own feelings, Sir William hit on an alternative solution. Peter was placed in a school in Schenectady, about 15 miles closer to Johnson Hall than Albany, probably allowing the little boy to be brought home more frequently.[14]

The question of how to educate his bicultural children was much on Sir William's mind. The year before, he had sent William of Canajoharie, then about 15, to Reverend Wheelock's school in Connecticut. It was not going well. The boy was struggling with his identity and responding angrily to Wheelock's methods. During his off-and-on residence at Fort Johnson and Johnson Hall as a boy, William had come to understand that his father was a great man and that in the British system the sons of great men were treated with deference. Wheelock, however, held the Congregationalist view that young people should engage in significant amounts of servile labor to take the pride out of them. He certainly was not going to make an exception for a boy he thought of as Sir William's half–Native American bastard. William, like other students at the school, was assigned substantial chores. Matters came to a head when Reverend Wheelock's son, Ralph, ordered William to saddle his horse. William refused on the grounds that his father was a gentleman. When Ralph sarcastically expressed doubt that he knew what a gentleman was, William retorted, "A gentleman is a person who keeps race horses and drinks Madeira wine, and that is what neither you nor your father do. Therefore, saddle the horse yourself!"[15]

Sir William's initial reaction was that William must obey the rules of the school but, upon reflection, made the decision to send him to study in Lancaster, Pennsylvania, with Reverend Thomas Barton, a man of gentler methods and with a deeper sympathy for William's unusual situation.[16] At first, things went very well: "And I have now the Pleasure to assure you that his Behaviour has given me entire Satisfaction—He is learning Arithmetick, & the Progress he makes is really surprising. He will soon write a Hand fit for any Business.... I have the most favourable Expectations of him, & shall be very happy if I can make him answer yours."[17]

Reverend Barton was candid with Sir William about the challenges his bicultural son was struggling with: "In his Disposition, he is naturally obliging, generous & good-natured, tho' he appears to have Something of the sullen, reserved & unsociable in his Temper—He has a Kind of rustic Diffidence or Bashfulness, which is injurious to him." As Sir William had feared, young William was also encountering the bigotry of the local citizenry. Reverend Barton was trying to teach him to ignore it: "Upon his first coming to Lancaster he challenged almost every Person he met with; & box'd half the Young Dutch Men in Town.... I have prevail'd upon him to lay them aside, So that he is now as peaceable a Lad as any in the Place."[18]

Sir William responded gratefully: "I am also well pleased that you have weaned him from those Athletick Exercises which I know he was fond of, and which in the present Age intitle the Champion to no other Prizes than such as you mention."[19]

Despite William's academic progress and his efforts to ignore personal insults, Lancaster was a frontier town, and it was impossible to shield the boy from knowledge of the grave injustices regularly meted out to other Native Americans by the settlers. Only two months after Sir William's letter to Reverend Barton, William left school: "I am sorry that William should be the Bearer of this Letter—But since the turbulent & disordered State of the Back Counties, occasioned by the Murder committed upon several Indians by one Stump, & the rescue of that Villain & the lawless insolent Behaviour of some of the Inhabitants, in Consequence thereof, he has relaxed in Application to Study, been uneasy in Mind."[20]

Barton, a decent man, recommended some time at home, and then a return to school. Sir William undoubtedly expressed his disgust at the actions of the settlers when he talked to his son in person but also told him that the colonial governments, not the superintendent of Indian affairs, controlled justice in such matters. Whatever Sir William said was not enough to make the young man feel comfortable with his ambiguous status.

It probably did not help that William's half brother, John Johnson, had recently returned from his two-year visit to Britain. Knighted by the king shortly after his arrival, as another mark of the king's continuing desire to honor Sir William, young Sir John was now ensconced as the master of Fort Johnson, a substantial estate worked by 10 to 15 enslaved people.[21] William did not return to school. Soon he was drinking heavily and causing disturbances in the neighborhood. After "repeated admonitions" and "assurances of amendment," it became clear that young William was happier with his mother's people than he could ever be at Johnson Hall.[22] His father would leave him a substantial bequest in his will, and William would retain his affection for his stepmother, Molly, who leaned on him in widowhood, but William would live the rest of his short life at Canajoharie.[23]

William's tortured adolescence had a profound effect on Sir William's thinking about the education of Molly's children. They would of course maintain loving family relationships with their mother's relatives and speak fluent Mohawk, an invaluable skill in the family business, but they must identify primarily as European Americans. Their mother's people continued to diminish in numbers. Their father's people continued to increase. It was essential that Molly's children be able to accept the world as it was while helping to create a buffer for their mother's people in the Mohawk valley. Sir William's vision was a future in which Molly's children would each be significant landowners, with bequests carved out of the Kingsland patent. They would be good neighbors to the Mohawks. The boys (George came along in 1769) would also engage in the fur trading business, as Sir William had done, a further source of prosperity for them.[24] The girls would have dowries sizable enough to attract decent and talented European Americans such as Daniel Claus as husbands.

Sir William now realized that he had waited too long to begin William's English education. Of course, William's situation had been different, because his dead mother's relatives had always expected to have him at Canajoharie for substantial periods during his childhood. In the stable home that Sir William and Molly were creating, their children's English education could and should begin much sooner. That was why, hard as it was for both him and Molly to send precious little Peter to boarding school, it had to be done.

Molly probably did not disagree with Sir William's assessment of their children's situation. She had shared in Sir William's unsuccessful struggle to give William of Canajoharie peace of mind. After Sir William's death, when she returned to Canajoharie, she would send Elizabeth and Magdalene to boarding school in Schenectady, and after Molly's flight from the Mohawk valley, she would sadly accept Daniel Claus and Frederick

Haldimand's advice to send the younger children to a boarding school in Montreal. Throughout the war years, Molly repeatedly brought the loss of her daughters' dowries to the attention of British officials.[25]

* * *

The choices that Sir William was making for his own children did not mean that he believed that Native Americans should be forced into rapid assimilation. His views on Native American assimilation were nuanced. With respect to the western tribes, "They cannot be brought under our laws for some centuries."[26] The Mohawks, Oneidas, and Tuscaroras, who had experienced close European contact for more than a century and were increasingly Christian, should be encouraged to send their best young men to British schools. These young men would slowly convince other members of their tribes of the benefits of adopting European forms of agriculture and property ownership. The three other Six Nations tribes—the Onondagas, Cayugas, and Senecas—were much less Christian than the Mohawks, Oneidas, and Tuscaroras and were probably decades away from having any interest in reorganizing their societies. A slow conversion to Christianity, gradual European settlement near them, and the passage of time were the means by which this would be accomplished, not by force.

In a long letter to Reverend Charles Inglis, a prominent New York City Anglican minister who was convinced of the need to promptly "civilize" the native populations, Sir William did his best to educate the minister as to the practical reasons this was not a good idea: "If the Indians are to be Civilized in order to be made Christians, which is generally deemed the best, Method to pursue, They would be apt to take the Alarm, being much more averse to that way of Life, than they are to Christianity, and the public would in a little time if the plan should meet success, and be carried on Extensively lose the benefit of the Furr Trade."[27]

Sir William described for Reverend Inglis his long conversations with gifted Six Nations people on the subject and conveyed the respect he held for their concerns about assimilation: "They say that it appears to them to have been ordained from the beginning that the White People should cultivate the Arts, and themselves pursue hunting, that no other Way of Life is agreeable to them, or consistent with their Maxims of policy and the frame of their Constitution." These people saw no benefit to adopting European ways: "They find all those Inds. who from their situation and our endeavors are become Civilized ... are poor, abject, full of Avarice, Hypocrisy, & in short have imbibed our Vices, without any of our Good Qualities."[28]

Sir William was unwilling to engage in the hypocrisy of denying the truth of these arguments or fail to acknowledge the reason why Europeans were so anxious for assimilation to occur: "and I am sorry to say that they are in General too well founded & these with the additional Apprehension that their adopting such a plan would be followed by their Annihilation as a people cause them to be extremely Jealous of any Endeavors to promote such a design."[29]

In his diplomatic but direct way, Sir William suggested that Reverend Inglis should drop his preconceived notions and accept that assimilation would take decades and would only succeed if the hearts and minds of Europeans changed: "I am persuaded it must one day take place, but … the Notion must flow from themselves, & that they must fall into it when our increas'd Numbers place them more in our Neighbourhood, & that they discover Superior Advantages in our Way of Living than in their own. … [T]he implacable resentment of the frontier Inhabitants of wch they are daily giving proofs, forbids that reliance on our Motives of Action & that Harmony which shod. Be the foundation of our hopes with them."[30]

* * *

As Sir William penned these thoughts, Molly's brother, Joseph, was living out his own complicated balance between the world of the Mohawks and the world of their European American neighbors. After a year at Oswego as an Indian Department interpreter, Joseph returned with his wife and baby son to Canajoharie in the spring of 1767. Traditionally, the family would have lived at Oquaga, the home of Peggie's family. Instead, they followed the European custom of living with the husband's family. Joseph's mother, Margaret, welcomed them joyfully. Joseph had arranged for Reverend Chamberlain to board with her in his absence. That had not gone well. Delivering "hellfire" sermons on Sundays, Reverend Chamberlain also ran a school for the village children. The Mohawks, who did not believe in corporal punishment, were shocked to see him chasing young children with a horse whip, an acceptable means of chastisement to some Europeans.[31]

Upon his return Joseph, now 24 years old, was among the most prosperous men of the village. Although the Mohawks continued to hold most of their land communally, he had used his share of the Kingsland money to purchase 80 acres in fee simple from the tribe. Sir William had augmented Joseph's holdings with a gift of 512 acres, probably as a wedding present.[32]

Joseph, Peggie, the baby, and Margaret lived in the house Margaret had shared with Brant Kanagaradunkwa. It was furnished with two beds, a table and 12 chairs, fireplace implements, and a cabinet. When not hunting or fishing, Joseph often dressed in English clothing, as did his wife. He owned a wagon, a plow, a harrow, and both a hauling sled and a pleasure sled. His fields grew wheat, corn, beans, and squash, and he raised cattle, sheep, and pigs. He employed hired men to perform the heavy labor. He continued to supplement his income with interpreting assignments from the Indian Department. Only about two miles from Joseph's farm was that of Nicholas Herkimer, grandson of one of the original German Palatine settlers at German Flatts. Within a decade, Joseph and Herkimer would find themselves contesting for ownership of the Mohawk valley.[33]

Margaret was delighted to have at least one grandchild living with her at Canajoharie. In the Mohawks' matrilineal society, she would have more likely expected it to be her daughter's children who resided with her. Molly gave birth to a fourth child in 1767, whom she named in honor of her mother, but she and her children continued to live 50 miles away at Johnson Hall.[34]

* * *

Molly was an increasingly prominent figure at the numerous Indian conferences held at Johnson Hall during these years. Justice Thomas Jones described her as "political" and as having "great art" in advancing Sir William's agenda at these conferences.[35] Molly's role was that of engaging in quiet conversations with influential matrons and sachems. Sir William did the orating at public councils. Molly also played a role in the distribution of food and gifts. Her diplomatic skills and her status as Sir William's partner were sufficient to cause her to be named senior matron of the most prestigious society of Six Nations matrons, a position normally reserved for a woman of more aristocratic lineage than Molly.[36]

For Molly, the busy, happy days at Johnson Hall continued to be tinged with concern about Sir William's serious health issues. One day in the summer of 1767, he collapsed unconscious to the floor. Having tried a variety of European remedies that had proved useless, he acceded to the urging of Molly and other Native American friends that he try Native American methods. Escorted by a group of Six Nations companions, he was taken by boat to Schenectady. He was then carried by litter deep into the woods to New Lebanon Springs, New York, where he bathed in and drank from the spring waters.[37] He was also treated with medicinal roots: "There are many simples in this country which are, I believe, unknown to the learned, notwithstanding the surprising success with which they are administered by the Indians."[38]

Although probably providing some temporary relief to Sir William's tortured body, the spring waters and herbs did not cure him. Back at Johnson Hall late that fall, he described a litany of health problems to his friend Samuel Johnson, the president of King's College: "My Complaints unhappily are many and attack me often together—The Ball which was Lodged in my thigh in the Battle at Lake George in 1755 becomes daily more troublesome to me, insomuch that I can very rarely attempt to Sit on a horse or take my usual Exercise." There was also a condition that may have been a parasitic disease but, given his rather heavy drinking, could also have been a liver ailment: "The Disorder you speak of which is much more Dangerous & troublesome is very difficult to describe as the Doctors are at a Loss what to call it, it first attacked me in 1761. put me to the most Excruciating torture." The symptoms were truly alarming: "during which I became delirious, its duration about 4 or 5 days, since which Time I have had Several returns of the Like sometimes Thrice in a Year but at Very irregular & uncertain periods. It seems seated near the stomach which Swells much during the Paroxysm of the Disorder attended with a Jaundiced Countenance the Eyes being particularly discoloured."[39]

Sir William was determined to continue his demanding work as superintendent of Indian affairs, despite his severe health problems. Shortly after his return from New Lebanon Springs, he set off for a conference at Onondaga, a journey of more than 100 miles lasting several weeks.[40] For the next several years he would continue a pattern of completing exhausting frontier diplomatic missions, only to return home in a state of collapse.

* * *

In March 1768 Sir William and Molly hosted a Native American conference at Johnson Hall attended by 700 people. The violence committed by settlers in western Pennsylvania against the Native American tribes there was a major topic of concern.[41]

In Sir William's mind, the solution was obvious. Where settlements already existed, the colonial governments needed to take strong action against criminality: punish those who murdered and robbed the neighboring tribes in the same manner as they punished miscreants when the victims were European Americans. Sir William also believed deeply that a permanent border between the British colonies and the western tribes needed to be established and enforced. The boundary set by the Proclamation of 1763 had been viewed by the governments in both London and the colonies as a wartime expedient that the colonial governments were taking no action to enforce. There were already significant encroachments.[42] In Sir William's view, these encroachments would inevitably lead to trouble. There was plenty of land east of the boundary that settlers could fill in. Only when that land was completely occupied decades hence should the western tribes be approached about land sales, which should then be executed through lawful procedures conducted by the Crown.

These opinions fit in with the orderly world Sir William was trying to establish in the Mohawk valley. Great men formed consortiums to obtain large tracts of land from the Crown. Tenant settlers were then recruited to farm these lands. Sir William believed that the landlords had a moral obligation to treat their tenants well. He also believed that it made sound business sense to do so because tenants felt loyalty to a good landlord.

For his part, Sir William was regarded as an excellent landlord, as he gave his tenants generous terms. Tenants were charged no rent for the first five years, when they were occupied with the arduous task of clearing the land. For the next 10 years, the rent was below the market rate elsewhere. His leases were two or three lifetimes in length. Sir William tended to recruit groups of tenants from Ireland and the Scottish Highlands who were used to a semifeudal society with landlords far harsher than him. His tenants came from the kind of place Sir William had come from, and they did not mind that no one but Sir William could operate a sawmill on his lands or that any ores discovered on a tenancy belonged to Sir William. Accustomed to a hard life in the old country, his tenants were grateful that they had 15 years to get on their feet in a new land.[43]

But there were other people coming to America who wanted to own their own land and resented the large landlords. These immigrants believed that any rent was "tribute" and that land should belong to the man who worked it. To their way of thinking, Native Americans did not work the land. These settlers had no problem with occupying land they viewed as vacant even though it had been Native American hunting grounds from time out of mind.[44]

By the time of the March 1768 Johnson Hall conference, Sir William had obtained permission from the Crown to negotiate with the tribes for a permanent boundary that theoretically was to be firmly enforced by the Crown and the colonial governments. He announced a meeting to be held at Fort Stanwix in the fall, to be attended by all interested tribes and by representatives of the affected colonies.[45]

It was essential that Sir William get agreement from the Six Nations before making his proposals to tribes such as the Delawares and Shawnees with which he did not enjoy the same close relationship. The Six Nations believed themselves to be the overlords of the Delawares and Shawnees based on wars that in many cases had been fought seven or eight decades before. The Six Nations sometimes accepted payment for lands occupied by the Delawares and Shawnees on the basis of this overlordship, although they did not occupy these lands in the sense that the United States occupied Japan and West Germany after World War II. Instead, the Six Nations exercised their suzerainty by hunting in these territories and by sending out an occasional war party if these hunting expeditions encountered any resistance. As the Six Nations continued to experience reductions in numbers due to disease and war, the Delawares and Shawnees were becoming louder in their insistence that the Six Nations had no right to sell their territories.⁴⁶

Sir William set out on September 15 for Fort Stanwix, located at present-day Rome, New York. The journey was about 75 miles. He brought with him 20 boatloads of presents. There is no record of whether Molly traveled with him, but given the importance of the conference, her position among the Six Nations matrons, and the size of the Mohawk delegation (238 people), it is likely that she did.⁴⁷

Governor William Franklin, Ben Franklin's son, represented New Jersey. The governor of Virginia sent a commissioner. As always with large conferences, it took more than a month for all of the Native Americans to arrive. On October 13, Sir William wrote to General Gage that 900 were assembled but that he expected a total of 3,000.⁴⁸

As they waited, bad news arrived from home. Daniel Claus, having stopped at Williamsburg on his way to Fort Stanwix from his annual Canadian business trip, found Anne nursing their critically ill third child, a toddler named after her mother. Four days later Daniel sent word that the little girl had passed away, dying in her mother's arms: "Her Mother bears the loss of her child [with] more Fortitude and Resignation than I expected."⁴⁹ On October 5 at 5 p.m., representatives of the Six Nations, the Delawares, the Nanticokes, the Conoys, and the Munseys gathered outside Sir William's quarters at Fort Stanwix "and in a very handsome manner performed the ceremony of condolence." By October 24, the bereaved father had arrived to assist his father-in-law in the Indian Department's most important negotiation.⁵⁰

The government in London had authorized Sir William to conclude a treaty that formalized a boundary at the junction of the Ohio and Kanawha Rivers. The deal Sir William actually finalized with the tribes pushed the boundary 400 miles farther west so that most of the land in present-day West Virginia and Kentucky was included. The total cost to the Crown was about 13,000 pounds, including both cash and presents.⁵¹

Sir William's justification for this change was that Pontiac had agreed in 1766 that traders who had been damaged by Pontiac's War would be compensated with land. Sir William's Pennsylvania deputy, George Croghan, received 100,000 acres, and a syndicate of wealthy traders led by Samuel Wharton received 2.5 million acres. Sir William participated in the Wharton syndicate, probably because his own trading business had been affected by Pontiac's War, but his participation can also be construed as a commission for getting the western tribes to agree to the land sale.⁵²

Sir William's efforts at Fort Stanwix were temporarily disrupted when he admitted Reverend Jacob Johnson to the conference based on a letter of recommendation from Reverend Eleazar Wheelock, Joseph's former schoolmaster, who claimed that Reverend Johnson wanted to use the large conference as an opportunity to proselytize Christianity to the assembled Native Americans. Sir William soon discovered, however, that Johnson was actively trying to convince the Oneidas not to cede the Wyoming valley to Pennsylvania on religious grounds, despite Pennsylvania's willingness to pay the Oneidas $10,000 Spanish dollars for the land. Wheelock stood to lose land equal to three or four townships promised him by Connecticut and on which he hoped to place a school if the land went to Pennsylvania. The exhausted Sir William was outraged at this abuse of his trust. It took him days to repair the damage and convince the Oneidas to proceed with the Pennsylvania cession. The incident resulted in a complete break with Wheelock and in Sir William becoming convinced that the Church of England needed to be strengthened in the northern colonies as a bulwark against the radical ideas of the dissenting Congregationalists.[53]

In a letter to General Gage soon after his return to Johnson Hall at the conclusion of the Fort Stanwix conference, Sir William warned of the need for good enforcement of the boundary by the colonies "by a Vigorous Exertion of these Laws against the first Offenders" and of the danger posed by the Congregationalists, because "the Civil & Religious preeminence they are gradually establishing demands the timely attention of those whose business it is to promote the National Church & secure its Rights and Privilidges."[54]

* * *

Sir William did not limit his views about the dangers of Congregationalism to mere words. A town was growing up around Johnson Hall. In 1766 Johnstown consisted of 10 houses. By 1771, it had doubled in size and consisted of a grid of four north/south streets and four east/west streets. In addition to the approximately 150 people who lived in the town, hundreds of local farmers, many of them Sir William's tenants, traveled to Johnstown's weekly market and its two annual fairs. In 1766, Sir William built St. John's Episcopal Church and a "snug house for a clergyman" in Johnstown. In 1772, he erected a much larger building for the church, capable of holding 1,000 worshippers and equipped with an organ that cost Sir William 100 pounds. He also supported the upkeep of the Anglican Queen Anne's Chapel in Fort Hunter and was the largest benefactor of St. George's Anglican Church in Schenectady. When the Canajoharie Mohawks raised $100 for the construction of an Anglican church at Canajoharie, Sir William contributed the remainder needed for construction. St. John's Episcopal Church and the Canajoharie church still stand today.[55]

Shortly after their return from Fort Stanwix, Sir William was able to make another improvement to Johnstown that brought joy to both his and

Molly's hearts. A fellow Irishman, Edward Wall, presented himself to Sir William and convinced him that he had "received a liberal education in Europe" sufficient to qualify him as a schoolmaster.[56] This was the answer to Molly and Sir William's strong desire to educate their young children at home rather than send them to boarding school. Mr. Wall soon found himself running a schoolhouse in Johnstown, provided by Sir William, which 45 children attended free of charge. Mr. Wall was a stern taskmaster who required students to bow when addressing him. He was, however, no fool. Nine-year-old Peter, seven-year-old Elizabeth, and five-year-old Magdalene were treated "with kind partiality and pointed indulgence."[57] Sir William and Molly regularly received glowing reports of their progress. Pampered they may have been, as befit the children of a baronet, but Sir William was an educated man who expected results. Master Peter, Miss Betsey, and Miss Leney learned to read, write, and do arithmetic. They were beginning their journey to the comfortable future their father was planning for them.

In June 1769, Sir William received word that his long quest to have the king confirm the Canajoharie Mohawks' gift to him had finally met with success. The Crown issued deeds to Sir William for 99,000 acres, or 154 square miles of verdant territory, most of which was located between Johnstown and Canajoharie. There was now plenty of land to distribute to both Catherine Weisenberg's and Molly Brant's children upon his death.[58]

At the same time, Sir William continued to take those actions that made the Mohawks feel he was their ally and brother in a harsh world. An early frost in the fall of 1768 had destroyed the Six Nations' fall harvest and placed them on the verge of starvation. They appealed to Sir William. He had 2,000 bushels of corn sent up from New York City for their relief. In the spring, he wrote to General Gage requesting additional food when the initial relief supplies were exhausted.[59]

Sir William and Molly continued to entertain both high-ranking European Americans and distinguished Native Americans at Johnson Hall almost continuously. Judge Thomas Jones painted a vivid picture of their hospitality: "He had besides his own family, seldom less than ten, sometimes thirty. All were welcome. All sat down together. All was good cheer, mirth and festivity. Sometimes seven, eight, or ten, of the Indian Sachems joined the festive board." Guests were well fed: "His dinners were plentiful. They consisted, however, of the produce of his estate, or what was procured from the woods and rivers, such as venison, bear, and fish of every kind, with wild turkeys, partridges, grouse and quails in abundance. … Each guest chose what he liked, and drank as he pleased." Although Johnson Hall was not large by modern standards, there was no regimentation to make things more convenient for the family: "The company, or at least a part of them, seldom broke up before three in the morning. Everyone, however, Sir William included, retired when he pleased. There was no restraint."[60]

Sir William and Molly were not often among the late-night revelers. Both had significant responsibilities to attend to in the morning, and Sir William sometimes continued to work at a desk in their bedroom after having bid good night to their guests. In March 1770 he wrote to Henry Van Schaack requesting nominations for officers of his militia regiment: "Excuse the Hurry I write in being 11 at night, & Just Stole away from a large Company."[61]

Molly had a substantial household staff to assist her with this constant flow of guests. Among them was a German butler named Frank and several household slaves.[62] Sir William continued to buy and sell slaves throughout the 15 years that Molly was his partner. The wife of a slave merchant wrote Sir William in 1768: "I received from Mr. Wetherhead a few days ago wherein he desires me to send the wench and two children which you spoke for some time ago and accordingly i have sent her and she bears a very extraordinary character which I hope she will turn out a good servant to so worthy a Master."[63]

In the fall of 1769 Sir William purchased Abraham and December from Peter Remsen, another New York City merchant. Sir William paid 90 pounds for the two young men, "both about 24 years old," who had been trafficked north from St. Croix. Abraham would be one of the three slaves who accompanied Molly and her children in their flight from the Mohawk valley in 1777 and was still with her on Carleton Island in 1783.[64]

7

Gathering Clouds

Molly and Sir William's family continued to grow despite his frequent bouts of ill health. After George's birth in 1768 or 1769, three more daughters, Mary, Susanna, and Anne, came along in 1771, 1772, and 1773.[1] Some believe that there may have been a ninth child, a girl, born sometime between 1764 and 1769. This is based on a letter written by Captain Norman Macleod, then in New York City, to Sir William Johnson at Johnson Hall in March 1770. In that letter, Macleod quotes from a letter he had received earlier from the commissary officer at Fort Niagara, Mr. Maclean, stating that an elderly Seneca sachem who had just heard of the death "of your little Girl" sent Sir William his condolences.[2] This is the only reference to such a child in the historical record. Sir William was a fond (and unashamed) father of Molly's children, and the Mohawks were very conscientious about performing condolence ceremonies whenever Sir William sustained a family loss.

It is unlikely that there would be no reference to a condolence ceremony for such a child in Sir William's papers or at least to expenses incurred for mourning clothing for Sir William and Molly. It is more likely that the child referred to as "your little Girl" was Anne Claus, the child of Anne and Daniel Claus, who died during the Fort Stanwix conference in the fall of 1768. Her death was elaborately condoled at the Fort Stanwix conference and would have been the subject of news brought back home to the elderly sachem. Maclean, the commissary officer, may himself have been unsure of Sir William's precise relationship to the child and therefore settled on the phrase "your little Girl" to handle it. If this interpretation is correct, although Molly may have miscarried a baby during her bout with smallpox in 1765 and would later lose three children in their adulthood, she had a far luckier experience than many other women of the time in seeing all of her eight children survive to maturity.

As their family grew, Sir William, although somewhat removed from the increasing agitation between the Crown and the American colonies playing out in places such as Boston, New York, and Philadelphia, kept well

7. Gathering Clouds

informed of current events through newspapers brought up weekly by boat from New York and by contact with well-placed correspondents throughout the colonies and in London. In May 1770 James Rivington, the Tory New York bookseller, wrote to Sir William reporting the appointment of Thomas Hutchinson as the royal governor of Massachusetts in the aftermath of the Boston Massacre.[3] Earlier that spring, both Rivington and Sir William were shocked by the spectacle of a British officer, Captain Preston, on trial for his life in Boston, because he had stood up to the mob the night of the massacre. Neither of them had any doubt about the source of the trouble: "The Representation of the ugly affair in Boston, last March, from the inflammatory accounts signed by Hancock, Adams, Cushing & c. &c. made much impression upon the minds of the people, which was highly enlarged upon and supported by the whole puritan or republican faction."[4]

Convinced that Eleazar Wheelock and Samuel Kirkland's Puritan Congregationalism was doing much harm among the Oneidas, Sir William concluded that it was imperative that the Congregational form of Christianity spread no further among the Six Nations. His effort to recruit Church of England missionaries to the Mohawk valley was not, however, meeting with the success he thought essential. The Society for the Propagation of the Gospel sent to Fort Hunter one young minister, John Stuart, whom both Sir William and Molly liked, but Sir William thought that several more missionaries were needed.[5] Sir William's former correspondent on the subject of Native American assimilation, Reverend Charles Inglis, the rector of Trinity Church in New York and a leading member of the Society for the Propagation of the Gospel, wrote him apologetically in the spring of 1770 about the dearth of additional young volunteers: "Dr. Blackstone has lately published a Commentary on the Common Law of England; a Work which is executed with great Perspicuity & Judgment, & has made the Study of the Law easy & agreeable, instead of being dry, disgusting & intricate as formerly. So that Numbers of young Gentlemen at the Universities chuse to study the Law instead of going into Orders."[6]

Undeterred, Sir William invited Reverend Inglis and Reverend Myles Cooper, the president of King's College, to Johnson Hall to discuss the problem. The visit couldn't have gone better. Sir William arranged for prominent Mohawks to be present, probably including the very well-educated Joseph Brant, and for the Mohawks to personally request the posting of an Anglican missionary at Canajoharie and elsewhere in Six Nations territory. Meeting these people was a revelation to Inglis, who prior to his correspondence with Sir William held the worst possible prejudices against the "savages." Now he wrote glowingly to Reverend Daniel Burton, the head of the Society for the Propagation of the Gospel in England: "Their Zeal & Anxiety to have a Missionary, their Behaviour

& the Character I had of them from those who knew them well & whose Veracity I could depend on, gave me much Pleasure; & induced me to stand Sponsor for a Child of one of their principal Sachems which was baptized by Dr. Cooper."[7]

Sir William impressed on Inglis during his visit how important the alliance between the Six Nations and the Crown was at this critical juncture: "It is of the utmost Consequence ... to secure their Friendship & attach them to our Interest."[8] Like Sir William, Inglis now believed that it was essential that funds be procured in England from the Crown and private donors for the recruitment and support of additional Anglican missionaries in Indian country: "And altho the Indians discover a greater Inclination to be instructed by the Society's Missionaries or Clergy of the Church than by these; yet if the latter continue among them, & none of the former visit them, Wheelock's Missionaries will succeed; & I can aver on the best & most authentic Evidence, that the Principles inculcated by them are by no Means favourable to Government."[9]

In a thank-you note written to Sir William a few days later, Inglis also regurgitated some of the points Sir William had made to him and Cooper about the need for prominent Anglicans "to remove some popular Objections lately propagated by Dissenters, with Regard to the first Emigrants to America, as if they were all Dissenters who fled from Episcopal Persecution & that the Dissenters are the only People of Consequence at present in the Colonies."[10] Sir William understood the existential threat to royal authority posed by the Whigs, who were now beginning to style themselves as Patriots, and he was doing all in his power to mobilize members of the colonial establishment to recognize and defeat that threat.

On the personal side, Inglis thanked Sir William "for your very polite Treatment when I had the Honour of waiting on you." It was customary in such letters to also thank the hostess. This was more than Inglis could bring himself to do. In order to avoid insult, Reverend Inglis decided not to mention Anne Claus and Mary Johnson who, under the rules of etiquette of the time, would be deemed to have presided at table for their "widowed" father. Reverend Inglis solved the problem by referring only to the male members of Sir William's family: "My best Compliments wait on Sir John Johnson, Colonel Clause & Colonel Johnson."[11]

Sir William would have smiled at this diplomatic treatment of his situation, and he would have told Molly how much the two ministers enjoyed their hospitality. This and the ministers' polite treatment of her at her table would have given Molly some comfort that Sir William was correct. As a leader among his people he could not marry her, but men of God accepted their union. It was certainly far different treatment than her mother, Margaret, had received from Reverend Ogilvie 16 years before.

7. Gathering Clouds

* * *

Meanwhile, as the Patriots flexed their muscles in Boston and to a lesser extent in New York City, Sir William's grip on the Mohawk valley and surrounding regions remained strong. In March 1770 he wrote to his ally Goldsbrow Banyar, undersecretary of state of the colony of New York, enclosing a revised list of judges and magistrates for the city and county of Albany. The original list sent for his approval had named his son-in-law, Guy Johnson, and his close friend, George Croghan, as magistrates. Sir William added his son, Sir John Johnson, and his other son-in-law, Daniel Claus, to the revised list and deleted the names of several Patriots, all to ensure that the judiciary of the region was composed of royal sympathizers and Johnson family loyalists.[12]

Sir William's growing concern about the political situation in America's major cities was not an abstraction. The importation boycotts were beginning to have a direct effect on his ability to administer the Indian Department. The annual summer conference was scheduled for July 16–23, 1770, and Sir William was having great difficulty obtaining the presents that annually reconfirmed the alliance between the Crown and the Six Nations.[13]

With General Gage's intervention, goods were finally procured, and the conference went off as scheduled. Molly attended and probably brought her children with her, since German Flatts was a stone's throw from Canajoharie, and Margaret would have expected to see them. In attendance were 2,500 Native Americans. Most were members of the Six Nations, but there was also a large contingent of Canadian Native Americans.[14] Although usually a happy time, when friends and extended clan members could visit together while doing business with the Indian Department, it was also a time when disease could easily be communicated to large numbers of people, especially small children who lacked the protection of modern immunizations for diseases such as diphtheria and whooping cough. To Sir William's dismay, many members of the Canadian tribes insisted on traveling back with him to Johnson Hall on their return trip to Canada. At some point, the Johnson family got very sick. On August 22, 1770, Sir William wrote to General Gage: "My Situation as mentioned in my last Surrounded by some Hundreds of Indians who followed me to this place on the private Affairs of Each Nation, & a Severe Indisposition in my Family rendered it impossible for me to transmit the Proceedings herewith inclosed until this time."[15]

Molly's children survived. A small daughter of Mary and Guy Johnson, who had attended the conference in his capacity as Indian Department deputy, died on August 3 or 4. The minutes of the Indian conference noted that "at 12 the Cheifs of the Mississageys & Abanakis came & condoled with Sir Wm. on the loss of his Grand child, a Daughter of Col. Johnsons who was buried yesterday."[16]

As Molly's children recovered from their summer illness, her brother and his family grappled with an even more serious disease. Late in 1769 Joseph's wife, Peggie, gave birth to their second child, a healthy daughter they named Christina. Within months of the child's arrival, Peggie contracted tuberculosis, and by December 1770, Reverend John Stuart described her as being near death from consumption. The once healthy young woman, who two years before had carried Isaac on a cradleboard when she accompanied Joseph as he guided a group of European Americans down the Susquehanna River, lingered until the following March. As an expression of family solidarity and sincere personal affection, Sir William contributed to Peggie's funeral expenses, describing Joseph in the accounts as a "True Friend."[17]

Perhaps as a way of diverting his mind from his grief, Joseph soon accepted an invitation from Reverend Stuart to take on a major project. Leaving little Isaac and Christina in the care of their grandmother, Joseph spent substantial periods of time at Fort Hunter. Living at the parsonage, he taught Stuart the Mohawk language. Together they developed a Mohawk translation of the Gospel of St. Mark as well as the Anglican catechism and a short history of the Bible. Stuart later wrote that Joseph was probably the only man in America capable of the task.[18]

Despite his gratitude for Joseph's invaluable assistance, Stuart soon refused Joseph a very important request. Margaret was doing her best to care for Joseph's two children, but it was Six Nations custom that the widowed father of young children marry his wife's sister after the mourning period elapsed. Six Nations children belonged to their mother's clan, and traditionally they lived in the mother's village. Joseph had convinced Peggie to live with him in Canajoharie on his substantial farm, but she had an unmarried sister, Susanna, and everyone expected him to marry her. From the perspective of Native Americans, this tradition made excellent sense. There were no stories about wicked stepmothers in Six Nations lore. Indeed, the Mohawk word for "mother" and for "mother's sister" is the same. Children were raised by the woman who would treat them as her own.[19]

Conversely, the Anglican faith had come into existence based on an Old Testament passage that seemed to forbid the marriage of a widow or widower to a sibling of the deceased spouse. Henry VIII had divorced Catherine of Aragon and broken with the Catholic Church on the strength of this biblical interpretation. Other denominations were less strident on the point.

7. Gathering Clouds

Joseph, who would continue to spend his life negotiating the divide between Native American and European American customs, now displayed the intellectual and spiritual independence that would characterize the rest of his life. Determining that there was a split of opinion on the question among Christians, Joseph had the marriage performed by an elderly German clergyman, Reverend John Jacob Ehle.[20] Stuart, who respected Joseph and depended on Sir William as the Fort Hunter chapel's biggest benefactor, remained on friendly terms with Joseph. Molly registered her opinion on the matter by naming her seventh child, born the year of the marriage, in honor of her new sister-in-law.

* * *

In addition to the annual summer conference attended by 350 members of the Six Nations, Sir William and Molly also hosted John Murray, fourth earl of Dunmore, at Johnson Hall in the summer of 1771.[21] Lord Dunmore, who was briefly the governor of New York before his more famous role as the last colonial governor of Virginia, was anxious to meet one of the most famous and eminent men of the American colonies.

Like most distinguished visitors to Johnson Hall, Dunmore was grateful "for the many Civilities & kindnesses you was so good as to shew me." Unlike most such visitors, he took note of the services of the enslaved people who made many of these civilities and kindnesses possible: "nothing could behave better than John & Abraham did whom you were so good as to name for my guid's, they have been perfectly sober, faithfull, & indefatigable, & I do assure you I think myself obliged to you, for their services." After less than two years in his service, Abraham had sufficiently impressed Sir William with his intelligence and loyalty that Sir William was willing to entrust Lord Dunmore to his care and allow Abraham to journey to Albany in the company of only one other enslaved man.

Lord Dunmore also tried to show some sensitivity to the Native American members of the Johnson family. Like Charles Inglis, Dunmore handled the complexity of Sir William's personal life by including in his thank-you note "my best Respects" to named male members of the family, Sir John Johnson and Guy Johnson, but, unlike Inglis, also mentioned "all the Rest of your family."[22]

Molly's satisfaction at having successfully entertained the governor was as usual mixed with anxiety about Sir William's health. The strain of his summer workload once again caused a severe onset of his various maladies. By early September, he was on his way to a newly discovered spring "Northward of Schenectady," probably Saratoga Springs.[23]

The treatment did no good, and when he returned to Johnson Hall a few weeks later, everyone was deeply concerned. When Sir John and

Guy took a business trip to New York City that fall, they expressed their fears to Sir William's close friend and business associate, Hugh Wallace. Alarmed, Wallace wrote immediately to Sir William suggesting a visit to New York City for a rest and to consult doctors.[24] Although returning from a Six Nations trip in early November "much fatigued," Sir William did not accept Wallace's invitation. Sir William had much to do, and perhaps he was beginning to realize that he did not have a great deal of time left to do it.[25]

* * *

Sir William decided it was time for the Mohawk valley to be split off from Albany County and become a separate county. The new county would be named for William Tryon, the man who had just succeeded Lord Dunmore as governor of New York, and the county seat would be Johnstown. Sir William's decision to push this proposal was based on several factors. The European population of the Mohawk valley had mushroomed over the prior three decades, so it was legitimate to argue that it now possessed a large enough population to support its own local government. Also, Sir William had never had a very friendly relationship with the Dutch merchants who controlled the city of Albany. They had always resented him as an interloper who had disrupted their monopoly of the fur trade. Now, in addition to the antipathy arising from competing business interests, Sir William increasingly saw the Albany merchants as antiroyalists, sympathetic to the radicals in New England who were seeking to destroy the bond between the mother country and its colonies. Looking toward the future, Sir William viewed his son, Sir John, and his sons-in-law, Guy Johnson and Daniel Claus, as the natural leaders of the Mohawk valley after his death. Their positions would be far more secure in a county where Johnson tenants were a very significant portion of the population, and where appointment to the major governmental posts for Sir John, Guy, and Daniel would not be questioned.

James De Lancey, the dominant figure in the New York Assembly and one of the most powerful men in New York's colonial government, assured Sir William that "you may rely on my Friendship in this and every other Matter wherein I can be of Service and my Friends are all strongly inclined to Assist me."[26]

By the spring of 1772, all was arranged. Sir William's friend Hugh Wallace wrote to him triumphantly: "All the Judges & Justices you recommended are fixt.... I have no doubt you will get both Sheriff & Clark fixed next year to your Mind."[27] Sir William responded enthusiastically: "I am now carrying on a handsome building intended for a Court House towards which I shall contribute 500 [pounds]."[28] Near the courthouse,

7. Gathering Clouds

Sir William also constructed a county jail. He could never have imagined some of the people who would occupy it in five years' time.

Sir William was already a member of the New York Council, the upper house of the New York legislature, although he avoided attending its meetings. He now nominated his son-in law Guy Johnson and his business associate Henry Frey to be Tryon County's representatives in the lower house, the New York Assembly. They were soon elected at a county meeting filled with Johnson loyalists. Johnson was pleased that the election "was unanimous, and will, I hope, always be such, as making Partys or Divisions amongst the Inhabitants can never be for their interest."[29]

* * *

As Sir William moved to secure the future of Catherine Weisenberg's children, the future of Molly's children was also very much on his mind. In the spring of 1772 Molly's eldest, Peter, was 12½ years old. Like his sisters, he was still in school at Johnstown, where a new schoolmaster, John Cottgrave, had succeeded Edward Wall.[30] As Sir William contemplated his own mortality, he reflected on the grave responsibilities that were likely to fall upon Peter at a young age. In English law and custom, upon a father's death it was the eldest son who became the head of the family. In particular, he was the protector of his widowed mother and the surrogate father of his unmarried sisters and brothers. As the eldest of six siblings, with a seventh to come the following year, Peter would carry a heavy load. Fortunately, the boy showed every sign of being able to handle it. Quick at his lessons, musical, fluent in both English and Mohawk, and like both of his parents possessed of high social intelligence, he was capable of becoming a successful and prominent man in the Mohawk valley if properly educated.

Peter had now reached an age when Mohawk boys were expected to spend most of their time with male relatives and friends hunting and trapping. Molly could not object when Sir William told her it was time to step up his education so he could fulfill his potential. It may have been at this time that Sir William first seriously discussed with Molly what life would be like for her and their children after his death. Johnson Hall would immediately become the property of Sir John; she had always understood that. But what was possible, now that the Kingsland patent had finally been approved, was a string of land grants for her and each of their children between Canajoharie and Johnstown. Her grant would be closest to Canajoharie so she could be near her mother. Peter would have a store on the land that would be a fur trading outpost and also a general store for the Canajoharie Mohawks and the German Flatts farming community. It was how Sir William had gotten his own start, and Peter, with his language and social skills, would do just as well. But Peter would also have an advantage his father lacked: a large farm inherited from Sir William. The girls would each have a substantial farm as a dowry and would attract fine husbands. Little George would have an excellent farm, too. Molly could spend her days helping Peter in the store if she wished or visiting her other children, all of them living nearby and financially secure.

It was hard for Molly to contemplate her beloved Sir William's death as she held the youngest of their babies at her breast, but for a woman who lacked the legal protections of marriage, it must have been comforting to know that Sir William would keep his promises to her. Peter had obtained as much learning as was available in Johnstown. Sir William wanted him to go to school in Montreal, because knowledge of the French language was an important asset for a man in the fur trade. Lightly populated Canada was also more accepting of bicultural children such as Peter than were New York City and Philadelphia. Eventually Peter would have to go to one of those cities for his business education, but first Sir William wanted to send him to a place where he would encounter little prejudice. Molly consented. In the spring of 1772, Peter set out for Montreal escorted by Major Augustine Prevost, a son-in-law of George Croghan, Sir William's Pennsylvania deputy and longtime friend.

It had been a long time since Sir William had last visited Montreal. Prevost was authorized to place Peter in whatever school he thought best upon their arrival. Sir William had high hopes for this new phase of his son's life, bidding Prevost to tell Peter, "I wish for nothing more than his Improving himself."[31]

Apparently, the school Prevost initially selected proved to be unsatisfactory. Fortunately, the Johnson family had contacts in the area. Doctor R. Huntley, a close friend of Sir William's nephew and Peter's favorite cousin, Dr. John Dease, visited the boy. Huntley made the decision to withdraw Peter from the school and place him at a school 33 miles from Montreal. Sir William later thanked Huntley profusely. In his new surroundings, Peter proved to be a talented student, although the separation from his family was difficult. Daniel Claus checked on him during his annual summer business trip a few months later, bringing the homesick boy news of his family. When Claus returned to the Mohawk valley, he was able to personally assure the anxious parents that Peter was well.[32]

* * *

Among Sir William's other projects in spring 1772 was a long letter to Dr. Arthur Lee, a London academic. In response to a number of questions about the Six Nations' language and culture, Sir William wrote an erudite letter in which he discussed, among many things, the grammar and syntax of the Six Nations' languages and the government and laws of the Six Nations confederacy. In response to a query about the Six Nations' ethics, he said that "unless heated with Liquor or inflamed by Revenge their ideas of Good & Evil & their practices in consequence thereof wod. if fully known, do them much honor. Tis true that havg. Been often deceived by us in the Sale of Lands & in Trade & many of them begin to act the same part but this Acquirement Reflects most on those who set the Example."[33]

As usual, the summer of 1772 was a time of furious activity at Johnson Hall. That year the new governor, William Tryon, and his wife were Sir William and Molly's guests. The purpose of the visit was twofold. Governor Tryon "perfected the purchase of sevl large tracts" for business associates of Sir William and personally listened to formal complaints from the Canajoharie Mohawks about George Klock's predatory land claims.[34]

Joseph Brant, fast becoming a leader among the Canajoharie Mohawks and with excellent English-language skills, was one of the primary spokesmen. Joseph had deep personal cause for concern about Klock's claims as well. The 80 acres he had purchased from the tribe with his share of the Kingsland money were part of the land claimed by Klock.[35]

At about this time, Sir William also instructed Guy Johnson to file a court statement on behalf of the Canajoharie Mohawks in their continuing battle with Klock: "Their fidelity, and Attachment to the English intitles them to strict Just[ice] Protection of Government, & that for the Considerations before mentioned their ... Slender Remains of their Property, is now reasonable and their Desire moderate."[36] Sir William consistently rejected the theory then being floated that the Six Nations had somehow ceded their territory to the king by allying themselves with him and calling him "Father" in various treaties. This theory would gain greater currency with the victorious Patriots after the American Revolution. Johnson thought it was nonsense and firmly told General Gage, now a significant landholder in upper New York that "our Right depends on purchase."[37]

* * *

During the last few years of his life, Sir William periodically escaped to a hunting lodge he had constructed 14 miles from Johnson Hall on the Sacandaga River. Accompanied by male friends, he was briefly free from the stress of diplomatic and business concerns. In the decades after Sir William's death, a local tradition arose that he may have had sexual encounters with two daughters of a local farmer, Susannah and Elizabeth Wormwood, during his stays at the hunting lodge.[38] If it is true, no children came from the relationships because no child of either woman was mentioned in his will, a document in which he dutifully made bequests to a number of illegitimate children, including Mary McGrah, putatively the daughter of Christopher McGrah, but conceived by Christopher's wife and Sir William while Christopher was a prisoner of war in Canada.

If a sexual relationship existed with the Wormwood sisters, it was not a commentary on Sir William's continuing attraction to Molly Brant, who bore him three children in the years 1771, 1772, and 1773. It is more likely that given the well-deserved reputation Sir William had earned in earlier years for his libidinous nature and with the Johnson family driven out of the Mohawk valley during the Revolution, the people who took the Johnsons' land were anxious to believe ill of the family patriarch, so a salacious rumor grew into a tall tale, which continued to be passed on long after Sir William's death.

In Montreal, Dr. Huntley continued to be a friend and mentor to Peter. In January 1773, Huntley was able to report to Sir William that Peter was rapidly learning French: "He now speaks the Language with the greatest Ease & Elegance."[39] Sir William wrote to Peter and said that he also wanted him to learn to dance and to fence. The obliging Dr. Huntley soon informed Sir William that "I have in Consequence of your Letter to Him, ordered Him a dancing and fencing Master, in the latter Accomplishment his Master informs Me He has made considerable Progress."[40] Peter was on his way to becoming a gentleman, although like most 13-year-old boys, he wasn't too pleased to be told he must learn ballroom dancing.

During this same period, Sir William convinced his daughters Anne Claus and Mary Johnson that they should allow their eldest daughters, Catherine Claus and Mary Johnson the younger, to attend boarding school in New York City. Boarding school for girls was a new idea, but Sir William was a fond grandparent who foresaw excellent marriages for his two eldest granddaughters if they acquired the necessary polish and contacts. Catherine Claus was almost 10 and Mary Johnson was eight and a half, but it was not too soon to begin making fine ladies of them and introducing them to the distinguished New York City families who had sons who would later be excellent marriage prospects.

In November 1772 their uncle, Sir John Johnson, escorted the two girls to New York City.[41] Hugh Wallace soon reported that "Yr young Lady's seem very happy & I hope their Mothers will believe they shall not want for Care & affection from us.... Mrs. Wallace desires her Complts. We have paid the 40 [pounds] on your Account which she will lay out for the Young Ladys as you desire."[42]

The obvious question is why Molly's two oldest daughters, Elizabeth and Magdalene, were not included in this plan. Magdalene was about the same age as Catherine Claus, and Elizabeth was two years older. At a time when Sir William was arranging dancing and fencing lessons for their brother Peter in Montreal, why were Elizabeth and Magdalene still attending the little schoolhouse in Johnstown?

One reason may be that as Sir William's brother, Warren Johnson, had long before recorded in his journal, Six Nations women had complete control of their daughters' upbringing. While Molly certainly had to make some concessions to British patriarchal ideas about the father's role, Sir William understood that she and all the Mohawks believed that the mother had a pivotal role in deciding her daughters' future.

Who could blame Molly if she did not want to send Elizabeth and Magdalene someplace where many people harbored deep prejudices against Native Americans, a place Molly might not feel comfortable visiting? Who could blame her if she did not want husbands for them who would regard her as an embarrassment?

And most likely, Sir William himself did not want Elizabeth and Magdalene to go to school in New York City. If there had been a girls' boarding school in Montreal, that would have been worth discussing with Molly, but it was better if his English and Native American children did not tread too closely on each other's heels. The boarding school in New York City, described by Hugh Wallace as "the best School in America," was extremely exclusive. The headmistress of the school, Madame Blanche Bayoux, had at first told Hugh Wallace that there was no room for Catherine and Mary even though they were the granddaughters of New York's only baronet. Wallace had had to enlist the aid of Reverend Ogilvie, formerly the pastor of the Fort Hunter Chapel and now a distinguished Anglican minister in New York City, to convince her otherwise. Ogilvie, the minister who had humiliated Molly's mother Margaret 20 years before, was certainly not going to assert his influence on behalf of Sir William and Molly's illegitimate children.[43]

Moreover, having Elizabeth and Magdalene in New York City could have proved detrimental to another goal vitally important to Sir William. As Sir William stared death in the face, he was becoming increasingly uncomfortable that his eldest son and primary heir, Sir John Johnson, was not yet settled in life. When Sir John returned from England in 1767 at age 25, his father had allowed him to set up a separate household at Fort Johnson. That was certainly more comfortable for Sir William and Molly, who were raising their family at Johnson Hall, and for Sir John as well. It had, however, made it easier for Sir John to conduct his private life with substantial independence.

Shortly before his trip to England, Sir John had formed a relationship with Clarissa Putman, a local farmer's daughter, in her midteens at the time. The result was a pregnancy and the birth of a baby girl she named Margaret. Soon after Sir John returned from England, Clarissa came to live with him at Fort Johnson, and by 1772 she had presented Sir John with a second child, William.[44] Sir William knew that what he had been able to conceal a generation before could not possibly be concealed by Sir John. Without telling Sir John of his own illegitimacy, Sir William made it clear to his son that he must marry a woman capable of being a baronet's wife and produce a legitimate family. Having spent two years in England moving in the highest social circles, Sir John himself was under no illusion that the relationship with the uneducated Clarissa could be permanent. Otherwise, he would have married her prior to the birth of their second child. Since he had not done so, it was legally impossible for Clarissa's little boy to succeed to the baronetcy. Things had been comfortable enough with Clarissa, however, that Sir John had delayed displacing her. But now, Sir William was sure that the time had come for action. He undoubtedly told Sir John that he had a moral obligation to permanently provide for Clarissa's children, but also told him that they should stop living at Fort Johnson and that he should find himself an appropriate bride. Sir William knew from personal experience that, as Sir John and Clarissa's children grew, this decision could only become more difficult. Sir John finally acceded to his father's wishes and found a house for Clarissa and their children in Schenectady.

The trip to escort Catherine and Mary to school was an excuse to get Sir John to New York City for the winter social season. Although "he wod lay no force on a Young Mans inclinations," the anxious father went so far as to obtain from the mayor of New York, Thomas Moncrieffe, a list of the most eligible young ladies in the city for his son's perusal.[45]

Having Sir John take Elizabeth and Magdalene along with Catherine and Mary to school in New York would have set off a round of gossip among the very families Sir William was hoping would produce a bride for Sir John. Probably neither Sir William nor Molly wanted Elizabeth and Magdalene to attend Madame Bayoux's school, each for their own reasons.

After Sir William's death, when Molly moved to Canajoharie she sent Elizabeth and Magdalene to boarding school in Schenectady. This may have been the fulfillment of a promise to Sir William, but it is just as likely that Molly herself understood the importance of doing so. After Sir William's death, when Molly's own voice appears in the public record, she consistently expressed a concern that her daughters have the opportunity to find substantial marriage partners. They had been raised at Johnson Hall as the daughters of a baronet. She wanted them to marry distinguished European American men. Eventually most of them would do so, but they would find their husbands far from the Mohawk valley.

8

The Worst of Times

Life at Johnson Hall continued its frenetic pace. In February 1773 Molly gave birth to their eighth and last child, a daughter she and Sir William named Anne in honor of Sir William's mother and the child's much older half sister, Anne Claus.[1] Within two months of the birth, Molly and Sir William found themselves unexpectedly entertaining 206 Six Nations people who came "to lay before me proceedings at the late Congress at Onondaga." High on the agenda were the visitors' assurances that they would "refrain from associations with nations unfriendly to the English" and their complaints about "the misdeeds of traders." Molly and Sir William scrambled to provide food for their late winter guests, their arrival being "very inconvenient, as provisions are extremely scarce."[2]

In January, Guy Johnson went down to New York City to take his Assembly seat. He was worried about leaving Mary and their two younger daughters at Guy Park for almost two months in the dead of winter. Mary, of course, was not alone. She had an overseer, servants, and enslaved people with her. Nevertheless, Sir William, though in ill health, made the 11-mile journey from Johnson Hall to Guy Park to check on her and the children. Guy thanked his father-in-law and reported that Sir William's two eldest granddaughters "are well in health & remr. you with tenderness." A few weeks later the girls were "eager still to hear from you." Hugh Wallace chimed in that young Catherine Claus was "much admired & thought by most people she will be the Belle of the Province."[3]

In late February came the news that Sir William had been waiting for. Sir John had asked Mary Watts to marry him, and she had accepted. Mary was the daughter of John Watts, a prominent New York City attorney and a member of the Governor's Council. Her mother was a sister of James De Lancey, current master of the Assembly. It was exactly the kind of match Sir William had dreamed of for his son. Mayor Moncrieffe's letter of congratulations exulted, "I think she was in the first class of those I sent you a list of."[4]

It must of course have crossed Molly's mind that the next mistress of Johnson Hall had just been selected. Nonetheless, Molly primarily focused on Sir William's health and the demands of her large family. She had long ago come to terms with the parameters of her partnership with Sir William, and he had likely explained to her that under the British system, even a legally married second wife would be required to move to her dower house upon the death of her aristocrat husband so that the firstborn son and his wife could occupy the manor house. Molly would have the equivalent of a dower house on the Canajoharie farm Sir William was planning to bequeath to her.

Whether Molly acknowledged to herself how soon this change might come is unknown, but others close to Sir William certainly were doing so. His heavy workload and the inadequacies of 18th-century medicine were now causing his maladies to plague him unrelentingly. In March, Peter Silvester, his Albany lawyer, wrote to Sir William about being "uneasy at the long continuance of your Indisposition."[5] Shortly after the April Indian conference Sir William suffered two more attacks, and by mid–May he confessed to General Gage that he was "scarcely able to hold a pen."[6]

Before he left Johnson Hall that summer for a rest cure, Sir William made some important decisions. He sent a letter to General Gage recommending that in the event of his death, Guy Johnson should succeed him as superintendent of the Indian Department. Guy had 17 years of experience among the Six Nations, and Sir William was confident that Guy could do the job: "the Interest of the public shall be the primary inducement as well as the first Consideration with me." A man of the world, Sir William knew that he needed General Gage to put Guy's case before the king and his chief advisers at the appropriate moment: "I am aware that Such an Office may probably be conferred on a person in nowise qualified for it, but who has Confidence enough to pass for a Man acquainted with these matters & a few friends to Countenance & recommend the Application."[7] The stability of the Mohawk valley and the happiness and safety of everyone Sir William cared about depended on the most competent man succeeding him. Yes, Guy was his nephew and son-in-law, but he was also the man Sir William had trained for the job and the man Native Americans looked to as his successor. Gage, who thanks to Sir William now had significant landholdings in the Mohawk valley, would see that a grateful king was apprised of Sir William's choice.

The other matter on Sir William's mind that summer was the next step in Peter's education. It was now becoming obvious that it would be Peter who would have to assist Molly in the upbringing of his younger siblings. Sir William wanted the boy to undertake a business apprenticeship in Philadelphia so that he would soon be competent to become a merchant in the Mohawk valley. Daniel Claus was again heading to Montreal for his annual summer business trip with the Canadian tribes. Sir William asked

8. The Worst of Times

Claus to confirm with Dr. Huntley that Peter's French was satisfactory and then to arrange for Peter's return to Johnson Hall. Molly and Sir William had not seen their son in 16 months. Peter would have a little time at home before heading to Philadelphia in the fall.

When Claus arrived in Canada, Huntley concurred that Peter "can't make any more Improvements at Montreal." As for Peter, he "longs to go down [back home]." Claus arranged for Peter to be escorted to Albany by Lieutenant Hastings of the 26th Regiment, "who I am persuaded will take Particular care of him as an intimate Acquaintance of mine."[8]

After Sir William's departure for the seacoast, Guy Johnson returned the favor of checking in on Molly and the children at Johnson Hall despite the work of rebuilding Guy Park, which had been struck by lightning and burned to the ground in mid-June. On August 26, Guy was able to report to Sir William that work on the courthouse and jail in Johnstown was nearing completion, that the "Harvests [are] well secured," and that "Peter is come from Canada, he is grown very much."[9]

Molly's heart must have been very full upon reuniting with her eldest child. He had left in the spring of 1772, age 12½, still clearly a boy; now a few weeks from his 14th birthday, he was almost fully grown. She knew the reason Sir William was hastening to complete Peter's education, but Sir William had battled ill health for years. This hadn't stopped him from running the Indian Department and his large estate or from continuing to beget children with Molly. Did she realize that his huge reserves of energy were nearing exhaustion, or was she only relieved that when he returned to Johnson Hall in September, the family would be together again?

* * *

The vacation by the sea did Sir William some good. Molly and the rest of the family were overjoyed to observe that for a few weeks at least, he seemed like himself again. But the press of work resumed almost immediately. Sir William and Molly hosted sachems of the Canadian tribes at Johnson Hall in the latter part of September and early October.[10]

Then, crushing news came from New York City. Young Catherine (Katty) Claus and Mary (Polly) Johnson had spent the summer at home with their parents. In September they returned to Madame Bayoux's school. Hugh Wallace assured their grandfather that "the two young Ladys are very well & seem pleased with their return."[11]

In late October, Robert Adems, a Johnson tenant and Johnstown storekeeper, traveled to New York City. He promised Sir William that he would pay a call on the girls. When Sir William opened Adems' letter from there a few days later, he no doubt expected a lighthearted report of his granddaughters' doings:

> I arrived here last Tuesday Afternoon and next Morning paid the Children A Visit who I found very well.... Polly with another Young Miss came a Friday Evening not seeing Katty I ask'd where she was, she told me she had got A Sore throat.... I then Enquired of the Madams If a Doctor had been sent for.... Doctor Bruce ... had been to see her Twice, and had sent some Medicine which they had given the Child a little before I came. I ... promised to call in the Evening when I hoped to see her better, (little thinking next Visit would see her a pale, Breathless Corpse) but had not been long gone when she got worse & a few Fitts carried her off in less than an hour. Her disorder was the same kind that Polly had, whose Behaviour on her Cousins death would have drawn Tears from the most hardned of Hearts.[12]

Catherine Claus, alive and well on a Wednesday and dead on Saturday, was just short of her 11th birthday. She was probably the victim of diphtheria, the killer of countless children before a vaccine became available in the early 20th century. Sir William had doted on his eldest grandchild and held great ambitions for her. The idea that she would go before him was probably unthinkable.

For Molly, too, Katty's death was a terrible shock. Katty had been a playmate of Elizabeth and Magdalene, and Molly was genuinely fond of Anne and Daniel Claus. Throughout the American Revolution, Daniel would show solicitude for Molly's welfare, and they would work together to keep the Six Nations loyal to the king.

On a personal level, the news came to Molly as she prepared Peter for his departure to Philadelphia, where he was shortly to begin the next phase of his education. Sir William had arranged for Peter to stay with the family of Francis Wade, a prominent Philadelphia merchant, while completing his business apprenticeship. Now as she packed Peter's trunk, Molly was faced with the reality that an intelligent, charming, and promising child could be snatched away by death in a distant city as the child prepared for the happy future of his or her parents' dreams.

Family tragedy notwithstanding, Peter left for Philadelphia about two weeks after Katty's death, escorted by Joseph Chew, a former militia officer and soon to be one of Sir William's secretaries. Peter and Chew took one of the boats that plied the Hudson River between Albany and New York City, a journey of about two and a half days. They stayed overnight in New York City, where they dined with Hugh Wallace, and then took the stagecoach to Philadelphia.

Sir William and Peter had apparently had a serious father-son talk before Peter left home. The 14-year-old's first letter from Philadelphia displays his intelligent and lively nature, some homesickness, and a sincere desire to meet his father's expectations and fulfill his potential: "I like the Place Very well as Yet & hope I Shall much More when I be Settled wrightly to Business.... I shall write you a Longer Letter by the next Oppertunity as I know but little of the Place Yet—I hope you will write by the next Post & Should be Extremely happy to hear from home as Soon as Possible. I shall write to Mr. Dease this Day & to my Mother." For diversion, Peter planned to turn to his music, but he knew that he was in Philadelphia to prepare for an adult life that would soon be upon him: "Please to let me know [as to] where I shall have a good Fiddle as it is a great Deal of Pleasure to Play at Leasure Ours.... I shall Please God, do all that lies in my P-Power to Please You & all persons here,—I suppose I shant Stay Long here, for the Sooner I can be Settled the better for me, & I Shall Like it the Better."[13]

The words "the Sooner I can be Settled the better for me" are almost certainly the regurgitation of his father's concern that Peter become established in life before his father's death. But why worry so much about this when Sir John Johnson, 17 years his half brother's senior, would be present to assist him? Peter's deep fondness for Dr. John Dease, the son of Sir William's sister Anne, may offer a clue to Johnson family personal dynamics. Throughout his time in Philadelphia, Peter repeatedly asked for letters from this favorite first cousin but never asked for letters from Sir John. Dease had come to live at Johnson Hall when Peter was small, and it is he, rather than Peter's actual older brother, Sir John, who seems to have been the object of Peter's hero worship. This may not be surprising given that Dease lived with Peter's family, while Sir John was living in England and later had his own establishment at Fort Johnson. It may, however, also be a sign that Catherine Weissenberg's only son resented at some level the obvious fact that Peter had been conceived in the months just prior to his mother's death. Sir John behaved politely to Molly and her children throughout his father's life and beyond, but Sir William, socially astute and a keen observer of human nature, may have detected a certain formality in Sir John's relations with Molly's children. When Sir William drew his will in January 1774, he named John Dease, not Sir John, as one of their six guardians.[14]

* * *

In addition to figuring out his estate plan, there were many other problems to engage Sir William's mind that winter. Much of his attention was directed to helping the Mohawks fight off bogus claims to their land. In December, he wrote urgently to Frederick Haldimand on behalf of the Canajoharie Mohawks. George Klock had taken it into his head to bring one or two alcohol-addicted Canajoharie Mohawks with him to London to argue Klock's case to officials there: "I must request you will give the earliest intelligence which yr situation at New York will best enable you to do to his Majesty's Ministers that the Conajoharees & lower Mohocks are highly exasperated at this fresh Instance of his behaviour and have entreated that he may be punished & the Indians sent back to them."[15]

Molly, as usual, was occupied with the running of their large household. In addition to their own children and numerous guests, Molly was caring for the half–English, half–Seneca son of Captain James Stevenson, formerly the commander at Detroit and now stationed in Albany. Stevenson wrote to Sir William in the late winter of 1771 about a problem he hoped Sir William would understand: "I have a fine Boy amongst the Senecas & would be glad to get him from them, altho it should be attended with some expence—now I should be glad of your advice & assistance in this matter, for I cannot think of leaving him amongst them."[16]

It would have been interesting to eavesdrop on the conversation that Sir William and Molly then had. The child was two or three years old. He would need the care of a foster mother for several years before he was old enough for his father to send him to boarding school. Would Molly be willing to do it? Molly must have winced as she considered the mother's situation. Why couldn't she live with Captain Stevenson at his post, just as Molly and baby Peter had come from Canajoharie to live with Sir William at Fort Johnson? Did Sir William tell her frankly that Captain Stevenson did not love the woman as he loved her? Subsequent letters make it clear that Stevenson continued to occasionally have sexual relations with his son's mother. Did Molly know that? It may have mattered to Molly that few of the Senecas were Christians at this time, and those who were Christian had been converted by French priests and were Catholics. Apparently, the child's mother was reluctant to make a quick decision. When Stevenson was transferred to Albany about two years later, the matter came to a head, and the mother and her family finally agreed to let the boy go in exchange for a financial settlement: "I believe they are well satisfied with the presents I have made them, & I assure you that the family have cost me 250 [pounds] 'tho she was with me but one year which was the time I commanded at Niagara."[17]

Sir William probably did not share Stevenson's comments with Molly. If he had, she probably would have disliked Stevenson as much as do most modern readers of his words. In any event, the mother's acceptance of the settlement was decisive for Molly, and she agreed to foster the little boy. Stevenson was grateful: "I beg my compts. To Molly & thank her for the pains she has taken relative to the child."[18]

* * *

Meanwhile, Peter was having a productive experience in Philadelphia and impressing everyone he met. Francis Wade had agreed to host him because Sir William was a significant client of his trading house. (Among other items, Wade frequently sold Sir William enslaved people and the contracts of indentured servants.) Although he had felt compelled to host Peter for business reasons, Wade became genuinely fond of the boy: "I have had several of my fri[e]nds Children, I never had one of a better disposition with which he seems to have an ambition to improve himself in anything he is put to."[19]

Wade was so impressed with Peter that he wanted to clarify the type of apprenticeship Sir William intended. Sir William's instructions seemed to imply a retail apprenticeship, but Peter was so intelligent that Wade thought an apprenticeship with one of the large Philadelphia wholesale firms was more appropriate. This would allow Peter to become a successful import merchant in Philadelphia or New York City. Sir William must have smiled with pride as he read Wade's letter, but there was no question as to what answer Molly wanted him to give or what Sir William himself understood to be necessary. He told Wade to place Peter in the retail apprenticeship. When it was finished, he would be coming home to his family and to his inheritance in the Mohawk valley.

Wade still couldn't bring himself to put Peter in a common retail apprenticeship. Instead, he placed Peter with William Barrell, "the genteelest man in the wholesale & retail business but he is the most Capable of improving him & Imports the largest of any in that way in the City."[20] Despite his affection and regard for Peter, Wade apparently preferred not to think too much about Peter's maternal ancestry. Rather than close his letter with respects to the boy's mother, Wade closed it with compliments "to Sr. John Colnl. Johnson [Colnl.] Claues & their ladys in which Mrs. Wade Joins."[21]

For his part, Peter was very open about, and not the least embarrassed by, his mixed ethnicity, and mentioned to Sir William that he had written to his mother asking her to send him some "Indian Curiositys As there are Gentlemen & Ladys here very desirous of Seeing them." From his father, he wanted "an Indian Book, for I am Afraid I'll lose my Indian Toungue If I don't practice it more than I do." Peter's letters to Molly, probably in Mohawk, have not survived.[22]

Although working at William Barrell's business during the day, Peter was continuing his academic studies, learning more mathematics with the Wade family tutor in the evenings and polishing his French with an instructor Wade had found for him.[23] Peter was also keenly observing life in America's largest city, reporting to his father that he had recently witnessed a public hanging: "I think it's the Most Dismal sight I ever Saw."[24] Peter was also becoming aware of the political situation, informing Sir William of rumors that William Franklin might lose his New Jersey governorship because of his father Benjamin's politics, and reporting that the shops of Philadelphia were to close on June 1 as a show of support for the city of Boston.[25]

Peter continued to be homesick, although he tried to be brave about it. He frequently expressed his love for both parents in his letters and urged Sir William to write as frequently as possible. Peter also wanted to hear from his 12-year-old sister Elizabeth but didn't want to admit he missed her: "pray tell Betsy to write me oftener as it will improve us both."[26]

* * *

Peter was the youngest of several correspondents passing on political news to Sir William from major cities. In London, the merchant John Blackburn reported reactions to the Boston Tea Party and gave Sir William details about the Port Bill and other sanctions that would become known in America as the Intolerable Acts.[27]

Sir William had confidence that General Gage would put matters to right in Boston. An experienced and highly successful militia commander, Sir William could not visualize colonial resistance so determined and widespread that it could possibly be any match for General Gage's regulars.[28]

Sir William's correspondents in New York City believed that the problems in Massachusetts were specific to that colony. As late as the end of June, Hugh Wallace predicted that New York's "Violent Libertines" would only go "as farr as talking & resolving at Town Meetings &c—but I am sure no farther."[29]

But as usual, Sir William was primarily focused on Indian Department business. One of his last letters to Gage in early July described an atrocity in the Ohio Country. Settlers thought to have been led by a man named Michael Cresap had murdered 30 Shawnees and Six Nations people: "The Irregularities committed on the Frontier since You went to England were indeed so many & increased so fast that they alone would be sufficient to bring on a War without the recent provocation the Indians received from Cressop."[30]

Two of the victims of the massacre were the brother and sister of one of the leading Cayuga sachems, Logan. Logan declared that he would seek revenge and asked for assistance from the other tribes of the Six Nations confederacy. Feelings were running so high that Sir William had to convene a conference at Johnson Hall to address the outrage of his closest Native American allies.[31]

By July 4, 600 Six Nations people had assembled on the grounds of Johnson Hall. In addition to the atrocity against Logan's family, George Klock and his land claims were on the minds of the Mohawks who were present. Although Klock had received no help from the authorities in

London, his land claims were still rattling around the New York courts. Perhaps with a wink from Sir William, the Canajoharie Mohawks decided they'd had enough. In May, a group of about 20 Canajoharie Mohawks, led by Joseph Brant, Brant Johnson, and Paulus Peters (the son of the sachem Hendrick), went to Klock's farm and demanded he drop the court case. Joseph Brant and several others physically assaulted Klock when he refused. Legal documents were taken from his house as well as some property the Mohawk who had accompanied Klock to England claimed had been stolen from him. The group promised they would return with a release of his claims for Klock to sign. When they returned in June with the release, Klock was wisely absent. The group left after making some threats to Klock's family and killing some of their sheep. On July 8 while most of the Canajoharie Mohawks were at Johnson Hall, Klock swore out a complaint naming Molly's brother Joseph Brant as "the ringleader" of the May assault.[32]

* * *

The pressure to address Six Nations' grievances in a manner that would keep war from breaking out was once again putting severe strains on Sir William's health. Sir William confessed to Gage that "so much trouble & attention has greatly effected my Health which was much improved last Summer, but I must make a Sacrifice to the Urgency of the times."[33]

Did Sir William understand how near the end was? A letter he wrote to one of his militia comrades the week before was still full of his paternalistic but generous plans for his Highland tenants and the further development of the Mohawk valley: "should they prove industrious, & get forward, it would heighten my happiness, there being nothing upon Earth delights me more than to see the rude woods made cultivable, and afford Sustenance to the poor & distressed."[34]

Sir William's last report about Peter was, as always, a good one. At the end of June, Hugh Wallace wrote, "I saw your Son Peter at Philada. last Wednesday. he was verry well & I think is a verry sober good Lad. he has a verry good Name from his Acquaintance."[35] Perhaps the happy memory of those words of praise for his loving and precocious son helped Sir William to heave himself out of bed on the morning of July 11.

It was a hot day, and Sir William confessed to family members that one of his fits might be coming on. He could feel "a sense of compression and tightness across the stomach," which was sometimes a harbinger of worse to come.[36] The conference had been going on for a week, but many of the Six Nations people were still very upset. Sir William was expected to give an oration late that afternoon; it was important that he go through with it.

Sir William stood under the arbor of his garden and began his speech. All around him were familiar faces: Molly, proud of him as always but deeply concerned; Guy Johnson and Daniel Claus, the sons-in-law he had trained in Indian diplomacy for so many years and who the Six Nations and Canadian tribes looked upon as his successors; and hundreds of Six Nations people, some who were among his closest friends and others who respected him as an ally and a protector.

At first the speech possessed all "the spirit, activity and energy" that the Six Nations expected of a great orator.[37] Sir William apologized for settler encroachments into Native American territory and for the crimes they committed there. He assured them that "these men will be sought after and punished."[38] But then, under the pounding rays of the sun, he began to sway. He had the presence of mind to rapidly conclude his remarks: "Whatever may happen, you must not be shaken out of your shoes." Sir William ordered pipes, tobacco, and liquor to be distributed. Then he asked for help. He was near to fainting. He told Molly and the others he could not breathe. They helped him to a chair in the room he shared with Molly. He drank a little water and wine, but this did not revive him. Dr. John Dease, his beloved nephew, was sufficiently concerned that a messenger was sent to Fort Johnson telling Sir John to come with all speed.[39]

Sir John mounted his best horse. At some point during the 11-mile gallop to Johnson Hall, the horse collapsed. Sir John hurriedly walked the rest of the way, but he was too late. At 8 p.m. as the last rays of light left the skies of the Mohawk valley, Sir William suffered the last of the many "fits" that had haunted him for the past 13 years of his life. As Sir John approached Johnson Hall, he could hear the mourning songs of the Six Nations.[40]

Sir William died at age 60, a normal lifespan for the time. Throughout his 15 years with Molly, he had willed himself to fight off the effects of his war wound and his other maladies. Now the battle was over, and Molly faced the future that their 23-year age difference had always portended. The first few days were filled with comforting their children and receiving the condolences of the hundreds of Six Nations people present at Johnson Hall when Sir William died. Then came the funeral.

The procession that took Sir William away from Johnson Hall for the last time wended its way down a hill to St. John's, the Anglican church he had built for the town. As was customary, the men of the family walked directly behind the coffin. Sir John, Guy Johnson, and Daniel Claus sincerely loved and respected Sir William. Now as they followed him down the hill to his final resting place, they must have wondered if they could hold together the legacy of leadership in the Mohawk valley that he had bestowed upon them.

Behind Sir William's male European heirs came the rest of the family: Anne Claus with her sole surviving little boy, Sir William's namesake; Mary Johnson with her three daughters; and Molly with all of her children except Peter. Brant Johnson and William of Canajoharie walked with them, too. Brant, raised by his Mohawk mother, accepted that he was of his mother's clan, not of his father's. William, motherless, angry, and conflicted about his identity, followed the English funeral customs in silence out of respect for his father's memory and for Molly, who had always been kind to him.

Sir William's will specified that the Mohawk sachems should be invited to his funeral and given a place of honor. In the outpouring of emotion following his death, the entire Mohawk nation walked behind Sir William's family singing the Mohawk mourning songs for their brother.

Behind the Mohawks came 2,000 European American settlers of the Mohawk valley. Hundreds of them were tenants of Sir William. They sincerely mourned a man who had given them a start in the New World on terms that could only be dreamed of in the Old World. Many others were not his tenants. Small landowners and militiamen, they respected his military leadership during the French and Indian War and his uncanny ability to preserve peace with the Six Nations, whose land they were encroaching upon. But quite a few of them saw Sir William as part of an old order they were chafing against. These were the people who would soon be at loggerheads with the surviving members of Sir William's family.

Behind the settlers came hundreds of representatives of the other five tribes of the Six Nations. Unlike the Mohawks, their warriors were more allies than brothers to Sir William. It would be Molly and her brother Joseph's strenuous task to keep them loyal to the king when the final breach between Britain and her American colonies came.[41]

The mourners laid Sir William to rest beneath the altar of the church. His will suggested that if her children so desired, "the remains of my beloved wife Catharine Johnson" should be removed from her grave near Fort Johnson and laid beside him. Catherine would have the respectability in death she had craved in life. Posterity would have no reason to question Sir John's right to the baronetcy or the right of the baby son Mary Watts Johnson would soon give Sir John.[42]

* * *

As for Molly, although according to Daniel Claus she never ceased to mourn Sir William, her job was to shepherd their eight children, now ages 17 months to 14 years, to adulthood. Back in 1763 when their three eldest children were babes, a close friend of Sir William died. Sir William's condolence note to the widow, Catherine Corry, summed up what Molly knew Sir William expected of her now and what she expected of herself:

> Having always considered you to be a Lady of good sense I shall not attempt to offer you the usual consolation on such occasions, convinced your direction will enable you to support a loss which is at present irretrievable especially as the care of your Family is now become your sole & particular charge for the Welfare of whom prudence demands the utmost Extension of those Abilities of which I know you to be Mistress.[43]

Molly's own "Abilities" would now be put to the test, not just as the well-off mother of a large family of young children, but soon also as a war refugee struggling to preserve a future for her own children and her nation. In the beginning, though, there was some assistance. A woman could not be the legal guardian of her children in 18th-century America. Sir William named the following guardians for Molly's children: his nephew John Deese; John Butler, Sir William's Indian Department interpreter and the son of his first British friend in the Mohawk valley; James Stevenson, who had a half–Native American son himself and was beholden to Molly for the child's care; Henry Frey, whom Sir William had designated to hold one of two Tryon County seats in the provincial assembly; and Joseph Chew, Sir William's Indian Department secretary and the man who had escorted Peter to Philadelphia.[44] Sir William's last charge to these men was heartfelt. Invoking "the long un[in]terrupted friendship" between him and "Mary Brant my present Housekeeper," they were to guard the legal interests of their eight children and oversee the enforcement of the financial plan for their benefit set forth in the will. "They will strictly and as Brothers inviolably observe and Execute this my last charge to them. The Strong dependence on & expectation of which unburthens my mind, allays my cares & makes a change the less alarming."[45]

Sir William had given considerable thought to the estate plan for his complex family, drafted six months prior to his death. The beneficiaries included his three "legitimate" European American children by Catherine Weissenberg, Molly and her eight children, and three other natural children: Brant Johnson and William of Canajoharie, described as "Half bred Mohocks" and as "two Mohawk Lads," and Mary McGrah, described as "Daughter of Christopher McGrah."[46]

Unlike Brant Johnson, William of Canajoharie, and Mary McGrah, Sir William specifically acknowledged Molly's children as his own in the will. The claiming of Molly's children was intended as a public acknowledgment of his special relationship with and love for Molly. The failure to acknowledge the other three natural children probably was not because he doubted paternity, at least in the cases of Brant and William, but instead was the result of his desire to prevent the will from becoming a source of scandal by admitting in a public document that he had begotten children by so many different women.

The property division was not equal. British wills of the time almost always favored the eldest son over younger sons and all sons over daughters. Illegitimate children were often omitted entirely, but a decent man such as Sir William provided something for them:

> And First To the children of my Present House Keeper, Mary Brant the Sum of One thousand pounds sterling, viz to Peter my natural son by said Mary Brant the sum of Three Hundred pounds Sterlg. And to each of the rest, being seven in number, One Hundred pounds each.[47]

Brant Johnson and William of Canajoharie, who were already of age, each received 100 pounds in New York currency rather than pounds sterling, an indication that there was no expectation they would ever travel or have interests beyond Indian country. Sir John, "my Dearly beloved son," was to receive one half of the remaining money after other bequests were paid, and Daniel Claus and Guy Johnson, on behalf of Anne, Mary, and their children, were each to receive one fourth of that same amount.[48]

As for Molly, "To my prudent & faithfull Housekeeper Mary Brant, mother of the before mentioned Eight children, I will and bequeath the Lot No. one being part of the Royal Grant now called Kingsland ... which she is to enjoy peaceably during her natural life, after which it is to be possessed by her Son Peter & his Heirs forever."[49] Touchingly, Sir William did not require Molly's land inheritance to revert to Peter should she marry, as was often done. She did not take advantage of that opportunity, and perhaps Sir William knew she never would.

Sir John received most of his father's real estate as was customary: Johnson Hall, Fort Johnson, and 100,000 acres of land. Daniel Claus, in right of his wife, received their house, Williamsburg, as well as another house in Albany and 13,000 acres of land. Guy Johnson, in right of his wife, received Guy Park, a house in Schenectady, and 13,000 acres of land. In addition to their cash bequests, Molly's children received real estate grants that were side by side in the Kingsland patent. Peter received 6,000 acres (roughly one half what his "legitimate" half sisters Anne and Mary received via their husbands). Molly's younger son, George, then about five years old, received 3,780 acres. Her six daughters received between 2,300 and 3,000 acres each.[50]

Sir John was bequeathed the library and furniture at Johnson Hall except the contents of Sir William's room and the nursery, which were bequeathed to Molly. Sir John, Anne Claus, and Mary Johnson each received one-fourth of Sir William's slaves and one-fourth each of his cattle:

The other fourth of my Slaves and Stock of Cattle of every kind I give & Bequeath to the Children of Mary Brant my Housekeeper, Or to the survivors of them, to be divided Equally amongst them, Except two Horses, two Cows, two breeding sows & four Sheep which I would have given (before any Division is made) to young Brant & William of Conajohare.[51]

In addition to the enslaved people Molly could take with her as the property of her minor children, she was personally bequeathed "One Negroe Wench Jenny the sister of Juba."[52] Jenny was the young enslaved woman whom Molly had apparently prevented from being sold in the mid–1760s at the behest of Juba, Jenny's sister. Both Jenny and Juba would accompany Molly and her children into their Canadian exile.

9

The Lonely and the Brave

Just two weeks after Sir William's death the probate of the will was completed, and it was time for Molly and her children to vacate Johnson Hall in favor of Sir John and Lady Mary. The two oldest girls, Elizabeth and Magdalene, were sent off to boarding school in Schenectady. Peter was summoned home from Philadelphia. All the comings and goings and the departure from Johnson Hall must have been difficult to explain to the five younger children. Molly and her family probably lived at Joseph's house in Canajoharie while her own home was being constructed nearby. Also being constructed was the store that Peter was to operate with his mother's help.

General Gage accepted Sir William's recommendation that Guy Johnson succeed him as superintendent of Indian affairs. Within a week of Sir William's death, Gage named Guy acting superintendent and wrote to the Earl of Dartmouth, the king's minister for the American colonies, requesting a permanent appointment for Guy.[1]

Guy confirmed Joseph Brant's position as an interpreter in the Indian Department and asked him to be present for all negotiations. This increase in Joseph's responsibilities meant that Molly, although now residing in Canajoharie, could easily continue to keep abreast of both sides of the diplomacy between the Six Nations and Britain.[2]

Guy needed the help and support of all experienced Indian Department personnel, because just as was happening throughout the rest of the American colonies, political events were coming to a head in the Mohawk valley. On August 27, 1774, only six weeks after Sir William's death, the Tryon County Committee of Safety[3] held its first meeting at a farmhouse in the hamlet of Stone Arabia, close by the farmlands Sir William had bequeathed to several of Molly's daughters. The committee issued a declaration that decried Parliament's attempt to tax their colonies as an "obvious Incroachment in the Rights and Liberties of the British Subjects in America." The declaration condemned the closure of the Port of Boston as "oppressive & arbitrary" and promised to send aid to the inhabitants of

Boston. The signers endorsed the five delegates selected in New York City to attend the first Continental Congress, and while claiming to continue their allegiance to the king, the declaration's signers nonetheless promised to "abide by ... such Restrictions and Regulations ... agreed upon by the said Congress." A committee of correspondence was established to communicate with the Committees of Safety in Albany and New York City.[4]

The 12 members of the standing committee were a collection of small landowners. Not surprisingly, George Klock's son Jacob was one of them, but in a sign of the fissures soon to appear in the ordered world Sir William had known, so was John Frey, a son of Henry Frey, Sir William's close friend, Guy's colleague in the provincial assembly and one of the guardians of Molly's children.[5]

The Johnson family's first reaction to the changing political landscape was to wait and see what transpired at the Continental Congress in Philadelphia. Sir John did not enjoy politics. Shy and retiring by nature, he had steadfastly refused his father's attempts to invest him with political offices. Sir John had, however, accepted his father's request that he succeed Sir William as military commander of the region. Sir John was now major general of the Tryon County militia, whose membership included hundreds of Johnson tenants and allies.

Guy Johnson, outgoing and a ready student of all that his uncle had to teach about diplomacy and power, was the political arm of the family. In addition to being the superintendent of Indian affairs and a member of the provincial assembly, he was also a county judge and an adjutant general of the militia.[6]

Although wary of the new assertiveness of some of his neighbors, as evidenced by the formation of the Committee of Safety, Guy still couldn't believe that men of substance at the Continental Congress would throw away their association with the mother country. In mid-September he wrote to John Blackburn, Sir William's favorite London agent: "The Delegates are sitting at Philadelphia I really cant forsee what it will end in; but I hope the event will rather be productive of harmony rather than disunion."[7]

As the fall wore on, it became clear that the proceedings of the Continental Congress were not going to "be productive of harmony." With Joseph's help, Guy discovered that Reverend Samuel Kirkland was actively informing the Oneidas of the proceedings at the Continental Congress and encouraging them to believe that the king meant to make war on both the colonists and Native Americans.[8]

At a meeting of the Six Nations confederacy in November, Joseph and probably Molly were able to line up allies to dispute the Oneidas' charges. Guy reported gratefully to Gage: that "some persons of Influence exerted themselves at Onondaga and observed that it would be time enough to suspect us when we proceeded farther."[9]

Guy held conferences with the Six Nations at Guy Park on December 1–8, 1774, and January 20–28, 1775. Joseph attended both conferences, and although only Indian Department employee names are mentioned in the minutes, Molly probably came down from Canajoharie for these important meetings as well. Guy pointed out to the Six Nations that it was the colonists who constantly encroached on their land, while the king's deputies sought to hold the colonists back. Guy also openly denounced Samuel Kirkland for the first time.[10]

Guy and Sir John realized that Patriot sympathies were increasing in the Mohawk valley and that they could not let the activities of the Committee of Safety go unanswered any longer. The magistrates of Tryon County were all Johnson men, and the grand jury was handpicked by the magistrates. At Guy and Sir John's behest, the magistrates and the grand jury of Tryon County signed a declaration denouncing the activities of the second Continental Congress and declaring the county's loyalty to the king.

As the winter of 1775 gave way to spring, there were persistent rumors that Massachusetts militia companies were planning to march into the Mohawk valley and arrest Guy Johnson, the ranking British official in upper New York. Guy was sufficiently alarmed that on March 20 he made a formal complaint to the magistrates of Tryon County.[11]

Guy and Sir John began fortifying Guy Park and Johnson Hall. Using his power as a judge, Guy had the Tryon County sheriff stop suspicious persons on the roads, searching them for correspondence with the Massachusetts rebels and the Albany Committee of Public Safety.

* * *

Meanwhile in Canajoharie, Molly went anxiously about her business. She and 15-year-old Peter operated the store that Sir William had envisioned. Like all merchants, they found that trade goods were harder to come by because of the boycott of British goods that was in effect. Several of her children attended the grammar school at Canajoharie with their cousin Isaac, Joseph's son. The older ones still cried for their father. The baby did not remember him. The adjustment to the loss of her life partner and the strain of parenting eight children alone would have been enough to fill her heart with pain, but now she also had to contemplate the likelihood that war was imminent.

There was no question as to whose side Molly was on. Sir William's memory required loyalty to the king who had honored him, but so did her children's future. For that matter, so did the future of the Mohawk nation.

Molly firmly believed that the Oneidas were fools to think that the colonists were their friends. The colonists would soon try to gobble up Six Nations territory if the king's officials, the men of the Indian Department, were not there to deter them.

Molly knew that if war broke out, Joseph and most of the Mohawk men would stand with Guy, the man they had given Sir William's Mohawk name, Warraghiyagey. Peter would go too. There was really no question about that either. Sir John had accompanied Sir William to the Battle of Lake George at age 14. Joseph had accompanied Sir William to Ticonderoga at age 15. Joseph would look out for Peter as best he could, but Peter would join all of his male kin, both Mohawk and British, in the defense of the Mohawks' ancestral lands and the Johnson family's patrimony.

* * *

Shortly after the Battles of Lexington and Concord, the Mohawk valley Patriots called a public meeting to stir up support for the rebel army forming on the outskirts of Boston. The interpretation of what transpired at that meeting depended very much on one's politics. As the notes of the Committee of Safety described it, "This Country has for a series of Years been Ruled by one family, the different Branches of which are still strenious in dissuading people from coming into Congressional Measures." From the Committee of Safety's point of view, the Johnsons were illegally suppressing the liberties of the people "and even have last Week at a numerous Meeting in the Mohawk District appeared with all their Dependants armed to oppose the people from considering of their Grievances, their number being so large and the people unarmed, struck Terror into most of them, and they dispersed."[12]

Guy and Sir John's view, of course, was that they were the ranking political and military officials of the king in Tryon County and that General Gage had instructed Guy to take all necessary measures to keep the rebellion from spreading. When Guy, Sir John, and Daniel Claus strode to the front of the meeting that May night and threatened with arrest all those who did not peaceably disperse, they did so in the name of the king and to uphold what they believed to be the lawfully constituted government.

Although forced to back down at the public meeting, the firebrands of the Committee of Safety were undeterred, vowing "it is our fixed Resolution to support and carry into Execution everything Recommended by the Continental and provincial Congress, and to be free, or die."[13] Political opinion in the county at the time was divided into three camps: Johnson tenants and allies, firmly on the side of the king; Patriots determined

9. The Lonely and the Brave   109

to establish a republican government; and a third to a half of the population who either didn't care or were biding their time to see how events played out.

Despite the Committee of Safety's complaints that its letters were being seized by Guy Johnson, the committee was also in the business of seizing letters. On May 21, the committee's minutes reported that two letters had been "intercepted," one from the Mohawks to the Oneidas, urging them to remain loyal to the king or at least to maintain neutrality, and the other from Guy Johnson to the magistrates of the county.[14]

The letter from the Mohawks to the Oneidas was signed by Joseph Brant and the leading sachems of the three Mohawk clans. Molly, as one of the most influential Six Nations matrons, together with the three Mohawk clan mothers, probably also played a role in the authorship of the letter.[15]

Members of the Committee of Safety deeply feared Sir John's ability to rouse his tenants and Guy's ability to call upon the Six Nations. The committee countered by actively negotiating with the Oneidas with the help of Reverend Kirkland and by procuring powder and flints from Albany.[16]

The summer was the traditional time for Indian conferences. The Patriots were concerned that their situation would become much more perilous if Guy Johnson was left at liberty to invite hundreds or thousands of Six Nations people to Guy Park in the coming months. At the end of May, the Committee of Safety took two actions. In order to force the unaligned colonists of the county to take a stand, it issued a proclamation forbidding any signer of its "Association" "to have any Dealings or other Connections in the Way of trade with any person or persons whatsoever, who have not signed the Association.... Anyone breaking these Resolutions ... will be dealt with as Enemies to the District and to their Country."[17]

The Committee of Safety's second measure was to write Guy Johnson a lengthy letter making several demands, including that he hold the summer's Indian conference at Onondaga rather than invite the tribes to Guy Park, that he persuade the Six Nations to remain neutral in the dispute between Great Britain and the colonies, and that he disarm because he was in no danger from his political opponents. But despite this assurance, there was a thinly veiled threat: "We cannot think, that as You and your family possess very Large Estates in this County, you are unfavorable to American Freedom, altho' you may differ with us in the Mode in obtaining a redress of Grievances."[18]

Nicholas Herkheimer (Joseph Brant's neighbor) and Edward Wall (Peter, Elizabeth, and Magdalene Johnson's former fawning schoolmaster) were the Committee of Safety members who hand-delivered the letter to

Guy Johnson at Guy Park on Saturday, June 3, 1775. He told them he would respond by June 12.[19]

* * *

The moment of decision was now upon the Johnson family. The Johnsons knew that the colonial army around Boston was growing by the day and that General Gage was in no position to assist them. The defense of the Mohawk valley was in their hands. The Mohawks were loyal to them, and although some of the older sachems still hoped that the situation could be resolved peacefully, many of the young men, led by Joseph, were prepared to fight.

The Oneidas and the tribe with whom they shared their land, the Tuscaroras, were at best neutral and probably pro–Patriot. The three western tribes, the Onondagas, the Cayugas, and the Senecas, were on the fence. There was little European settlement as yet in their territories, and some of their number saw no reason to involve themselves in the Englishmen's disputes. Nevertheless, they understood that Guy Johnson was their link to the king, who had sometimes been a restraining force on the colonists and whose annual gift of trade goods was a significant part of their economy. Guy thought he could raise a substantial number of fighting men from their ranks if he invoked their alliance with the king, but they would need some convincing. Asking the three western tribes to travel through Oneida territory to discuss their entry into a war the Oneidas opposed was awkward. Perhaps the Patriot demand that the annual conference be held west of Oneida country was a gift in disguise. The western tribes could meet with him in Onondaga country without difficult conversations with Oneida hosts on the way to the conference.

While Guy was pondering all this, a message arrived in cipher from Gage. Guy was to muster as large a force of Native Americans and loyal militia as he could and proceed to Canada, where he was to join General Guy Carleton's forces for the relief of Boston. This order made it imperative that the conference occur at Fort Ontario, also known as Oswego, on the southern shore of Lake Ontario in Onondaga country.[20]

Once Guy Johnson convinced the Six Nations to aid the king, an open state of war would exist in the Mohawk valley. What did this mean for the rest of the family and their property? It was decided that Sir John would remain at fortified Johnson Hall, surrounded by dozens of armed tenants who lived in the vicinity of Johnstown. This would hopefully deter the Patriots from attempting to seize Johnson property, but everyone understood that Guy Park and Williamsburg, 11 miles distant from Johnson Hall would be in an exposed position once Guy and Daniel Claus departed with their militiamen and Mohawk allies for Fort Ontario.

9. The Lonely and the Brave

Should Mary Johnson, Anne Claus, and their children move to the relative safety of Johnson Hall and their brother's protection? Both elected instead to accompany their husbands to Fort Ontario and from there to go with them to Canada. For Mary Johnson, the decision was a particularly serious one because she was eight months pregnant. Once hostilities began, it might be months or even years before the families were reunited if the women and children did not leave with Guy and Daniel. Still, for Mary it would mean a 95-mile journey in an open boat to Fort Ontario, with portages through the woods made on horseback in the last month of her pregnancy. Mary and Guy Johnson's union was a love match (even though Mary's father had been delighted by it). Mary could not bear the idea of the separation. She chose to take the risk. In the long years that followed, Guy would have much time to ponder the correctness of the decision.

* * *

They set out shortly before the deadline expired for Guy's answer to the Patriots. In addition to Guy and Mary, Daniel and Anne, and their children, dozens of Fort Hunter Mohawk warriors and about 120 European American militiamen were members of the party. Acting as officers for the militiamen were Indian Department interpreter John Butler and his son Walter. The Johnsons and some of the militia traveled on bateaux loaded with supplies and with gifts for the other Six Nations tribes. Other militiamen marched along the road that ran beside the river. Most of the Mohawks traveled in canoes. The flotilla was not inconspicuous as it poled and paddled its way westward up the Mohawk River. The travelers stopped at Canajoharie, where Joseph, Peter, and William of Canajoharie, together with dozens of Canajoharie Mohawk fighting men, joined the expedition. There were now about 90 Mohawk warriors ready to fight beside the Johnsons and their militiamen.[21]

Molly and the rest of her children remained at Canajoharie, as did her mother Margaret and Joseph's wife and children. Worried that Elizabeth and Magdalene could be seized as hostages at their school in Schenectady, Molly summoned them home. They would help her run the store in Peter's absence and assist her in caring for the five younger children. Although it must have been somewhat unnerving to know that most of Canajoharie's men of military age were departing, Molly was shrewd enough to understand that the Patriots were afraid of the Mohawks and would probably do nothing to the Canajoharie and Fort Hunter settlements that would spark Mohawk revenge. It was probably young Peter on whom her anxieties settled. Like all mothers who watch a son go off to war, she repressed the thought that it might be the last time she would ever see him.

* * *

The Mohawks' letter to the Oneidas had done some good. When the expedition arrived at Fort Stanwix in Oneida country, many of the Oneidas announced that they would remain neutral, despite Reverend Kirkland's Patriot sympathies. The party then proceeded to Fort Ontario, arriving safely on June 17. Within the next few weeks, a total of 1,458 Native Americans, mostly members of the Six Nations but also some Shawnees, Caughnawagas, and Hurons, assembled there to receive the king's presents and to listen to Guy's exhortations. After days of meetings, almost all of those present except the Mohawks decided to remain neutral. This was a blow to Guy, but worse was to come.[22]

Shortly before Guy's force of Tryon County militiamen and Mohawk warriors was to set off across Lake Ontario for Canada, Mary Johnson went into labor. We do not know whether it was an army doctor at the fort or an experienced Six Nations midwife who attended her. Her sister, Anne Claus, was certainly present. Whatever help she received was not enough. She and the baby died on July 11, 1775, the first anniversary of her father Sir William's death. There was no choice but to bury her at the fort. Anne took charge of Mary's three young daughters, the oldest of whom was 12. Guy would never fully recover from the shock of Mary's death. He outlived her by 13 years but did not remarry. The heartbroken family and their 220 followers set off across Lake Ontario within a few hours of her burial. They arrived at Montreal on July 17, 1775.[23]

Shortly after the Johnson flotilla's departure from the area, the Tryon County Committee of Safety decided to tighten the screws on all those colonists who had not yet declared themselves for the Patriot cause: "Resolved That it be Recommended ... That the General Association be tendered to such, as have not signed it, and that exact Lists of such persons in each District who shall refuse or neglect to sign the same, be Returned to this Committee by the first Day of July next, or sooner."[24]

The Committee of Safety, still trying to convince the Mohawks to remain neutral, parleyed with the few Canajoharie sachems and older men who had not departed with the Johnsons and Joseph Brant. The Mohawks used their standard method of temporizing with opponents. The old men of the village wanted peace, but they could not control the young men. The local colonists certainly noticed how empty the vicinity was of military-age Mohawk males.[25]

Meanwhile, the Tryon County Patriots were extremely anxious about Guy and Joseph's activities and believed themselves to be in desperate need of assistance: "All our Enemies in this County will appear in arms against us as soon as the Indians are nigh to us[;] ... ammunition is so

9. The Lonely and the Brave

scant that We cannot furnish three hundred Men so as to be able to make a Stand against so great a Number."[26]

In response, the Continental Congress decided to send commissioners to Albany to meet with representatives of the Six Nations for the purpose of formally requesting their friendship. Prior to the conference, the commissioners traveled to German Flatts to urge the Canajoharie Mohawks to attend the meeting, and to request that they send messengers to the Canadian tribes asking them to attend as well. When the congressional commissioners arrived at German Flatts in mid–August, Molly was among those who met with them. The commissioners were under no illusions as to where Molly's loyalty lay. Lieutenant Colonel Tench Tilghman, the secretary of the delegation, and later an aide to George Washington, wrote in his journal on the night of the meeting that "the Indians pay her great respect and I am afraid her influence will give us some trouble, for we are informed she is working strongly to prevent the meeting at Albany, being entirely in the Interests of Guy Johnson."[27]

With Guy Johnson and the rest of the Indian Department in Canada, Molly understood the importance of projecting strength and confidence to the Patriot delegation: "She saluted us with an air of ease and politeness, she was dressed after the Indian Manner, but her linen and other Cloathes the finest of their kind."[28]

Reverend Kirkland accompanied the commissioners. This man who had been her brother's friend, and had received hospitality and help in the early days of his ministry from Sir William and from her, now stood before her trying to undo Sir William's life work. She decided to shame him in front of the other Mohawk elders and remind them that he was behaving dishonorably and was unworthy of their trust: "Upon seeing Mr. Kirkland an Oneida Missionary, she taxed him with neglect in passing by her House without calling to see her." Playing the widow card in a way that would have been poignant to the other Mohawk elders, "she said there was a time when she had friends enough, but remarked with sensible emotion that the unfortunate and the poor were always neglected."[29]

Although at one level Molly would have preferred that no Canajoharie representatives attend the Patriots' conference, she understood that with so many Mohawk fighting men accompanying Guy Johnson and Joseph in Canada, it was best to temporize for the present. Also, if some Canajoharie Mohawks attended the conference, they would give her intelligence about what occurred there. Sending messengers to the Canadian tribes to urge their attendance was another matter. That would be a confusing signal to the Mohawks' Canadian relatives. Molly and her allies firmly exerted their influence to have this Patriot request rejected. In the end, all the Patriot commissioners achieved at the Albany conference was more promises of neutrality, with the Mohawks still pro–British, the Oneidas still pro–Patriot, and the other tribes waiting for events to unfold.[30]

Although Molly put on a brave face and did what she needed to do during the negotiations with the Patriot commissioners, the toll of the last year was apparent to those who had known her in happier times: when "one of the Company who had known her before told her she looked thin and asked her if she was sick, she said sickness had not reduced her, but it was the remembrance of a Loss that could never be made up to her, meaning the death of Sr. William."[31]

* * *

As summer turned to fall, Guy Johnson's militiamen and their Mohawk allies rendezvoused with General Carleton's forces in Canada. Johnson's forces took part in actions at Chambly, St. Johns, and Montreal. Their resistance to the invading Patriot army would help preserve Canada for the king. It was in an action just outside Montreal that Molly's son Peter established his military reputation in a manner that would have made Sir William proud.

Ethan Allen, who had already earned his own considerable renown at Ticonderoga, was secretly advancing toward Montreal with a force of 110 men (part of a larger force commanded by General Richard Montgomery), on September 25, 1775, when his movements were detected by a Loyalist scout. The British forces in the vicinity consisted of about 500 men, including 40 regulars. The remainder of the British forces consisted of British American militiamen and Native Americans from Canada as well as Guy Johnson's Tryon County militia and their Mohawk allies.[32]

Once the British commander knew Allen's position, he was able to use his superior numbers to begin flanking Allen. As Allen and his men became aware of what was happening, the Canadian Patriots, who had been ordered to resist the flanking operation, slipped off into the woods, leaving Allen with about 45 of his Green Mountain Boys in a dense forest and in imminent danger of being surrounded. Allen and his men began retreating through the woods as fast as they could. According to Allen's account of the battle, they ran a full mile, with the Loyalists in hot pursuit. The regulars, unused to woodland conditions, could not keep up. It was the Mohawks and the Tryon County militiamen who bore down on 37-year-old Allen and his men, with 16-year-old Peter Johnson in the vanguard.

As Allen tells it, "I expected in a very short time, to try the world of spirits; for I was apprehensive that no quarter would be given to me, and therefore had determined to sell my life as dear as I could." It was Peter, dressed as a British militia officer, who was closest to Allen: "One of the enemy's officers boldly pressing in the rear, discharged his fuse at me; the ball whistled near me, as did many others that day. I returned the salute, and missed him, as running had put us both out of breath; for I conclude we were not frightened, I then told him that inasmuch as his numbers were so far superior to mine, I would surrender, provided I could be treated with honor, and be assured of good quarter for myself and the men who were with me, and he answered I should."[33]

With admirable self-possession and accompanied by only one other militiaman, Peter "directed me and my party to advance towards him, which was done, I handed him my sword." The Mohawks had by now caught up, and some wanted to take immediate revenge on Allen. This practice was not regarded as dishonorable among the Six Nations and may have been one of the reasons Allen wanted to surrender to a British officer. As Allen tells it, he had to hide behind Peter, actually twirling him around in a circle, as two Mohawks menaced him with their rifles. Since Peter was armed and Allen was not, Peter apparently was willing to serve as Allen's shield until an "Irishman" arrived and convinced the Mohawks to desist.[34]

This man was probably one of Sir William's stalwarts from Johnson Hall. In any event, young Peter was given full credit for taking Allen prisoner. Guy, reporting to the Earl of Dartmouth, wrote, "Col: Allen being vigorously pressed by those of my Corps surrendered to Mr. Johnson one of my officers."[35]

Both Allen's and Guy's accounts make it clear that Peter participated in the battle as a British militia officer, not as a Mohawk. Although he was living with his Mohawk mother at Canajoharie, the store he operated with her there, patronized by both European American settlers and Mohawks, was intended to give him the opportunity to become one of the leading merchants of the Mohawk valley. Together with his land inheritance, the store was meant to ensure that he would be looked upon as a man of substance by the British and German settlers in the valley. His Mohawk connections would make him useful in helping to run the Indian Department, perhaps as a possible successor to Guy, who had no sons, and to help protect the Mohawks from further incursions on their territory. But Peter was being presented to the wider world as British, as his father intended.

* * *

While Guy Johnson, Daniel Claus, and their men were helping to hold Montreal for the king, alarming news came to them from London. After extensive lobbying, Major John Campbell had managed to get himself appointed superintendent to the Canadian Indians. This cleaved off a substantial portion of Guy's Northern District and meant that despite his 20 years of service, his command of native languages, and his ability to convince the Canadian tribes to support the king's cause, the role that Sir William envisioned for Daniel Claus had suddenly evaporated.[36]

Guy and Daniel decided that they must go to London to lay their case directly before the Earl of Dartmouth, secretary for the American colonies. Guy had recently received a request from the Earl of Dartmouth that he send Dartmouth a summary of all Native American grievances. Guy and Joseph Brant quickly realized that this was a remarkable opportunity. Why not have the highly articulate and well-educated Joseph describe the Six Nations' grievances to the Earl of Dartmouth personally? At the same time, Joseph could drive home to him the unique trust the Six Nations reposed in the Johnson family and the importance of retaining the Johnsons as the king's sole representatives for Indian diplomacy in the northern half of the American colonies. John Hill Oteronyente, a Fort Hunter Mohawk, would also accompany the group.[37]

With the approach of winter, many of the Mohawks, including William of Canajoharie, were planning to leave Canada and return to the Mohawk valley. Peter Johnson could easily have accompanied them home to Canajoharie. It was decided instead that he would accompany Guy, Daniel, and Joseph to London.

While Molly undoubtedly would have loved to see her son, there were good reasons for him to go to London, reasons with which Guy and Joseph thought Molly would agree. The group was to travel on the same ship that was transporting the famous Ethan Allen for trial in Britain. It would have been foolish not to let Peter capitalize on his having taken Allen prisoner. This was the sort of thing that could secure a young man's future. It is touching evidence of the love Guy bore Sir William that he wanted the boy to have full credit for this deed rather than try to take the credit for himself. With the Mohawk valley about to erupt into warfare, Peter would not be a merchant again for a long time. Some kind of military appointment was what he needed, and it was much better to be an officer in a regular army unit than in the colonial militia. The trip to London would also allow him to meet important people, and in a world where favors were bestowed upon people who knew people, these connections could later prove invaluable to him. Moreover, now that he had famously captured Ethan Allen, it wasn't at all clear that Peter could simply go home and live quietly with his mother and siblings. The Committee of Safety might feel compelled to arrest him. William of Canajoharie was taking some risk by returning home, but he identified as a Mohawk, and the Patriots were still trying to negotiate with the Mohawks. Peter, who was holding himself out as a British subject, was at greater risk, particularly as Allen's captor. And, of course, Peter wanted to go to London. What an adventure!

Both Guy and Joseph were in favor of Peter accompanying them, and Joseph's consent was important. Men were deemed to be responsible for their sisters' sons in Mohawk culture. Unlike a father and son, they belonged to the same clan, and clan offices were passed down from maternal uncle to maternal nephew. It was often the maternal uncle as much as the father who taught a Mohawk youth how to be a man, regularly taking him along on hunting and raiding expeditions. This was absolutely the case when a boy's father was dead. Although Peter was being presented to the world as British, he was close to his mother and spoke fluent Mohawk. Joseph would have felt very responsible for the welfare of his only sister's eldest son. Joseph was important to the success of the London venture. Guy could not have brought Peter along if Joseph thought he should be sent home. Instead, Joseph concluded that it was safer and more advantageous for Peter that he accompany his elders on the journey across the ocean. The choice that Molly had made in taking Peter from Canajoharie as a baby to grow up at Fort Johnson and Johnson Hall with his father's people was playing out to its logical conclusion.

On November 11, 1775, Guy's party boarded the *Adamant* at Quebec and sailed for Falmouth, England. The party consisted of 14 people: Guy Johnson and his three daughters, Daniel and Anne Claus and their son, Joseph Brant, John Hill Oteronyente, and Peter Johnson, as well as Walter Butler, Joseph Chew, Peter's cousin Dr. John Dease, and Gilbert Tice (a former Johnstown innkeeper). Butler, Chew, Dease, and Tice were all Indian Department employees who had departed the Mohawk valley with Guy and fought for the king in Canada. None of them would be safe if they returned to the Mohawk valley.[38]

10

The Land of Their Fathers

Back in the Mohawk valley, the Tryon Committee of Safety alternated between boldness and panic. In the last week of October, it was decided that three members of the committee, one a member of the Klock family, would pay Sir John a visit at Johnson Hall and in effect demand that he choose sides.

Although not a gregarious man like his father, Sir John now showed himself to possess his father's intelligence and resolve. Disdaining to ask for time to reply, Sir John told the committeemen that "he never had denied the Use either of the Court-house or Goal to any Body, ... for the Use, where these houses have been built for, but ... the Courthouse & Goal be his property, till he is paid 700 [pounds] ... being out of his pocket for the Building of the same." Sir John then cannily told the committee representatives that he had never forbidden his tenants to join the Patriot militia, "as they may use their pleasure, but we might save ourselves the Trouble he being sure that they would not."[1]

As for himself, the man who had been personally knighted by George III told them "that before he would sign any Association, or would lift up his hand against the King, he would rather suffer, that his head shall be cut off." Sir John concluded the interview by telling the delegation that it was common knowledge that people in New York City had been forced to sign the Association on threat of exile and "that likewise two thirds of the Conajohary and German flatts people have been forced to sign."[2]

The Committee of Safety decided to ask the provincial congress how it should proceed with respect to Sir John, but the day following the visit to Johnson Hall, the committee voted to send a letter to the Canajoharie sachems requesting that they not allow men of military age such as William of Canajoharie "who have acted inimically against us, and fought against our united forces near the Fort St. John," to return to their homes in Canajoharie. The letter to the sachems was likely spurred by the committee representatives who visited Sir John seeing William of Canajoharie

10. The Land of Their Fathers

at Johnson Hall. He had stopped there on his way back from Canada to deliver messages from Guy Johnson to Sir John.[3]

William of Canajoharie soon returned home and decided that boldness was his best protection. He showed up at Jacob Klock's house (Klock had the good fortune not to be home) and told Klock's wife that the committee had better leave him alone. As Klock described the encounter to the committee, "He came there from John's town accoutered with two pistols, a gun and a Broadsword on his side, Saying 'I am a King's Man, who dare say anything against it; I have Killed so many Yankies at Fort St. Johns with this Sword of my Father, they are no Soldiers at all. I kill'd and scalp'd and kick-d their arses.'" Leaving nothing to Mrs. Klock's imagination, William continued: "The d---d Committee here have gone too far already, I will shew them better, and will cut some of their heads off by and by; I only pity the wives and children for I shall come with 500 Men which I have ready, to cut off the whole River and burn their houses this Fall yet."[4]

These statements sparked the rumor that John Butler might invade the valley with a force of Loyalist militia and Native American allies. Scouts were posted above German Flatts as a precaution.[5]

The Canajoharie sachems responded to the Committee of Safety's letter regarding William of Canajoharie with their usual position: The older people of the village could not control the young men's activities, but it was good that William had now returned from the war.[6] The committee, not willing to incite the Mohawks by taking any direct action against William, voted only to report his threats to the Patriots' agents for Indian affairs.[7]

Likewise, the provincial congress decided it would be "impolitic" to attempt to take possession of the Johnstown jail or to "molest Sir John while inactive" but applauded the committee's efforts to recruit Sir John's tenants to the Patriot militia.[8]

For the time being, it was a waiting game that was fraying everyone's nerves. At the end of December, William of Canajoharie got into an altercation with a Patriot sympathizer. William killed the man with a knife. It is not clear whether the Patriot was armed. The Committee of Safety entered evidence against William in its minutes, but William was not given any opportunity to respond. The committee again made the decision that it was prudent not to incite the Mohawks, and no further action was taken.[9]

For Sir John and Lady Mary, Sir John's encounter with the Committee of Safety made it likely that a time of frightful decision was coming. By now they were the parents of two small children, and Mary was soon to become pregnant with a third child. They had recently been informed of Mary Johnson's tragic death at Fort Ontario. Were they about to find themselves cast out of Johnson Hall or separated for some lengthy period as the battle for the Mohawk valley raged?

The marriage was a happy one. Sir William's instinct to suppress his impatience and give Sir John time to make his own choice had been wise. Having won Mary Watts's hand, Sir John proved to be a faithful husband. The break with Clarissa Putman was final. She and her two children continued to live at Schenectady in a house he provided. He paid their expenses and provided Clarissa with a living allowance, but he had no more children with her. Mary Watts Johnson would eventually bear Sir John 18 children, 11 of whom survived to adulthood.

* * *

The Adamant arrived in Falmouth, England, a few days before Christmas. Guy immediately set about preparing a detailed report for the new secretary for the American colonies, Lord George Germain, which he submitted on January 26, 1776. The report described the Six Nations' land grievances in detail, recounted the military accomplishments of the Tryon County Loyalists and their Mohawk allies in Canada the previous fall, and requested that Guy's temporary appointment as superintendent for Indian affairs of the Northern District be made permanent, as was desired by both Guy and the Six Nations.[10]

On February 29, Guy, Joseph, and John Oteronyente were formally presented to the king and queen at St. James's Palace. Joseph did exceptionally well, bowing to the king rather than kissing his hand to make it clear that he came as the emissary of an ally rather than that of a subject nation, but kissing the queen's hand as was expected of a gentleman when being presented to a lady.[11]

Two weeks later Guy, Joseph, and John Oteronyente sat down with Lord Germain for substantive discussions. Joseph made it clear that the Mohawks expected redress of their land grievances in exchange for their loyalty to the Crown. Joseph also insisted that the only person they trusted to execute the Crown's part of the bargain in America was Guy Johnson: "We have been often assured by our late great friend Sir William Johnson who never deceived us ... that the King and wise men here would do us justice.... We therefore hope that the Assurances now given us by the Superintendent may take place, and that he may have it in his power to procure us justice."[12]

Germain assured Joseph that if the Six Nations remained loyal, when the rebellion ended the Mohawks' land grievances would be favorably resolved. Germain also made Guy's appointment as superintendent permanent, but did not rescind Major Campbell's appointment as agent for Canada.[13]

Joseph also used his time in London to diminish British prejudices about Native Americans. He granted an interview to James Boswell, a writer for *London Magazine*. Boswell was impressed with Joseph's command of the English language and surprised by his refined manners, noting in his article that Joseph "had not the ferocious dignity of a savage leader."[14]

Joseph was invited to numerous society dinners and balls during his visit, where he made the acquaintance of many prominent aristocrats. He also used his time in England to do some sightseeing. He visited Newmarket, Windsor, Portsmouth, and the Tower of London. It would be through Joseph's eyes that Molly would gain her impressions of these places, for Sir William, before coming to North America, had spent the first 23 years of his life in Ireland, not England. Joseph would say in later years that although he had been impressed by England's technology, he had been shocked by the great disparities of wealth. A Mohawk counted himself successful if he had enough food and material possessions to distribute to fellow Mohawks in need. In London, starving children died in the streets as the coaches of the wealthy rolled past.[15]

During this period, Guy arranged for Peter to become an ensign in the regular army. A fee was normally paid for such an appointment. It is likely that the payment was made on Peter's behalf by Lord Adam Gordon, a friend of both Sir William and Guy.[16]

Daniel and Anne Claus decided to remain in London while Daniel attempted to secure some kind of appointment. Guy made the wrenching decision to leave his three young daughters in Anne's care.

Joseph, John Oteronyente, Guy, John Dease, Joseph Chew, and Gilbert Tice sailed from Falmouth on the *Lord Hyde* in early June. Since Peter's regiment, the 26th Foot, was already in the province of New York, it is very possible that Peter accompanied them. A spirit of optimism reigned. By now it was known that the American army, decimated by smallpox, had been forced to withdraw from Canada to Ticonderoga and that the British fleet was converging on New York. The *Lord Hyde*, a brig, was headed for New York City as part of a military convoy. Joseph and Guy expected to join General William Howe's army there and be part of a force that would move up the Hudson River to join with British forces moving south from Canada for the liberation of the Mohawk valley.

The *Lord Hyde* was armed with 12 three-pounder cannons. Near Bermuda, it was attacked by an American privateer. Male passengers were expected to help defend the ship, and Joseph in particular was reported to have displayed his marksmanship to good advantage. The *Lord Hyde* sustained significant damage, but the privateer was driven off. The *Lord Hyde* limped into New York Harbor on July 29, 1776, docking at Staten Island.

Across the harbor in Manhattan, Patriot officers were furiously trying to whip their forces into shape for the coming invasion.[17]

* * *

As Joseph and Guy conferred with government officials in London, Sir John's time as first citizen of the Mohawk valley was drawing to a close. In January, a force that Governor Tryon estimated as "near four thousand" marched to Johnson Hall under the command of General Phillip Schuyler, arriving on January 24. Sir John had some advance notice and was able to assemble 600 men "from his Tenants and neighbours[,] the majority highlanders." Although he had four small cannons at his disposal, it was clear that he faced overwhelming odds, so he elected to wait for a more favorable moment to resist. Some of his men were taken prisoner, but many others were able to slip away.[18]

Schuyler, probably fearing that the Mohawks would not allow him to take Sir John out of the county without exacting a heavy price, instead placed him under virtual house arrest and required him to sign a bond for 1,600 pounds sterling. The terms of the bond provided that Sir John was "not to aid the King's Service or to remove within a limited district from his house" or else the bond would be forfeited. The Patriots also seized 360 guineas from Sir John's desk. Governor Tryon viewed the seizure as theft. General Schuyler viewed it as money that could no longer be used to pay for Loyalist arms and ammunition.[19]

For the next week, Schuyler and his men conducted an operation in the Mohawk valley similar to one being conducted on Long Island. A number of Loyalist farms were either burned or plundered, including that of the McDonnell family, who had nine sons in the Loyalist militia, and that of Captain John Hare, an officer in the Indian Department who was then in Canada with John Butler. Mrs. Hare was forced to stand by and watch on a midwinter day as Schuyler's men took her farm equipment, cattle, household goods, and a silver watch.[20]

* * *

It was probably at this time that Molly Brant began actively aiding the Loyalist cause. With Continental troops searching for them, dozens of men decided that they must slip away to Canada to join John Butler. At least one group of them came to Molly's farm, and "she conducted them to a secure hiding place in the woods, and there took them food each morning and evening during a week." When the Patriot searches abated, she gave them each "a sack of provisions" and provided "an Indian guide to take them through the woods."[21]

Molly may also have sent a messenger to Governor William Tryon in New York City, relaying a message from John Butler at Fort Niagara and adding a personal message of her own. Molly and Sir William had entertained Governor Tryon at Johnson Hall on several occasions when he and Sir William conducted business with the Six Nations. Realizing that many Six Nations' leaders (including almost all who were not Mohawk) were still insisting on the Six Nations' neutrality, she probably believed it essential that she assure Tryon of the Six Nations' loyalty to the king. On February 8, Governor Tryon wrote to the Earl of Dartmouth (who he did not yet know had been replaced by Lord Germain): "By late Secret Intelligence from the Northward and as far Westward as Detroit, I have the agreeable information that the Indians are firmly attached to the King's interest." The same letter from Tryon to Dartmouth belatedly repeated the news of Peter Johnson's capture of Ethan Allen (who was currently languishing in a British jail) and asserted that the Indians "have chosen Peter Johnson, the natural son of Sr Wm Johnson (by an Indian Woman) to be their Chief." Tryon thought that "a Commission of General to Peter would be politic."[22] The message from "the Northward" was probably sent by word of mouth and may have been somewhat garbled in translation by the Native American messenger, thus the reference to Peter being chosen as chief, but it is very likely that the proud mother wanted to make sure the governor was aware of both the Six Nations' loyalty and her son's military exploits in the king's service.

On May 14, 1776, the Tryon County Committee of Safety took the same momentous action that was being taken by Patriot committees throughout the colonies: "Resolved, unanimously by this Board, that an Independence from Great Britain shall be represented by our Delegates at the provincial Congress."[23]

The spirit of independence wafting through the province had also finally emboldened the provincial congress to conclude that Sir John must be officially arrested and removed from the Mohawk valley. His continuing ability to raise hundreds of men for the king was a danger that could no longer be ignored. Colonel Elias Dayton, with a force of 350 men, was sent to perform the deed. One of Dayton's officers was 22-year-old Captain Joseph Bloomfield of the 3rd New Jersey regiment. Bloomfield would go on to serve as governor of New Jersey and as a brigadier general in the War of 1812. His Revolutionary War journal is the best description we have of the events surrounding the attempt to arrest Sir John.

According to Bloomfield, on May 19 at 8 a.m. Dayton's force "passed by the elegant Buildings of Guy Johnson & Col. Daniel Claus Sons in Laws of Sr Wm. Johnson & now in England doing America all the Mischief in their Power." Friends in Schenectady, including a visiting Fort Hunter Mohawk, had already forewarned Sir John of the Patriots' advance. When Dayton's men arrived in Johnstown at 4 p.m. that day, they were informed "that Sr John Johnson had left John's Town with most of the Male Inhabitants & all the Highlanders, Dutch & Irish ... with 50 Indians, that they were.... Armed and intended to Attack us Very probably this Evening."[24]

Young Bloomfield was put in charge of a night guard of 68 men, which in three shifts surrounded the camp throughout the night. Although the threatened attack did not come, Bloomfield and his men were treated to the "War-hoop" of the Mohawks echoing throughout the forest "in a most hideous manner," and "this added to the Darkness of the Night, being in a strange Country surrounded with woods."[25]

Despite his tense night, when he went off duty in the morning, Captain Bloomfield was up for an adventure: "My curiosity induced me to pay a Visit alone this morning to Johnson-Hall, which is a Very beautiful large & elegant Build[ing]. ... My excuse to see the Hall was to wait on Miss Peggy Watts (a Sister of Lady John Johnson's & who I was formerly Acquainted with) & who I said I understood was at the Hall."[26]

Although Sir John had escaped, his wife, Lady Mary, then in her early 20s, was still at the mansion. In the end, Sir John had decided against taking his pregnant wife and two small children on what would be a 200-mile trek through the forests of northern New York to Canada. He preferred to rely on the honor of Patriot officers than subject Lady Mary and their children to risks that had killed his sister and her infant at Fort Ontario.

Now it was Lady Mary's role to claim the merciful treatment, under the European military code, that a lady of quality was entitled to at the hands of enemy officers. The cheeky young man at her door, who had danced with her sister at a New York City ball a season or two past, was an easy place to begin: "Lady Johnson received and treated me with the greatest Politeness talked freely upon the present unhappy Times & seemed to have the greatest fortitude for a Woman considering the situation her household was in. She shewed me Sir Wm. Johnson's Picture, which was curiously surrounded with all kinds of Beads and Wampum, Indian curiositys and Trappings of Indian Finery wh. He had received in his Treatys with different Indian Nations." Lady Mary had made, if not a friend, at least a sympathetic warden: "I returned pleased with my feigned Visit, greatly pleased with Johnson Hall and the worthy Lady indeed (though a Tory who is in Possession of it)."[27]

* * *

Lady Mary was not the only Mohawk valley resident who would execute a fine acting performance that day. At noon Abraham, chief sachem of the lower castle at Fort Hunter, arrived with a delegation of sachems and men of military age to parley with the Patriots. The parley was opened "by the Indians demanding in a haughty manner of our great Warrior (as they called Col. Dayton) what He meant by coming into their country with armed Troops & whether He was for Peace or War?"[28]

Dayton replied evenly that he had no quarrel with the Mohawks and instead was there "to suppress the Highlanders & others who had taken up arms against the Congress." Dayton urged the Mohawks not to interfere "in our Family Quarrel with Great-Britain." The Mohawks were not mollified, asserting that "we came to take Sr. John's Life their good old Friend Sr Wm Johnson's Son, That they loved Sr Wm. who was their Father, for his sake they would protect his son, that Sir Williams blood ran in their veins, was mixed with their Blood, and they would stand by him."[29]

Bloomfield, who was present with his commander throughout the meeting, appreciated the Mohawks' bravura: "They sett in their Indian painted warlike dress with their Indian Tomahawks with Pipes ... and smoking with such a confident air of Dignity & Superiority as if they were above all other beings mad[e] and their Authority extended over the whole Earth."[30]

The next day Dayton decided to take a more aggressive position, telling the Mohawks that "if they offered to take up the Hatchet or oppose his Warriors ... He would ... burn all their houses ... & Cast the Mohawks with their Wifes & Children off of the face of the Earth," but if "they would be still and let us alone in a Family Quarrel" no one would harm them. While he made his speech, "our Detachment with Drums & fifes were parrading & made a most martial appearance through the street."[31]

Abraham was in a difficult position. The Patriot force had just received reinforcements and was large enough to carry out Dayton's threats, but some of the lower castle's young men were in the woods with Sir John, and the family bond that Abraham felt for this half brother of Brant Johnson, William of Canajoharie, and the children of Molly Brant was very real. Abraham decided to de-escalate, telling Dayton that "all they wanted was to be assured Sr. John should not be killed. We might do as we liked with the Highlanders." Dayton assured Abraham that "not a hair of Sr. John's head should fall to the ground."[32]

Having established an uneasy truce with the Fort Hunter Mohawks, Dayton sent out a proclamation ordering the Highlanders to turn themselves in. One hundred ninety-five did so; roughly the same number of men were then making their way to Canada with Sir John, who planned to rendezvous with John Butler's forces.[33]

Accompanied by Bloomfield, Colonel Dayton himself soon inspected Johnson Hall: "We saw all Sr. William's Papers ... all the Treaties He made with the different Indian—Nations ... all of which placed Sr. William

Johnson's Character in a Very important station of life and greatly merited the warmest thanks of his Country." Bloomfield consoled himself with the ridiculous idea that Sir John's "foolish impudent, treacherous & base conduct" was at variance from the "Paths of his good old Father in supporting the Liberty of America," while the ghost of Sir William was doubtless hovering over the scene yearning to chase this pack of traitors from his house.[34]

A few days later, probably after consultation with General Schuyler, Dayton sent Captain Bloomfield to Johnson Hall to inform Lady Mary, then about five months pregnant, that she must go to Albany the next day, accompanied by an officer whom she could choose. It was quite clear from the wording of the letter that Lady Mary was in custody and that the officer who accompanied her was to convey her into the hands of the Albany Committee of Safety.[35]

Lady Mary, of course, selected Joseph Bloomfield to accompany her. On the morning of Tuesday, May 28, 1776, the Johnson family left Johnson Hall and Johnstown for the last time. Lady Mary and her housekeeper rode in a phaeton, with Captain Bloomfield on horseback beside them. Lady Mary's two children rode in a wagon with their nurse and two liveried servants (probably enslaved people) and the estate's overseer. They stopped for the midday meal at a Schenectady inn, "where a Pack of Tories came to Visit her Ladyship." On the road between Schenectady and Albany, Bloomfield had to brandish his pistol when Loyalist sympathizers tried to separate him from the rest of the party. That night, Bloomfield noted gratefully in his journal, "Turned her over to Walter Livingston Chairman of Com of Safety in Albany."[36]

* * *

Meanwhile, the Patriots tightened their grip on the Mohawk valley. Having sat in Sir John's pew at St. John's Church the previous Sunday, Dayton spent the rest of the week working with the Tryon Committee of Safety to seize the county's public records and to deal with dozens of Loyalists who still refused to sign the Patriots' Association.[37]

On June 5 Captain Bloomfield, on his way back from Albany, dined with Dayton's second-in-command "at the neat, curious & elegant Seat lately occupied by Col. Claus, a son-in-law of Sr Wm ... he being a Violent Tory & having fled & taken up Arms against us, without doubt has forfeited to this country all his Right to those Buildings."[38]

The Tryon Committee of Safety was worried about the security of German Flatts, just across the river and immediately west of Canajoharie. The committee requested that Dayton secure the Flatts as quickly as possible. Captain Bloomfield was part of a detachment of 220 men who marched out of Johnstown on the afternoon of Saturday, June 8, heading for the road that ran along the north bank of the Mohawk River.[39]

Messengers from the lower castle at Fort Hunter informed Molly and the leading sachems at Canajoharie that the Patriot army was marching toward them. The Canajoharie sachems realized that Dayton would take the same tack with them that he had taken with the Fort Hunter sachems: stay out of this family quarrel, and there would be no trouble. Molly's situation was different. She knew by now that Lady Mary and her children had been taken under guard to Albany and that Johnson Hall, Guy Park, and Williamsburg were all in Patriot hands. She also could be under no illusion that the Committee of Safety was unaware that she was actively aiding and abetting the Loyalist men of Tryon County. Clearly, the Patriots might decide to arrest her. What were the sachems prepared to do if they tried?

Sir William's long record of service had not prevented the Patriots from acting against his British family. Neither would it protect his Native American family. Molly's choice was to flee with her children ahead of the Patriot troops, abandoning the property that was to guarantee her children's future, or to stand her ground and rely on her identity as a revered Mohawk matron. The Canajoharie Mohawks had received back William of Canajoharie and the other warriors who had fought the Patriots in Canada, despite the importuning of the Committee of Safety. Although Dayton's army was a new wrinkle, Molly made the calculation that the Mohawks would shield her as well.

* * *

The Patriots' decision about Molly's fate was made above Captain Bloomfield's pay grade. His journal notes only that at 5 p.m. on June 9 the Patriot troops "passed by the Indian Castle called Fort Hendrick, in this place lives Miss Molly (the noted Indian Squagh kept by Sir Wm. Jonson) & her Eight Children who were all well provided for by the Vigorous old Baronet before his Death."[40]

Bloomfield and his men encamped at German Flatts on a site about 12 miles west of Molly's home. As the Patriots marched past Canajoharie in broad daylight, Molly must have heaved a sigh of relief, but she understood that the danger continued.

General Schuyler soon sent word to the Mohawks and the other tribes of the Six Nations confederacy that they should assemble for a meeting with him at German Flatts in mid-July. Schuyler and his Patriot Indian agents were boldly taking over the annual summer event that Sir William and Molly had hosted for many years, when gifts were distributed to the Six Nations and the alliance between the king and the Six Nations was reaffirmed.

For Molly, such a switch of allegiance was unthinkable. Her son and brother were in England even now pledging the Six Nations' loyalty to the king. If the Six Nations forsook the king and went over to the Patriots, what would become of her family? But the fear she felt was not only for her own relatives. The actions of George Klock and the City of Albany in the years before Sir William's death made it clear to her and to her brother Joseph that the Mohawks' survival depended on their alliance with the Johnson family's Indian Department and with the king. Molly and Joseph understood that the Patriots would use the Six Nations for as long as they needed them, but once the king's men had been driven away, they would turn on them and swallow up their remaining territory.

Word had already seeped into Canajoharie that the Oneidas had promised their beloved Reverend Kirkland that they would support the Patriots even if the other five nations decided to stand with the king.[41] It was incumbent upon Molly to make sure the Mohawks remained steadfast in their loyalty to the Crown. She did not dare personally appear at Schuyler's congress, but she needed to ensure that those Mohawks who did attend would serve as a counterweight to the Oneidas, convincing the Onondagas, Cayugas, and Senecas not to give way to Patriot blandishments and to at least remain neutral.

Meanwhile, the ever-curious Captain Bloomfield, having finagled entrance to Johnson Hall, was also determined to meet the famous Molly Brant. Returning to German Flatts from a meeting in Johnstown on June 17, he "called on the way at Hendrick Castle at the house of Miss Molly … who by the generosity of her Paramour Sr Wm. Johnson has every thing convenient around her & lives more in the English taste than any of her Tribe."[42]

Molly's blood surely ran cold as one of her slaves admitted the Patriot officer into her home. Was this the moment of reckoning? Had the Patriots sent this man to arrest her? The suave young captain doubtless said that he was there to present Lady Mary's compliments and to assure Molly that Lady Mary and her children were well. Molly played along. She had 15 years of diplomatic experience as Sir William's partner. She was used to chatting people up and determining what they wanted. As it turned out, all young Bloomfield desired, besides a look at her, was a pair of buckskin leggings "made in the Indian Fashion." Molly, a talented seamstress, sometimes took custom orders from traders and local settlers for such leggings as part of the mercantile enterprise she ran with her son. European Americans found the traditional Native American leggings to be very comfortable hunting garb.[43]

Molly quickly acceded to Bloomfield's request. She had little choice and realized it was perhaps a good thing to have a friendly acquaintanceship with one of the Patriot officers at German Flatts. Bloomfield returned on July 14 to pick up the leggings. This time Molly's two oldest daughters, Elizabeth and Magdalene, were present. Bloomfield was impressed with 15-year-old Elizabeth: "Had the pleasure of seeing the Young Ladys, one is Very handsome, both were richly dressed agreeable to the Indian—Fashion."[44]

Elizabeth's beauty, as reported by Captain Bloomfield, gives us some sense of how Molly may have appeared to Sir William when he first saw her so many years before. Young Bloomfield found Molly, now age 40, to have "the remains of a Very likely Person," although like most young people he had no ability to estimate age, guessing her to be "about 50."[45]

This was the last time Molly and Bloomfield would meet, although it certainly didn't have to be. The day before Captain Bloomfield picked up his leggings, the Tryon County Committee of Safety received additional information that Molly was actively aiding the Loyalists by forwarding to Sir John the loyalty pledges of local settlers. According to the testimony of George Walker, "Mr. Dellinbaugh Cautioned Mr. Walker to Keep it Secret unless to a good Friend who might be Depended upon that … Molly the Squaw could forward any association to Sir John Johnson at any time."[46]

Fortunately for Molly, with hundreds of Six Nations families assembling at German Flatts for Schuyler's congress, the Patriots decided it was no time to arrest the senior matron of the confederacy's female honor society. In a year's time the Patriots would regret this decision, but for now they desperately wanted at least neutrality from the Six Nations, and they were determined to take no incendiary actions.

* * *

The Indian congress was an education for Joseph Bloomfield, who had previously held the usual British prejudices about Native Americans: "They are grave even to sadness, upon any serious Occasion; observant of those in Company, respectful to the old, of a temper cool deliberate, by which they are never in haste to speak before they have thought well on the matter, & are sure the person who spoke before them has finished all he has to say."[47]

Bloomfield was similarly impressed with the behavior of the Christian Mohawks and Oneidas at Sunday services: "their devout Behaviour struck me with Astonishment & made me blush with shame for myself and my own People."[48]

The outcome of the congress was predictable. Individual Mohawks left no doubt that they were pro-Tory. Abraham, the senior sachem at Fort Hunter who spoke for them in official sessions, had the job of claiming that the Mohawks were neutral, but "His speech was full of trifyling

Evasive answers." The Onondagas, Cayugas, and Senecas seemed truly neutral, although all three tribes asserted that they could not take responsibility for the actions of their young men. Only the Oneidas and the tribe with whom they shared their land, the Tuscaroras, were sincerely friendly, although they too expressed a desire for peace.[49]

While Molly was relieved when the congress concluded and the Patriots came away not entirely satisfied, the Oneidas' pro-American tilt was nevertheless important, representing a very visible crack in the unity of the Six Nations confederacy. It had been unthinkable for 300 years that any of the Six Nations would go to war against any other member of the confederacy. But now, with one of the Oneida settlements only about 30 miles from Canajoharie, the Loyalist Mohawks had to wonder what would happen if the Englishmen's battles erupted in the Mohawk valley.

Molly, a widow caring for seven children ages 3 to 15 and whose brother and eldest son were far from home, must have felt particularly vulnerable. She nevertheless continued her pro-Loyalist activities. She was convinced there was no future for her family or her tribe in the Mohawk valley if the Patriots triumphed. Like Joseph and Peter, Molly would show great courage in resisting the tide that threatened to force them from their ancestral lands and to destroy the fruits of Sir William's lifetime of labor.

Lady Mary's plight surely increased Molly's conviction that she must throw all her energy into the Loyalist cause. The provincial congress denied Lady Mary's request to go to New York City, which by late September was in British hands. Instead, the congress sent her to the country seat of the Colden family, Coldenham, 12 miles west of Newburgh, in Ulster County. Although the son and grandson of Tories, Cadwallader Colden III was a Patriot, and as a result Coldenham was left in the family's possession. Although the conditions of her imprisonment were not currently unpleasant, Lady Mary was being held there as a hostage for Sir John's good behavior. Should he attempt to retake Tryon County for the king, that could change.[50]

Molly probably also knew that Sir William's good friend and her children's guardian, Henry Frey, had been banished to Connecticut. Forced from his comfortable farm, he was living there under very reduced circumstances.[51]

Molly's spirits rose in late November when she received word that her brother Joseph had made it safely to his father-in-law's village, Oquaga, located in the Susquehanna valley about 10 miles north of the New York–Pennsylvania border. Upon his return from England, Joseph had participated in the invasion of New York the previous summer. While quartered on HMS *Suffolk* off Staten Island prior to the British landing in Brooklyn

10. The Land of Their Fathers

on August 22 and then during the monthlong invasion, Joseph had won the respect and friendship of men such as General Clinton's aide-de-camp, Lord Rawdon, and Earl Percy, son of the Duke of Northumberland.[52]

Once New York had been secured, it was decided that Joseph should convey a message of friendship from General Howe to the Six Nations. Howe hoped that the Six Nations would seize control of the Mohawk valley as Howe's army moved north from New York City to rendezvous with British forces moving south from Canada. On November 16, 1776, Joseph and Gilbert Tice set out from New York City on the dangerous mission. Posing as an Oneida warrior and a Patriot militiaman on leave from Washington's army and later as a pair of hunters, they fooled Patriot sympathizers and patrols.[53]

With Dayton's army at German Flatts, Joseph did not dare return to Canajoharie, so he sent messengers to Molly and to the Fort Hunter Mohawks. He asked Molly and other prominent Mohawks to urge the men of military age to meet Joseph at Fort Niagara. By now, the Patriots were aware that he had made it to Oquaga, but Joseph, accompanied by his father-in-law Isaac and a few other Oquagas, made their way through Seneca country and arrived at Fort Niagara on December 28, 1776. Buoyed by Joseph's return, the taking of New York City, and the three-way British invasion of upper New York that Tories and Patriots alike believed was about to occur, Molly dared to hope that liberation was at hand.[54]

* * *

As Molly celebrated Joseph's return from Europe, Sir John plotted the rescue of his wife and children. Given that Lady Mary would be traveling with a newborn and two toddlers, the plan was bold, perhaps too bold. With the help of one of her husband's Loyalist tenants, who procured a horse and sleigh, Lady Mary and her sister, dressed as farmers' wives, slipped away from Coldenham and made their way to the British fort at Paulus Hook, where Sir John was waiting for them. From there, he was able to convey them safely to New York City. The family spent a few happy weeks there, but with the arrival of spring, Sir John needed to return to the Loyalist regiment he commanded in Canada.[55]

Lady Mary could have remained in New York but, like Anne Claus and Mary Johnson, feared months or years of separation if she stayed behind. The Johnsons' straitened financial circumstances may also have played a role in her decision. Lady Mary's father, John Watts, had fled to England and was not available to provide shelter to her and her children. The couple and their little ones sailed from New York City to Montreal on a freezing, windswept vessel. One child died on the voyage, and one of the other children died in Canada from an illness that may have been contracted aboard the ship. As Sir John contemplated the retaking of the Mohawk valley, there was probably not a great deal of mercy in his heart.[56]

Joseph returned to upper New York and spent the winter recruiting followers. Some Mohawks joined him, but the other five nations seemed determined to maintain neutrality in the Europeans' war. Joseph was more successful among European American Loyalists, many of them tenants of large landowners, but also among small landowners who believed that no good could come from defying the king. By the spring Joseph had recruited about 100 European American men. Dressed and painted like Native Americans to preserve their anonymity and increase the terror of their opponents, these men, together with 100 to 200 Native Americans, became known as Brant's Volunteers.[57]

11

Exile

In Canajoharie, Molly waited on tenterhooks. As the rumors of Joseph's activities permeated the region, her own danger increased. The Patriots continued to refrain from taking action against her, but European American allies were suffering greatly. The previous fall the Patriots arrested William Dillenbach, the Palatine farmer who made the mistake of telling a Patriot informer that Molly could get loyalty pledges to Sir John. When Dillenbach's 17-year-old son, Martinus, used a pair of blacksmith's tongs to fend off the men who were trying to take his father away, he was held on the ground by a militiaman and stabbed in the back with a sword by a Patriot militia officer.[1] In the spring as Joseph recruited his volunteers, more of Sir William's faithful tenants were expelled from his landholdings when the occupants of the small settlement of Johnson's Bush were declared to be enemies of the country by the Tryon County Committee of Safety.[2]

Soon, it was clear that Joseph needed to take more aggressive action to feed his hungry men as they waited to rendezvous with Howe's army. One day in early June, Joseph and his men walked into the European American settlement of Unadilla, 20 miles north of Oquaga, and demanded supplies. Telling the frightened farmers that John Butler would reimburse them when the king's men regained control of the area, Joseph and his men seized cattle, sheep, and pigs.[3]

Not surprisingly, the distressed settlers demanded that General Schuyler take action to stop such depredations. This posed a problem for Schuyler. He knew that most of the Six Nations were continuing to maintain neutrality. Unless he demonstrated to the confederacy that he had only acted against Joseph after extreme provocation, he risked pushing the Six Nations over to the British side.

Schuyler called upon Nicholas Herkimer, the commander of the Tryon County militia, to attempt negotiations with Joseph. Schuyler held little hope that Joseph would make peace, but the conference was necessary political theater to bolster the neutralists in the councils of the Six Nations after the Patriots dealt with Joseph Brant.

Herkimer sent a messenger to Joseph proposing a parley. Joseph's reasons for consenting to meet are more opaque. He certainly had no intention of making peace, and there was a chance of treachery if he agreed to participate. On the other hand, from his work as an interpreter for the Indian Department, he knew how deeply the settlers feared the ferocity of the Six Nations. Joseph probably hoped that by letting Herkimer see his volunteers, the Patriots would understand that the Mohawk valley would not be ceded to them without the shedding of much blood, and this would keep the Patriots from taking any action against Canajoharie and Fort Hunter until the Mohawks' upper and lower castles could be liberated by the king's armies.

On June 27, 1777, Joseph Brant and Nicholas Herkimer met in the central square of Unadilla. As agreed, each man brought only a handful of his officers into the square. Herkimer's force of 380 men waited at ease in an open field at one end of the town, while about 130 of Joseph's men watched the proceedings in a field on the other side of the small village. Joseph and his men appeared bare-chested to show they were unarmed. Herkimer and his men were also supposed to be unarmed. Nevertheless, several militiamen in the negotiating party were carrying concealed pistols and had been instructed to shoot Joseph and his lieutenants if Colonel Ebenezer Cox, a senior member of the Tryon County Committee of Safety, spoke the words "The matter is ended."[4]

Joseph and Herkimer had enjoyed decent relations for the past decade as the owners of neighboring farms in the vicinity of Canajoharie and German Flatts, but the choice of Colonel Cox to accompany Herkimer was certainly not intended to mollify Joseph. Cox was George Klock's son-in-law. The two men detested each other.[5]

Herkimer and Joseph shook hands. Herkimer said that he came in peace. Joseph observed that if that were true, it was strange that Herkimer had brought 400 soldiers with him. Herkimer asked Joseph if he and his people would remain at peace. Joseph replied that his fathers and grandfathers had always been in agreement with the king, and so was he. He asserted that the current trouble was caused by the "Boston people" and criticized General Schuyler and Herkimer for following their lead. Herkimer defended the new nation and the new government and said that opposing them would not be wise. Joseph angrily retorted that further discussion was pointless. Cox cursed Joseph and shouted, "The matter is ended." At this point, only one of the four armed militiamen thought it was wise to go for his weapon. At the sight of Joseph Waggoner fumbling inside his jacket, Joseph raised his right hand. Instantly, his men in the field began the war whoop, and dozens of others emerged from the woods that encircled the village, with their muskets aimed at the Patriot negotiating party.[6]

11. Exile

Joseph would later tell Daniel Claus that he had less than 200 men with him and that they had only about 20 pounds of gunpowder, which he had purchased on his own credit. Nevertheless, he was momentarily in control of the situation.[7] Herkimer repeated that he had not come to fight. Joseph responded that if Herkimer and his men wanted war, he and his men were ready. Both Joseph and Herkimer understood that no one in the two negotiating parties would survive if shots were fired. It was agreed that both sides would withdraw from Unadilla.[8]

* * *

Soon after this drama played out, Joseph received happy news. General John Burgoyne had been placed in charge of all British forces in Canada. King George had personally approved Burgoyne's plan to use a force of 7,000 men to proceed south on Lake Champlain to retake Ticonderoga and then march farther southward to Albany, while a smaller force of regulars, reinforced with Loyalists and Native American allies, crossed into the province of New York from Lake Ontario and marched eastward, first capturing Fort Stanwix and then proceeding to rendezvous with Burgoyne at Albany. The plan assumed that General Howe would leave a garrison to hold New York City, but would send a substantial portion of his army northward up the Hudson River to rendezvous with Burgoyne as well. Joseph was asked to bring his men to Oswego to participate in the western prong of the invasion.[9]

Joseph arrived at Oswego on July 23. He brought with him 300 men ready to fight.[10] He was happy to see there both Daniel Claus and Sir John Johnson. After much lobbying, Daniel Claus had been given an appointment by Lord Germain to command the Native Americans who were to be part of the western army commanded by General Barry St. Leger. Arriving in Montreal earlier in the summer, Claus now brought with him to Oswego about 150 Native American fighting men. Some were Misisageys; some were Fort Hunter Mohawks who had made their way to Canada after Dayton's invasion of the Mohawk valley; and others were Caughnawagas, Canadian relatives of the Mohawks. Sir John came to Oswego as commander of the King's Royal Regiment, the unit he had raised from the Johnson tenants and other Tryon County Loyalists who had fled with him to Canada.[11]

Joseph soon learned that there was significant softness in the force assembling at Oswego. In order to deal with the unfortunate reality of the Six Nations' neutrality, John Butler, in his capacity as Guy Johnson's deputy superintendent of the Indian Department, had sent messages to the Six Nations and the tribes west of Niagara telling them to assemble at Oswego for the annual Indian conference. Butler was hoping that the distribution of gifts by the Crown, together with the presence of St. Leger's regulars and the European American Loyalists, would convince the Six Nations and the western tribes that the king was serious about destroying the Patriots and that it was time for them to join the winning side.[12]

At least there was good news from the northern army. In June, Burgoyne's force had taken control of the high ground around Ticonderoga, forcing the Americans to abandon the fort in the dead of night. Realizing that the way southward was now open to the British forces, Philip Schuyler grimly sent word to his wife, Katherine, telling her to burn the wheat fields surrounding their summer home at Saratoga so the crop could be of no use to Burgoyne's men. This she did by her own hand, since it was a capital offense in New York for a slave to commit arson, and the slave accompanying her to the fields refused to execute her order.[13]

What Joseph and the others at Oswego did not know, and would only come to understand that bitter autumn, was that Burgoyne had unwisely decided to abandon the planned route to Albany in favor of pursuing the retreating Patriots. Even now, Burgoyne's army was bogged down in a swampy, dense forest, forced to build a corduroy road to transport artillery and supplies while Patriot snipers shot at them. They were making only about a mile a day toward the headwaters of the Hudson River, giving the Patriot army plenty of time to prepare for them.[14]

Daniel Claus and Joseph agreed that they must forge ahead, putting the best face possible on their many problems. Daniel gave an impassioned speech to the assembled Native Americans, asserting the strength of the king and his allies and urging those Six Nations men who were neutral to come along to watch the battle. Joseph worked the crowd, promising valuable booty to those who decided to join the fight. Emotions were charged. Rumors circulated that neutralist Senecas were threatening to assassinate Joseph for his role in trying to draw their tribe into the Englishmen's war.[15]

In the end, several hundred warriors decided to take Daniel Claus's invitation to observe the battle, with the option of joining in if things were going the king's way. Joseph, with a picked force of 200 Native Americans and European American volunteers who intended to fight, and a unit of 30 regulars commanded by Lieutenant Henry Bird, headed up the Oswego River in advance of the main force, with the object of cutting off communications between Fort Stanwix and the Mohawk valley. Joseph also planned to send a messenger to Molly in Canajoharie to obtain information about Patriot troop movements around German Flatts.[16]

* * *

Joseph and his men arrived at a landing at the head of the Mohawk River on August 2, and the messenger to Molly was sent on his way. St.

11. Exile

Leger and the main force of about 1,500, including regulars, Hessians, Sir John's King's Royal Regiment, and Daniel Claus's men, together with several hundred "observer" Native Americans, arrived on August 3 and quickly surrounded Fort Stanwix. The young commander of the fort, Colonel Peter Gansevoort, boldly rejected St. Leger's demand that he surrender the fort, which had a garrison at the time of 750 men.[17]

By the afternoon of August 5, Joseph's messenger to Molly returned. Molly sent her brother a warning that a Patriot force had departed German Flatts the previous day and would be within 10 to 12 miles of his camp that night. Molly's intelligence was accurate. Nicholas Herkimer was making his way westward with 800 men and 400 ox-drawn carts to relieve and resupply Fort Stanwix.[18] Although Herkimer was aware that St. Leger's force was at Fort Stanwix, he apparently did not realize that some of the king's forces were positioned well east of the fort.

Joseph and John Butler quickly selected a deep marsh-filled ravine, with a corduroy road running through it, located about six miles east of the fort near the Oneida town of Oriska, as an optimal site to ambush the Patriots. On the morning of August 6, Nicholas Herkimer, mounted on a white horse, entered the ravine at the head of a column almost a mile long. He and his men were accompanied by 60 Oneida warriors, who were escorting the Patriots through the heart of Oneida territory.[19]

Given the easy pickings that Herkimer's force had become, Joseph, thanks to Molly's intelligence, was able to convince many of the Six Nations neutrals to join his and John Butler's men as they lay in wait in the wooded high ground on both sides of the ravine.[20]

Once a substantial portion of the Patriot column was inside the narrow ravine, the troops were suddenly subjected to withering fire by Joseph and Butler's forces. Herkimer was wounded immediately; his left leg shattered below the knee, and his horse was shot dead. Herkimer's men somehow got him to a tree behind which he continued to issue orders, his leg propped up on his dead horse's saddle.[21]

The Patriots' initial casualty rate was frightful, but then fortune smiled on them. A sudden summer shower soaked everyone's musket primers, and the shooting briefly paused. Herkimer used the time to draw his men into a defensive circle. Suddenly it was Joseph and Butler's men who were being subjected to heavy, concentrated fire. Many of the Native Americans pulled back, but at about the same time Sir John's King's Royal Regiment arrived. The battle continued throughout the day. Hearing the nearby engagement, Colonel Gansevoort sent a unit out from the fort to attack St. Leger's depleted camps, causing chaos that prevented any further reinforcements being sent to Joseph and Butler.[22]

In the end, it was not clear who won the Battle of Oriskany.

Approximately 160 Patriot militiamen died, as did about an equal number of Tories and Native Americans allied with the king. Despite the murky outcome, the fallout from the battle was great. Six Nations fighting men, enraged by losses sustained in the battle, soon attacked and burned the nearby Oneida town of Oriska, destroying forever the unity of their confederacy. Herkimer's force limped back to Fort Dayton at German Flatts. The enmity between the Patriots and the Mohawks was now out in the open. Never again would the two groups be able to live together in the Mohawk valley.[23]

* * *

Molly was surely terrified as Herkimer's men returned to her vicinity, and news of the destruction of Oriska filtered into Canajoharie. Most of the Mohawk warriors were still with Joseph. Molly and her children waited for the next shoe to drop in a village populated by women, children, and old men. It would not take the Patriots long to figure out who had given Joseph the information about Patriot troop movements. Molly was already well known to the Committee of Safety as a Tory agent.

Fortunately for Molly, the Patriots were in disarray. Colonel Ebenezer Cox, a leader of the Committee of Safety and the man who had wanted to assassinate Joseph at Unadilla, had been killed in the battle. Henry Frey's son, John, another leader of the Committee of Safety, had been wounded and taken prisoner. General Herkimer would die of his wounds in a few days. The Committee of Safety was demanding help from the Continental Army. If St. Leger's force wasn't decisively defeated, Fort Stanwix would eventually have to surrender, and then the Tories would march down the Mohawk valley to German Flatts.[24]

Benedict Arnold was sent to German Flatts with a force of 900 men. As Colonel Gansevoort stubbornly held out inside Fort Stanwix, Arnold decided to bluff St. Leger. Arnold sent a Tory, whose brother Arnold was holding hostage at Fort Dayton, to convince St. Leger that Arnold was marching toward him with an army much larger than he actually had. Believing Arnold's ploy, St. Leger ordered a retreat to Oswego. Joseph, Sir John, and Daniel Claus were shocked. Joseph made it clear that he and his men would still try to rendezvous with General Burgoyne. Sir John and Daniel Claus requested permission to do the same, but St. Leger, unwilling to risk a decrease of his army, denied the request.[25]

The decision to bypass Canajoharie and attempt to link up with Burgoyne in the woods north of Albany was excruciating for Joseph. It meant leaving Canajoharie undefended now that hostilities between the Patriots and Mohawks had erupted, but Joseph understood that he could not protect the village against Arnold's force with only 200 or 300 men. Joseph

11. Exile

needed to assist Burgoyne and then persuade him to send a force west to liberate the Mohawk valley.

When news of St. Leger's retreat reached German Flatts, the elated Patriot militia commander told the Committee of Safety that as soon as they knew things were going well in the east against Burgoyne, a militia unit should march "to the castle" and demand that "they deliver up the Tories, and I should think Molly too; or to be taken as our Enemies."[26]

When Benedict Arnold and most of the Continentals were sent to reinforce Horatio Gates near Saratoga, the Committee of Safety began to dither about whether to arrest Molly and the other Tories at Canajoharie. The local militia commander tried some psychological warfare instead. He sent Molly messages threatening her with arrest and detention in Albany if she did not leave Canajoharie. Stalling for time, Molly sent replies insisting that she was neutral.[27]

The Committee of Safety felt bolder about acting against the wives and children of Loyalist militiamen who had retreated with St. Leger to Oswego. On August 25, the Committee of Safety ordered the arrest of John Butler's wife and 10 other women who were wives and daughters of Loyalist fighting men. The women were taken to Johnstown, where they were confined in a private home.[28]

* * *

Ratcheting up the pressure in the waning days of the summer, the Patriot militia commander decided to search Molly's house to see if Joseph was hiding there. The search also provided the commander with an opportunity to get a closer look at Canajoharie's by now nonexistent defenses. As Margaret, Molly's 10-year-old daughter, would recall as an adult, "The family ... were greatly alarmed one night soon after they had retired, by a loud & continued knocking at the doore." As Molly opened the door to several militiamen, she probably believed that the moment of her arrest was at hand. Instead, the surly men demanded to know if Joseph was in the house. She told them he was not. Summoning up every ounce of self-possession she could muster and hoping to gain a psychological advantage, she told them "they might Search the house if they pleased, which they did, commencing their examination of the sleeping rooms." The men's loud voices awakened the children. As Margaret recalled, "I was in one of the beds of which they drew back the Curtains, & seeing only Children in it, they declined ferther Search—& withdrew. I perfectly remember my alarm."[29]

Although Joseph was not in her house the night of the search, he had returned to the vicinity of Canajoharie and was hiding with his men in the woods. He and his volunteers had succeeded in making contact with

Burgoyne's forces in the forests north of Saratoga, but disturbed by what he saw, Joseph realized there would be no help for the Mohawk valley anytime soon. Reluctantly, he concluded that he must make the long journey to Fort Niagara in hopes of reuniting his volunteers with the other Loyalists who had retreated there.[30]

Canajoharie was on the way to Niagara. Joseph had already decided that his own wife and two children needed to leave the upper castle. He doubtless thought that his mother and Molly and her children should do the same, but he knew that Molly was resistant to removing her seven children from their comfortable home and marching them hundreds of miles through the woods.

Events would soon help him persuade her. A few days after the midnight search of her house, Molly received intelligence that she might receive yet another nighttime visit from the militia and that this time she would be arrested. Molly, perhaps hoping that if they were not in the house when she was taken away, Elizabeth and Molly's mother Margaret could bring the younger children back to their home when she was gone. Molly's daughter Margaret later wrote, "My Mother instantly Sent us to a Neighbour in whome she had confidance—My Mother would not leave her house the Servants were on the watch throughout the Night." As Molly and her slaves kept their sleepless vigil, "About two O'clock in the Morning Several persons were seen on the premises, but no one approached the house." Molly sent one of her two male slaves, Abraham or December, to tell her neighbor to hide the children. The sleeping children were awakened, and Margaret recalled that when they were told what was happening at their house it "occasioned us so great alarm that [we] were put in to the utmost confusion[;] having retired[,] we were each Scrambling for our Cloths. The person Who had the care of us sent us out in the adjoining nook where we were screened till My Mother sent for us on the following day."[31]

Molly had finally had enough. She sent Joseph word that she was ready to leave.[32] Her slaves, Juba, Jenny, Abraham, and December, helped her carry the smallest of her seven children as they met Joseph in the woods outside Canajoharie at night. Those who wanted Molly's home and possessions did not wait long. Decades later, Margaret remembered sadly that on their way west, they had to double back and "pass within Sight of our own House [and] our hearts ached as we discovered lights through the windows whilst we were stealthily wandering from our home."[33]

* * *

Members of the Committee of Safety and aggrieved Oneidas both had designs on Molly's home and possessions and the property of other Mohawks who were evacuating Canajoharie. The chairman of the

Committee of Safety, Peter Deygert, was observed making several trips to Canajoharie to remove plunder from Molly's home and the homes and fields of other Mohawks who had deserted the village, and his daughter was soon seen walking about town wearing one of Molly's silk gowns. Honyery Doxtater, an Oneida warrior who had participated in the Battle of Oriskany and whose home had been burned at Oriska, quickly moved his family into Molly's house.[34]

As more Mohawks left, the Committee of Safety decided it was safe to act against the few who remained. On September 17, 1777, Deygert ordered the militia to arrest William of Canajoharie, described by the semiliterate clerk of the Committee as "William Johnstown." "You are hereby Ordered ... to take a File of your Men, and take into Custody the Body of William Johnstown carry him down to Johnstown, there to commit him to Prison to remain till further orders from this Fort."[35]

Proud and stubborn, William may have resisted his captors. The warden of the Johnstown jail signed a receipt of custody for him, but from this point William disappears from the historical record. It is likely that he died of wounds inflicted during his arrest or during his imprisonment in the jail his father had built for Tryon County.[36]

As Molly and her younger children made their way through the woods to Onondaga, home of the Keepers of the Six Nations' council fire, she could not know that a second family tragedy was also unfolding. Although a small force was eventually sent from New York City in a last-minute attempt to rendezvous with General Burgoyne, General Howe took the bulk of his forces to Pennsylvania to capture the rebel capital of Philadelphia. As the British troops, including Peter Johnson's unit, waited in the last days of the summer of 1777 for General Washington to conclude that Philadelphia could not be defended, Molly's intelligent, musical, and courageous son Peter died due to either camp fever on the outskirts of fetid Philadelphia, or wounds sustained in a skirmish at nearby Fort Mifflin. He was 18 years old. It would be months before Molly learned of his death.[37]

12

Guerrillas and Refugees

After failing to prevail in two engagements in the vicinity of Saratoga, General John Burgoyne surrendered his army to General Horatio Gates on October 17, 1777. Burgoyne's surrender had a terrible impact on the Mohawks of the lower castle at Fort Hunter. Already subject to Oneida raids, the Mohawks now had to leave their homes. Forced to abandon all their possessions, they made the trek to Montreal, where they implored Daniel Claus to obtain relief supplies for them in the face of the coming Canadian winter.[1]

Molly and her party arrived at Onondaga, near present-day Syracuse, as rumors that things were not going well for Burgoyne were beginning to drift westward. Molly and Joseph both did their best to bolster support for the king. Appearing before a confederacy council, Molly demanded retaliation against the Oneidas for their actions against her and other Mohawks. As Daniel Claus soon reported to his superiors in London, "She always had a great sway during the late Sir Wm Johnson's life time, and even now, and I understand the Six Nations have decreed to render her satisfaction by committing hostilities upon that tribe of Oneida rebels that committed the outrage."[2]

Both the Cayugas and the Senecas soon became aware that the rumors of Burgoyne's defeat were true. When Molly arrived in the western territory of the Six Nations, she found both tribes "very wandering and unstable" in their loyalty to the king.[3] Molly understood that if the western Six Nations tribes switched their allegiance to the Patriots or even persisted in their neutrality, the allegiance of the dispossessed Mohawks would have little value to the Crown.

The Senecas, whose territory was the most remote from European American settlements, were the largest and most powerful tribe of the Six Nations confederacy at this time. The once powerful Mohawks had lost most of their territory to European American settlers, and had lost most of their population to wars and European diseases. Molly knew that the Onondagas and Cayugas were likely to follow the Senecas' lead. Traveling

12. Guerrillas and Refugees   143

to Canadesagey, the principal Seneca town, which was located in the Genesee River valley, "she had a pointed conversation in publick Council" with Sayengaraghta, head sachem of the Senecas, "reminding him of the former great Friendship & Attachment which subsisted between him and the late Sir Wm Johnson ... to whom ... he so often declared & promised to live and die a firm Friend & Ally to the King of England and his Friends." As Daniel Claus reported to Sir Frederick Haldimand, who had replaced Guy Carleton as governor of Quebec, Molly's appeal to Sayengaraghta's honor, together "with other striking Arguments and Reasonings[,] ... had such an Effect upon the chief and the rest of the 5 Nations present, that they promised her faithfully to stick up strictly to the Engagements to her late worthy Friend, and for his & her sake espouse the King's Cause vigorously."[4]

Among Molly's "other striking Arguments and Reasonings" was certainly the point that it was the king's Indian Department that had always stood between the Six Nations and the gluttonous land claims of the settlers. If the king's men were driven away, was there really any reasonable hope that the Patriots would cease their incursions into Six Nations territory?

In undertaking to publicly remonstrate with the Seneca sachem, Molly was relying on her position as the great Sir William's widow and on the right of senior matrons of the confederacy to urge peace or war based on their own assessment of what was the best course of action. The influence of senior women within the Six Nations' councils continually came as a surprise to Europeans. Daniel Claus, sophisticated in the culture of the confederacy, informed Haldimand that "she is in every Respect considered & esteemed by them as Sr Wms relict [widow], and one word from her is more taken Notice of by the five Nations than a thousand from any white Man without Exception."[5]

John Butler also understood the depth of Molly's influence. When Butler returned to Fort Niagara after the retreat from Fort Stanwix in the fall of 1777, he found that a refugee crisis was inundating the fort and the surrounding area. Hundreds of Native Americans sought refuge at the fort because their land was either occupied outright by the Patriots or their traditional hunting grounds had become unsafe. The resources of the fort were overwhelmed, and Butler feared that violence could break out unless someone of stature was present at the fort to urge the Native Americans assembled there to be patient. As Claus reported to Haldimand, "hearing that she was at Cayouga, he [Butler] sent her repeated & very pressing & encouraging Messages to come & reside at Niagara."[6]

It was a difficult decision for Molly. She and her children were ensconced in the home of the head sachem at Cayuga. It was crowded and less comfortable than her home at Canajoharie, but Butler was asking her to bring her seven children, the youngest of whom was four years old, and her mother Margaret, who was well into her 60s, a distance of 150 miles through the forests of western New York in late autumn. Molly's destination was an even more overcrowded frontier fort that was likely to be substantially less comfortable than her current situation. Nevertheless, she did not take long to make up her mind. If she hoped to ever see Canajoharie again or regain her children's patrimony, she must do everything in her power to keep the alliance between the king and the Six Nations strong.

It was probably Joseph who guided the family on its arduous journey.[7] At long last Molly set eyes on the fort Sir William had captured from the French in 1759 during that long ago summer when in the last stages of her pregnancy with their eldest child, Peter, she had told Sir William she wanted to join him. He had told her not to come. It was no place for a woman. Yet here she was 18 years later at the end of a long forest trek, accompanied by their six young daughters and small son. The comfortable life Sir William had provided for them had been ripped away, and Molly was determined to do everything in her power to get it back.

* * *

British authorities decided to use the winter to ensure that the Six Nations were firmly on the king's side. John Butler sent out invitations for a conference at Niagara indicating that many gifts would be distributed. The British were determined to demonstrate the continuing might of the British Empire and to reassure the Six Nations that it was no mistake to reaffirm their century-old alliance with the Crown. Gifts worth 34,000 pounds were shipped from Montreal and distributed to the more than 3,000 Native Americans who attended the conference.[8]

Joseph acted as interpreter for the event. The delighted British commander at Niagara wrote to his superiors that "Joseph ... has been of great service & deserves every favour I can shew him."[9] Molly played the role so familiar to her from the many conferences she had helped Sir William host; entertaining sachems and senior matrons while reinforcing all the points that the Indian Department speakers were making in the formal council meetings. General Frederick Haldimand, the new governor of Quebec, a man who had worked with Sir William over the years, was very pleased. In the spring of 1778, Haldimand ordered that a house be constructed for Molly near the fort. After a winter in very cramped quarters, Molly was relieved to finally have some living space for her family again and a place where she could better conduct her diplomatic efforts.[10]

The spring also brought some partings. Molly sent Margaret and George, now ages 11 and 9, to boarding school at Montreal. Daniel and Anne Claus were there and promised to look after them. Although Molly

12. Guerrillas and Refugees 145

hated to send them from the family circle, she knew that Sir William would have expected her to give them the education that would allow Margaret to attract a proper husband and George to manage his property and make his way in the business world.[11]

More worrisome, but equally necessary, was Joseph's departure to make war in upper New York. Joseph still expected that he and his men would soon rendezvous with a British force that everyone at Niagara believed would shortly be sent up the Hudson River from New York City by General Henry Clinton. While they waited, Joseph and his men intended to make life difficult for the settlers in the backcountry of upper New York.[12]

On May 30, 1778, Joseph and his men, together with a contingent of Butler's Rangers led by a Loyalist son of Henry Frey, attacked the settlement of Cobleskill, near Schoharie Creek. Joseph burned the settlement and some prisoners were taken, but most of the settlers were allowed to escape. The local militia made the mistake of pursuing Joseph's force. When the militia caught up with them a few hours after the attack, Joseph and his men killed almost all of the rebels.[13]

On July 18 Joseph attacked Andrewstown, five miles southeast of German Flatts, and nearby Springfield. The settlements were burned, and scores of cattle were driven to Joseph's headquarters at the now deserted Unadilla. Eight men were killed and 14 were captured during these engagements, but at Springfield Joseph prevented his men from killing or capturing any of the women and children.[14]

The people of the Wyoming valley in western New York were not so lucky. There, a combined force of European American Rangers and Seneca fighting men led by John Butler and Sayengaraghta destroyed eight forts, burned 1,000 dwellings, and took 1,000 head of cattle. Angry over the settlers' encroachment into their territory and about Seneca deaths at Oriskany, the Senecas took 227 scalps and only five prisoners. Unlike Joseph, John Butler was completely unable to prevent the carnage.[15]

* * *

While on campaign with his men, Joseph did not forget about his family at Niagara. On August 4 he sent a letter to Taylor and Duffin, the owners of the trading post at the fort, authorizing his wife to charge whatever she needed to his account and telling the merchants to give Molly 30 pounds of credit, also to be charged to his account.[16] Daniel Claus was thinking of Molly too. At the beginning of the summer, she received a small trunk of goods from him. She thanked him with the fervent hope that "the time is very near when we shall all return to our habitations on the Mohawk River."[17]

Information was spotty at Niagara. In the same letter, Molly told Daniel Claus that she had "a report of Joseph having had a brush with the Rebels, but do not know at what place." Rumors abounded: "its reported that Colo Butler, & Joseph have joined; Every hour we look for a confirmation of this news."[18]

By early fall, Molly received accurate information from a messenger sent to her by Joseph himself. Joseph wanted her to know that the attempt to reclaim Canajoharie was under way. He had attacked German Flatts and "did not leave a House, Barn, or Stable unburnt to ashes" except for the homes of two Loyalist families and the minister who had married him and Susanna. Molly asked Taylor and Duffin to pass this intelligence on to Daniel Claus, who reported it to General Haldimand.[19]

Joseph was uncertain about what his next move should be, since General Clinton had not yet sent his army from New York City: "Miss Molly says he has now thoughts of penetrating through to the Army at New York, with only three or four men[,] ... as he finds it impracticable with the whole of his Party.... Miss Molly however thinks the risk is to [sic] great, so Wishes, is not without hopes, that he may come in here." The same letter acknowledged a disbursement of 25 pounds to Molly per order of General Haldimand: "She desires you will thank his Excellency for her."[20]

Despite the occasional gifts from Joseph, Daniel Claus, and the British government, Molly and her family, having fled Canajoharie with little more than the clothes on their backs, were living in very straitened circumstances, and Molly was finding her diplomatic work very costly: "She desires Mr. Taylor to inform you the Manner She lives here is pretty expensive to her being obliged to keep in a manner open house for all those Indians that have any weight in the 6 Nations Confederacy."[21]

Molly found herself in a very difficult position. With Daniel Claus in Montreal and Guy Johnson still in New York City, she was the only member of the Johnson family at Niagara who could handle the diplomacy necessary to keep the Six Nations loyal to the Crown. She would have been much happier to go to Montreal, where she could reunite with Margaret and George and put her younger children in school, but her diplomatic duties prevented her from doing so. Conscious that Haldimand thought Molly was performing a valuable service at Niagara and confident that he would reimburse them, Taylor and Duffin assured Claus, "We have told her we will not see her in want."[22]

Daniel Claus was indeed relying on Molly to help keep the Six Nations confederacy loyal. That fall he reported to Haldimand that he had asked her to calm leaders of the Confederacy after news of the Patriot alliance with France reached Niagara. Claus's spin on the situation was that the Protestant New Englanders would soon tire of an alliance with French

12. Guerrillas and Refugees 147

Catholics and that the French admiral's spotty performance off the coast of Rhode Island the previous summer would speed their disenchantment: "Desiring her to communicate this Intelligence to her Brother & the Chiefs of the Six Nations ... with my Salutations and Request to persevere Faithful to their ancient Friend and Ally the Great King of England."[23]

* * *

By midfall, Joseph decided that an attempt to reach New York City with only a few men was pointless. He received word that John Butler's son, Walter, and Sayengaraghta, the Seneca sachem, were heading toward him with a force of almost 600 men, half European American Rangers and half Seneca fighting men.

Joseph and his men rendezvoused with the Butler/Sayengaraghta force on October 22, 1778. Joseph's meeting with young Butler and the Seneca sachem did not go well. Butler and Sayengaraghta were planning to attack Cherry Valley, population 300, the largest remaining European American settlement south of the Mohawk River. Butler asserted that the European Americans among Joseph's men were subject to his authority for this raid, a view that neither Joseph nor his men accepted. As Joseph learned more about the wholesale slaughter that had occurred in the Wyoming valley at the hands of Sayengaraghta's forces and the Rangers that summer, the more uncomfortable he became.

Joseph ordered his European American volunteers to disappear into the woods but told Butler and Sayengaraghta that he and the Native Americans with him would accompany them. Now Joseph was solely a Six Nations warrior with the same right to claim prisoners as any other warrior.

As the Rangers and Senecas swooped down on Cherry Valley, Joseph attempted to minimize casualties. He was able to protect 12 people he claimed were Loyalists, and according to witnesses, he attempted to save others, but Walter Butler proved as ineffectual as his father at preventing civilian casualties, or perhaps he simply didn't care very much about doing so. More than 30 women and children were killed at Cherry Valley. Butler's terror techniques were effective. Virtually all settlers west of Schenectady evacuated after what became known as the Cherry Valley Massacre. The settlers' departure was so complete that George Washington became concerned that the food supply for the Continental Army would be compromised. The Cayugas and Senecas would pay a brutal price for Cherry Valley the following summer.[24]

* * *

Walter Butler did take some prisoners at Cherry Valley. One was Lieutenant Colonel William Stacey, the second-in-command of the

Massachusetts regiment charged with protecting the settlement. When Stacey arrived at Niagara with Butler's Rangers in the late fall of 1778, Molly had only recently learned of the deaths of her son Peter and her stepson William of Canajoharie.[25]

When Molly encountered Stacey at the fort, it was probably the knowledge that William of Canajoharie had died while in Patriot custody, combined with the senselessness of young Peter's death in a faraway military camp where she could do nothing to save him, that caused Molly to temporarily cast away her persona as the Christian, acculturated partner of one of North America's leading European American men. Instead, for a brief time she became solely a Six Nations mother. It was traditional among the Six Nations for the mothers of dead fighting men to rule on the fate of prisoners. Young prisoners were frequently adopted and given the name of deceased warriors. Adult male prisoners were often tortured and executed as revenge for the dead. Molly may have been reminded of her right to decide Stacey's fate by other Six Nations women who commiserated with her at Niagara.

Not long after Stacey's arrival, Molly confessed to John Butler, one of young Peter's guardians, that she had dreamed twice of having Stacey's head and kicking it about the fort with members of her tribe. Perhaps she was merely blowing off steam with a man who was one of Sir William's closest associates, but Six Nations people held the belief that dreams were important and that it was unhealthy not to give them actualization. Butler interpreted the conversation to mean that she wanted Butler to turn Stacey over to the Mohawks.

John Butler may have been ineffectual or worse in the Wyoming valley as the Senecas killed scores of civilians the previous summer, but here in the precincts of a British fort, he was not willing to be responsible for a prisoner's death. He told Molly clearly that no British prisoner could be turned over to the Mohawks. Perhaps Molly was relieved by his unequivocal response—before her death she would become a founding member of the Anglican church at Kingston, Ontario—but Butler wasn't sure. If she talked about these dreams to the many Six Nations fighting men at the fort who respected her, might not one of them decide to fulfill the dream for her? Butler mentioned the encounter to Niagara's commander, and Lieutenant Colonel Stacey was soon transferred to Montreal. For her part, later in the war Molly would take into her home a 10-year-old Patriot boy who had been captured with his prisoner-of-war father. Close in age to her own surviving son, George, she raised young William Lamb to adulthood.[26]

* * *

The Stacey incident confirmed for Niagara's commander that he was uncomfortable having Molly at the fort. Like most Englishmen,

12. Guerrillas and Refugees   149

particularly military men used to command, Lieutenant Colonel Bolton had difficulty with the idea of a female political leader. He respected and perhaps even liked Joseph, but found having to deal with Molly unsettling. Bolton did not comprehend that Joseph, seven years younger than Molly and primarily a military leader at this time, did not have Molly's political influence among the tribes of the Six Nations. When John Butler asked Molly to come to Niagara to help keep the refugees in order, Bolton had happily accepted the positive consequences of her presence, but he did not really understand or accept that Molly had a constituency that expected results. Daniel Claus would shortly tell General Haldimand (a rare military man who accepted Molly's political role) that she had "prevented many an unbecoming & extravagant proposal to the Commanding officer at Niagara."[27] The flip side of this influence was that when Six Nations people came to Molly in crisis, she had to be able to produce some aid for them in order to retain her credibility. To Bolton, who was under pressure to reduce the expense of the refugees' presence, her demands were becoming a nuisance.

Governor Haldimand's first reaction to Bolton's suggestion that Molly take up residence in Montreal was to ask Daniel Claus to consult with Joseph about the idea.[28] Joseph was in high favor with Haldimand, who was impressed with Joseph's military performance during the 1778 campaign in upper New York. Haldimand had recently reported to Lord Germain that the success of the campaign "must be attributed greatly to the Indian Joseph Brant whose attachment to Government, resolution and Personal Exertion Makes him a Character of a very distinguished kind, & I humbly conceive entitles him to some particular Mark of the king's favor."[29]

Joseph and Daniel Claus both believed that under the right circumstances, Molly would be quite amenable to leaving Niagara and relocating at Montreal. Accordingly, Haldimand sent her a personal invitation. Molly and her children left Niagara on July 17, 1779. Her mother, Margaret, remained behind, probably to nurse Joseph's wife Susanna, who died at Niagara during this period.[30]

When Molly arrived at Montreal, there was a happy reunion with Margaret and George, and there were visits to Daniel and Anne Claus, Sir John and Lady Mary, and Guy Johnson, who had finally decided that he was doing no good in New York City and should make his way to Canada. Five years after Sir William's passing, Molly soldiered on. This was her fifth relocation since her departure from Johnson Hall. In addition to all the losses caused by the war, she had never gotten over Sir William's death. She tried to do her best for her children and her people, but the depth of her loss was always with her. Daniel Claus wrote that summer after seeing her again that even with the passage of time, Sir William's "Memory she never mentions but with Tears in her Eyes."[31]

* * *

Molly's stay in Montreal was to be a short one. After the Patriot settlements west of Schenectady were destroyed by Joseph, Butler, and Sayengaraghta's 1778 campaign, George Washington decided that the Six Nations loyal to the king must be driven from their homeland. In April 1779, he sent a force to destroy the three main villages of the Onondagas. At summer's end, he turned his attention to the Senecas and Cayugas. By mid-August, a force of 2,300 men led by General John Sullivan had entered Seneca country from the south, while a force of 2,000 men led by General James Clinton entered from the north.[32]

Joseph and Sayengaraghta cast aside their differences to oppose this existential threat to the confederacy, but together and joined by a contingent of Butler's Rangers and a small detachment from Sir John's regiment, they had a combined force of only about 600 men.[33] Daniel Claus received an urgent request for reinforcements from the Senecas. Claus was prepared to send a small force of Mohawks and Canadian Indians to their assistance, but he understood that there would soon be many more refugees at Niagara and that Molly's presence would be sorely missed. It was important to start readjusting Haldimand's thinking on this point.[34]

Molly's thinking required no readjustment. She knew that she must return to Niagara immediately. Claus explained her views to Haldimand on September 6. Molly believed that "her Staying away at this critical Time, may prove very injurious to her character hereafter, being at the head of a Society of six Natn Matrons, who have a great deal to say among the young Men in particular in time of War[,] … for if she was to forsake them now, they might impute it to Fear, and that she forsaw or knew of an impending Danger over the Confederacy which she kept concealed and went out of the way to avoid it, wch Reflection would be insupportable to her."[35]

Haldimand quickly acceded to Molly's judgment, instructing Guy Johnson on September 9 that "I have acquainted Colonel Claus that Miss Molly is to act as she thinks best, whether in remaining in this Province, or Returning to Seneca Country—and that you or Col. Claus will give her such presents as you may think necessary, and if she goes provide for her Journey as it Seems to be a Political one."[36]

Considering the difficult circumstances that Molly was likely to encounter at Niagara, Haldimand was concerned for her family and was willing to provide for them at government expense at Montreal: "I should imagine it will be more Convenient, and much more advantageous for her Children to leave them Settled either at School, or in some Comfortable

Situation in the Neighborhood of Montreal, in either cases, You or Col. Claus will do what may be need full in disposing of them as you may think most pleasing and Convenient to them."[37]

The news that Governor Haldimand thought Molly should leave all of her surviving children at Montreal was very unwelcome to her. She had certainly intended to enroll the youngest three, Mary, Susanna, and Anne, in school in the fall. That and reunion with Margaret and George were the primary reasons Molly had not been opposed to leaving Niagara. But the idea of having to be separated from all of them was more than she could bear. She understood that it was dangerous to refuse the governor's suggestion. She was utterly dependent on him for financial support. He thought he was being generous, and a rejection of his idea could offend him. Nevertheless, although she enjoyed the diplomatic work and felt it was her duty, it was her children who had kept Molly going for the last five lonely years, and the thought of being without all of them was intolerable.

Guy Johnson told Governor Haldimand frankly that Molly's "anxiety to have her Children with her seems insurmountable, however I shall manage about it in the best manner in my power."[38] The entire Johnson family needed to be in the good graces of the governor of the province at this time, and for that reason Guy and Daniel probably both guilt-tripped Molly a bit. They undoubtedly reminded her that the girls needed an education to be marriageable to the kind of husbands Sir William had wanted for them. There were no schools at Niagara. Guy himself had been making the same sacrifice for more than three years, letting Anne Claus raise his three daughters, and after an all too brief stopover at Montreal, he would do so again when he left for Niagara, now the base of operations for the Indian Department.

In the end, Molly negotiated a compromise. The two oldest girls, Elizabeth and Magdalene, now 18 and 16, had already received as much education as girls of quality were given at the time. Molly had no money to dress them for presentation in society, not even by the reduced standards of wartime Montreal, and she certainly had no money for dowries. It was better that they come with her until the war was won and their property was restored. She would leave two of the three youngest girls—Susanna, age 10, and Mary, age 8—to attend school with Margaret and George under Daniel and Anne Claus's supervision, but the youngest—little Anne, age 6—would remain with her mother.[39]

On September 13, Daniel Claus reported Molly's departure for Niagara and diplomatically finessed the compromise regarding the children: "Miss Molly ... requested me in a particular Manner to present her best Respects to Your Excell.cy ... most gratefully acknowledging Your Excellency's Kindness and Attention toward her and her Family, and recommending them to your Future Favor and Protection, she left her two youngest girls with me to send to School one is 10 the other 8 years old."⁴⁰

Molly and her other daughters traveled with 20 Mohawk warriors on their way to aid the Senecas. Guy Johnson, accompanied by 130 Native Americans and Indian Department men, departed at about the same time, as did Sir John and most of his regiment.⁴¹ Haldimand reported to Lord Germain that he had authorized Sir John to take 400 "of the best and, Most Active Troops" to go to the assistance of the Six Nations, explaining that "retaining the Indians in our Interest has been attended with a very heavy Expense to Government, but their Attachment has, alone, hitherto preserved the upper country and the Devastation they have made upon the Susquehanna and Mohawk Rivers has distressed the Enemy prodigiously."⁴²

Haldimand also used the occasion to discuss his handling of Joseph and Molly and to describe to Germain the state of Six Nations' politics. He acknowledged receipt of a commission for Joseph that would have made him "Colonel of the Indians," a promotion Haldimand had suggested after the 1778 campaign and a title Sir William had held during King George's War. Haldimand had been forced to withhold the promotion, he explained: "To speak in their stile, he [Joseph] has been but very Lately known in the War Path—He is now distinguishing himself in that Line but it will be Some time before he is acknowledged by them even upon a footing with very many of (as they Conceive) more experienced and greater Warriors."⁴³

Haldimand, though clearly impressed with Joseph's talents, was particularly concerned about the jealousy of Sayengaraghta and was not prepared to offend him: "the notice that has been taken of him [Joseph] by us in Consequence of his connection with Sir William—His being Civilized, and more Particularly for his good Services has from a Jealousy predominant in Indians, procured him as many Enemies of his own People, as friends with us—of this number is Schenderatchta (Sayengaraghta) King of the Senecas."⁴⁴

Having just decided to spend government money on Molly and her children, Haldimand decided it was time to make Lord Germain aware of her services and sacrifices as well: "His [Joseph's] Sister, who lived many Years with Sir William Johnson, by whom he had many children, and by whose Influence he was much indebted in his Successful management of the Six Nations, was driven from her home, and with her Family took Refuge at Niagara." Haldimand explained to Germain that Molly had come to Montreal at his invitation but returned to Niagara "thinking She Might be of use in encouraging the Indians to Preserve their Fidelity." Haldimand believed they were required to help Molly for both moral and practical reasons: "The Care of this Woman will necessarily be attended with Some Expense to Government, but whatever may be done for her is due to the Memory of Sir Willm. Johnson, to Her Services, and will be a handsome Mark of attention to Joseph."[45]

* * *

As Sir John and Guy Johnson rushed toward them with their insufficient reinforcements, the fate of the Senecas and Cayugas had already been determined. On August 29 near present-day Elmira, New York, Joseph's men, Sayengaraghta's warriors, and Butler's Rangers—outnumbered about seven to one—attempted an ambush of Sullivan and Clinton's combined force that would become known as the Battle of Newtown. Most of the Native Americans participating in the fight had never before experienced cannon fire. When the Patriots formed up their artillery and fired on them, many fled. Even Joseph's volunteers and the Rangers retreated a distance of 10 miles.[46]

In the days that followed, Joseph continued to organize some small ambushes, but they were pin pricks in the face of the Patriots' overwhelming numbers. By September 15, Sullivan had destroyed 40 Seneca settlements and the entire fall harvest, estimated at 160,000 bushels of corn. On the way back to Pennsylvania, he sent a force to Cayuga territory that destroyed all of the Cayuga settlements on both sides of Cayuga Lake.[47]

On September 26 when Sir John and Guy Johnson arrived at Carleton Island, located at the head of the St. Lawrence River near its junction with Lake Ontario, Sullivan had already left Seneca country. Sir John and Guy Johnson decided that they must nevertheless rendezvous with Joseph in order to demonstrate to the Senecas and Cayugas that they had tried to help them. They left Carleton Island with their combined forces on October 10 and met Joseph and his men at Oswego. The three men discussed the idea of a retaliatory raid on the Oneidas, but based on reports of a large Patriot force still in the area, a decision was made to proceed to Niagara for the winter.[48]

The group of Mohawk warriors with whom Molly had traveled arrived at Carleton Island on September 29. The nearly three-week journey from Montreal had been "tedious and disagreeable" for Molly and her daughters. The warriors were going to Oswego with Guy Johnson and Sir John and could be of no further assistance. Molly quickly realized that all available boats were being pressed into service for the Oswego venture and that none were available to take her farther west to Fort Niagara. She sent letters to Joseph and John Butler asking what she should do, but recognized that they were both fully occupied at Oswego. On October 5, she wrote to Daniel Claus telling him that she thought she might have to spend the winter at Carleton Island.[49]

Molly also wanted to apprise Daniel Claus of a developing problem she had observed since her arrival there: "the Indians are a Good dale dissatisfied on Acct. of the Colos. Hasty temper which I hope he will soon drop[.] Otherwise it may be Disadvantageous." The war years had taken their toll on the formerly charming and gregarious Guy Johnson. An able assistant to Sir William for almost two decades and a firm leader of the Indian Department in the early stages of the rebellion, four years since his forced departure from the Mohawk valley Johnson was still grieving the loss of his wife and the end of his happy family life. Compelled to once again part from his three children after a short visit at Montreal that summer and tasked with the impossible assignment of keeping Britain's Native American allies happy while reducing expenditures, Johnson was losing his political judgment and was beginning to drink too much.[50]

The Canadian Indians had always been Daniel Claus's responsibility, but now a contingent was about to accompany Guy to Oswego, and Molly was hearing complaints: "Those from Canada are much Dissatisfied on Account of his taking more Notice of those that are suspected than them that are known to be Loyal." Daniel was the only one who could head off the danger: "I tell this only to you that you Advise him On that head."[51]

As Molly suspected, the St. Lawrence River and Lake Ontario were soon full of dangerous ice, and there would be no boats going to Niagara from Carleton Island until spring. Fortunately, she also soon realized that she could be useful at Carleton Island and that the commander there, unlike Lieutenant Colonel Bolton, was a man who appreciated her services.

When Guy Johnson, Joseph, and John Butler arrived at Niagara on November 11, they found more than 2,500 refugees from Sullivan's campaign at the fort. Guy Johnson urged some of the Native Americans to go out hunting and to make their way to Carleton Island, where he hoped there were additional supplies. While a total of 3,000 Native Americans ended up wintering at Niagara, several hundred did make their way overland to Carleton Island.[52]

The commander at Carleton Island was Captain Alexander Fraser. Fraser had received reports that the Patriots might attempt a winter raid on Carleton Island similar to the one Washington had staged at Trenton at the end of 1776. Fraser needed scouts to keep a constant look out for the enemy throughout the winter in "uncommon depth of the Snows and constant severity of the Weather." At the end of the winter, Fraser was almost giddy with praise for the Native Americans who had performed these scouting services, for they "not only did this Service with chearfulness &

punctuality but have behaved better in every respect than ever I knew so great a number of them to do before."[53]

Fraser gave some credit for this happy outcome to Sir William's old friend, Captain Gilbert Tice of the Indian Department, and to the sachems present at the fort, "but their uncommon good behaviour is in a great Measure to be ascribed to Miss Molly Brants Influence over them, which is far superior to that of all their Chiefs put together."[54]

Molly had "done every thing in her power to maintain them strongly in the King's Interest." She had also encouraged the men to go out hunting, and according to Fraser, they brought in significant amounts of meat and fish that they shared with the British troops. For his part, Fraser had distributed what fresh venison he had in his stores to "sick Indians" and to "our own Hospital."[55] Fraser was happy to report that "tho we are composed of all Nations; of all Colours; & of all professions, there has not been during this winter the smallest disagreement between any two Individuals on the Island."[56]

Despite this wonderful result and his respect for Molly, Captain Fraser was still culturally taken aback by a woman who expected compensation for her services and wasn't shy about asking for it. Molly and her children had spent the winter in an army barracks. If she was to stay at Carleton Island, as she was now considering doing, she informed Fraser, she needed a house similar to the one she had at Niagara and a garden. Fraser was unsure what Haldimand's attitude would be, but wanted to lay the groundwork for the governor's approval of the expenditure by letting Haldimand know that Molly was an asset: "Tho she is insatiable in her demands for her own family, yet I believe her residence here has been a considerable saving to Government, as she checkd the demands of others both for presents and provisions."[57]

* * *

Spring brought Molly a welcome visit from Joseph, on his way from Niagara to upper New York for the 1780 campaigning season. There was much news. In late December, he had married for a third time. Catharine Croghan was Mohawk royalty. Her father, George Croghan, was Sir William's longtime deputy superintendent for Pennsylvania. Her mother, also named Catharine, was the senior matron of the Turtle Clan, and her mother's brother was Tekarihoga, the Mohawks' senior representative to the Six Nations confederacy council. Upon her mother and uncle's deaths, Catharine Croghan Brant and her half brother Henry would succeed to those positions.[58]

Joseph was a happy man. He had entered his second marriage to Peggie's sister, Susanna, for the sake of his children, but Catharine was his own choice. She was beautiful and intelligent. It was a love match that would last until the end of Joseph's life and produce seven children.

Joseph told Molly that John Butler would soon be arriving at Carleton Island on his way to Montreal. Butler would escort her if she wanted to visit her children there. She most certainly did.

When Molly departed for Montreal that summer, she—as a bargaining ploy—did not make it clear to Captain Fraser whether she would return to Carleton Island or go to Niagara as originally planned. She also implied that she might apply directly to the governor for help with her housing situation. Captain Fraser reported to Governor Haldimand on June 21, 1780, that "Joseph Brant's sister Miss Molly left this place yesterday along with Colonel Butler much against my inclination." Fraser informed Haldimand that she might be planning to go to Niagara after her visit to Montreal, "where she will be a very unwelcome Guest to Colo Bolton."[59]

Fraser did not want to appear a pushover to his boss. He wanted to make it clear he was a prudent servant of the Crown, not doling out government funds indiscriminately: "If she [Molly] is not humoured in all her Demands for herself and her Dependents (which are numerous) she may by the violence of her temper be led to create Mischief."[60]

Molly's demonstration of adamant resolution may have been surprising to Captain Fraser, but now that she was required to provide for her children, she was not in a position to display what Europeans regarded as seemly feminine reticence. Instead, she adopted the forceful negotiating techniques employed by men when they were bluffing their way out of a difficult situation. Molly's eldest child, Peter, had died at a military camp for want of proper care. Some of her remaining children, including two attractive teenage girls, were currently sleeping in a freezing army barracks adjacent to a room full of libidinous and sometimes sickly soldiers. She was not going to lose any more of her children. Something had to be done.

Captain Fraser wanted Molly to remain at Carleton Island, and in his heart he knew she wasn't being unreasonable: "In case Your Excellency would wish her to remain here it were good that some little box of a house were built for her as it would be more comfortable to her family than living in a Barrack Room." He was already trying to provide incentives for her to stay: "I have at my own expense made a tolerable good Garden for her."[61]

Hoping that Haldimand would not think him weak but not wanting to leave his superior in any doubt as to the preferred outcome, Captain Fraser wrote that "I had every reason to be satisfyd with her Conduct through the winter—and as I know herself and her family to be steadily attached to Government I wish them to be attended to."[62]

12. Guerrillas and Refugees 157

Captain Fraser could not know it, but Molly's good treatment had already been signed off on at the highest levels. Dissatisfaction with the war, especially the expense generated by the war, was growing in Parliament. The expenses related to Molly and her family were relatively minor, certainly an amount that could be approved by Lord Germain. Germain nevertheless feared some nasty accusation by the opposition about wasting government money on the Native American paramour of a dead official. When he received Haldimand's October 1779 report regarding expenditures for Molly, Germain decided to protect himself by gaining approval from an unimpeachable source. On March 17, 1780, he informed Governor Haldimand that "the Provision You have made for Joseph's Sister is approved by the King."[63]

When Haldimand received Captain Fraser's letter that summer, the Governor had no reason to hesitate. His aide-de-camp, Captain Robert Mathews, promptly replied, "I am commanded by His Excellency General Haldimand ... to signify to You, His desire that You will have built for Miss Molly such a House as will lodge Her and Family comfortably chusing a favorable Situation within a few hundred Yards of the Fort."[64]

Haldimand's decision had been made after consultation with Daniel Claus as to Molly's wishes: "Her inclination fortunately, leads Her to settle at Carleton Island, rather than return to Niagara." One can imagine the look of amusement in Captain Mathews's eyes as he wrote to the relieved Captain Fraser that "it is very probable You will soon see Her at Carleton Island."[65]

13

Winners and Losers

As Molly enjoyed the summer visiting her children at Montreal, the men of the family were making war in upper New York. Emboldened by the success of Sullivan's campaign, some settlers had returned to their farms in the Mohawk valley during the spring of 1780. Sir John and Joseph were determined to make it clear that no matter what had happened in western New York the previous summer, they would not allow the reoccupation of the Mohawk and Schoharie valleys by Patriot settlers. During May, Sir John brought a combined fighting force of 528 European Americans and Native Americans down Lake Champlain and raided the vicinity of Johnstown. He not only burned Patriot farms within a 12-mile swathe but also recruited 143 Loyalists for his regiment.[1]

In July and August, Joseph, at the head of 314 Native American fighting men, destroyed the Oneida village of Canowaraghere and the European American settlements of Cherry Valley, German Flatts, and Vroman's Land.[2] On September 24 Joseph, John Butler, and Sir John rendezvoused at Oswego. Their combined force was 657 men. Their mission, as ordered by General Haldimand, was to destroy the fall wheat harvest intended to feed the Continental Army. The campaign, which lasted a month, was successful. Governor Clinton of New York estimated the loss of 150,000 bushels of wheat and the destruction of 200 dwellings. Tryon County officials reported in December 1780 that 1,200 farms were currently uncultivated, as their owners were not willing to take the risk of occupying them.[3] Sir John praised Joseph in his report as one of those who "exerted themselves upon the Occasion in a Manner that did them honour and contributed greatly to our Success."[4]

All of this good news encouraged Governor Haldimand to send Joseph a written commission as a captain in the Indian Department. It was not the "Colonel of the Indians" title that Lord Germain had originally envisioned. He was only one of seven captains of the Indian Department under Guy Johnson, but was the only Native American to receive such a commission during the Revolutionary War. By December 1780, Joseph was officially in charge of 188 men (mostly Mohawks, loyal Oneidas, and Mohicans), and their dependents (276 women and 233 children).[5]

Molly returned to Carleton Island that fall and was able to install her children in their new home. Elizabeth, Magdalene, Margaret, and Anne were all with her. George, Susanna, and Mary remained at school in Montreal.[6] Molly's relief was palpable. A new commander, Major John Ross, was to take over at Carleton Island at the end of the year, but Captain Fraser assured Governor Haldimand that the transition would be smooth: "I gave particular directions regarding Miss Molly's treatment, she had got into her new house, and seemed better satisfyd with her situation than I had ever known her before."[7] The previous year, Guy Johnson had expressed concern to Daniel Claus that Molly might not understand the limits of government assistance: "She is certainly you know pretty large minded.... I fear that any Expense or Attention will fall short of her Desires tho' I wish to gratify them." His fears were unjustified. Like a good male politician, Molly knew when to insist on her bottom line and when to show appreciation for concessions.[8]

If things were looking up for Molly and Joseph, the same could not be said for Guy Johnson. Both Governor Haldimand and Lord Germain had lost confidence in him. On August 8, 1780, Germain wrote to Haldimand: "I agree with You in Col. Johnson's unfittness to Conduct the business of the five Nations, at the present Moment. ... I was Content he Should have remained at New-York." The outcry in Parliament about the expense of the war was escalating, and Guy was tone deaf to the demands for economy: "a very Ample Supply of Presents for them is now going Out, tho not So large as was demanded by the Agents, for the Whole was enormous, particularly Colonel Guy Johnson's Estimate."[9]

To some extent, Guy Johnson would end up as one of the British government's whipping boys for a failed colonial war. Guy possessed 20 years' experience dealing with the Six Nations, much of it at the side of Sir William, the greatest ambassador to the Native Americans of his time. Guy knew all of the sachems and senior matrons of the Six Nations personally. He knew what they had been through: the sons and the lands, homes, and crops they had lost because of their alliance with the king. Guy had heard it from them face-to-face upon his arrival at Niagara, and he lived through the refugee crisis that unfolded there throughout the bitter winter of 1779–1780. It was he, not Haldimand or Germain, who would have to personally deal with these people's anger if supplies for the coming winter were inadequate. Guy did his best to make his superiors understand.[10] But it is also true that the stress from his tragic private losses and his great public burden were beginning to undo him. Molly had noticed his displays of anger at Carleton Island, and now he was missing clear clues from his superiors that they faced political and economic exigencies at home that could not be ignored.

* * *

The winter of 1780–1781 would prove milder than the previous one. Molly took advantage of the late onset of the season to take a short trip to Niagara in November 1780, escorted by Walter Butler. Her reason for the trip was probably to visit her mother Margaret, who may have been in failing health. Margaret last appears in the historical record at the beginning of 1780 when Guy Johnson gave her a gift of clothing. Only an emergency would cause Molly to travel so late in the season, risking separation from her children for the winter. There was a new commander at the fort, so Molly was not unwelcome.[11]

An officer's wife, Matilda Scheifflen, who met Molly en route to Niagara describes her at that time as having "a sensible countenance and much whiter than the generality of Indians." Molly may have been offended by this woman's manner. Mrs. Scheifflin apparently viewed Molly as an object of curiosity but not as an equal. She referred to Molly in a letter to her father as "formerly favorite Sultana to Sir William Johnson." Although Molly spoke English very well and usually displayed an outgoing personality, she chose only to speak Mohawk to Butler during the meal they shared with the Schleiffens. Mrs. Scheifflin noted that the Mohawk language sounded musical on Molly's lips.[12]

After her return to Carleton Island, Molly received alarming news from Niagara. According to Mohawks traveling from Niagara to Carleton Island, her brother Joseph had been involved in an altercation with one of the European American officers of the Indian Department, and other European American Indian Department officers had jumped in to take the officer's side, restraining Joseph.

The cause of the fight was a disagreement over strategy. Joseph believed that additional raids should be undertaken against the Oneidas, but Guy Johnson was not willing to authorize them. Joseph was not alone in advocating a more aggressive policy against the Oneidas. John Deserontyn, a Fort Hunter sachem, was waiting at Carleton Island with 40 Six Nations fighting men who expected Joseph to bring a force from Niagara for an early spring campaign.[13]

Having led successful raids in upper New York for three successive years, Joseph felt that he had a perfect right to argue the necessity of an Oneida campaign over drinks with the other Indian Department officers. These men saw Joseph as at most a peer in the Indian Department, while he knew that he had been leading his own company of volunteers for most of the war. The officer he came to blows with apparently was offended by

13. Winners and Losers

Joseph presuming to strongly disagree with Guy Johnson's decision. Guy's initial reaction to the incident was to separate the two men. Joseph told Guy that if there was to be no raid against the Oneidas, he wished to take a contingent of men to Detroit, where it was rumored that a Patriot army led by George Rogers Clark was approaching. Guy agreed to this, and Joseph departed for Detroit on April 8 with 17 men and a mission to recruit fighting men from the western tribes for the defense of the areas surrounding Detroit.[14]

Joseph did not ask Molly to intervene, but when she heard what had transpired, she was determined to do so. She immediately wrote to Daniel Claus, formally requesting that he report the matter to Haldimand. She admitted that there was a personal element to her outrage: "It is hard for me to have an only Brother whom I dearly love to see him thus treated." But there was also a strong policy reason that this matter could not be ignored: "This usage of my Brother makes me dread the Consequences, as some of the six Nations were Spectators of it, and well remember what Genl Schyler told them that they would be ill used and despised by the Kings people for their Services, of which they have now a proof." She knew full well that racial prejudice was involved: "The officers at Niagara are so haughty & proud not knowing or considering that the Kings Interest is so nearly connected with that of the Indians." The unfairness of what had occurred was obvious to Six Nations people: "Being scarce returned safe from the Rebel Country he must be thus treated by those of the Kings people who always stay quietly at home & in the Fort, while my Brother continually exposes his Life in going against the Enemy taking prisnrs."[15]

John Deserontyn supported Molly's position, writing to Daniel Claus the same day: "I must entreat you to represent to the General Assaregoa [Haldimand] how the officers go on at Niagara that he may interfere and strife [strive] to preserve our mutual peace & Welfare."[16]

Daniel Claus must have groaned when he received these letters. There was already an inquiry under way about the Niagara traders Taylor and Forsyth's dealings with the Indian Department, and that combined with Guy's large requests for aid to the Six Nations had put him on the thinnest of ice with Governor Haldimand and Lord Germain. The tone of relations between some of the Indian Department officers and Joseph Brant had been set when John Butler was in charge and fending off Joseph's requests for ammunition in compliance with General Carleton's orders, but Guy Johnson, with so many other problems plaguing him, had failed to set matters right after his arrival at Niagara. Daniel and Guy had been brothers-in-law for close to 20 years. Guy's three daughters were being raised by Daniel and his wife, Anne. But there was no way Daniel could ignore this. He had an official commission from the government. Molly was a senior matron of the Six Nations, and John Deserontyn was a leading sachem. They were both making a formal request. Despite Guy's close relationship with Sir William, Molly had lost confidence in his ability to appropriately handle relations with the Six Nations: "I beg you will speedily let His Excellency General Haldimand hear of it, who alone can heal this Breach of peace & Friendship, by his order & reprimand as Commander in Chief."[17]

Governor Haldimand reacted exactly as Molly and John Deserontyn hoped he would. Haldimand sent an order to General Powell, Niagara's commander, instructing him to investigate the matter and to ensure that Guy Johnson "gives that support to Joseph which his services & attachment to Government really merit."[18]

But by now, Guy Johnson was in the last stages of his tenure as Indian Department superintendent. While Joseph and a contingent of western Native American fighting men he raised at Detroit defeated a Patriot army led by Colonel Archibald Lochry 11 miles below the Great Miami River, Guy was being humiliated at the trial of Taylor and Forsyth in Montreal.[19]

Although never charged with wrongdoing, Guy was made to look at least incompetent and at worst possibly dishonest during the proceedings. He protested to Governor Haldimand: "Your Memorialist ... is now Constrained to represent to your Excellency how much he is hurt as an officer, and a man of Honor, at some Expressions reported to him to have been dropped lately in a Court of Justice maliciously intending to insinuate Collusive dealings." The Six Nations people were aware of the trial and believed him "disgraced," "all tending most generously to injure the reputation and destroy the influence of Your Memorialist."[20]

Guy had said it himself. His usefulness was at an end. He had seen his wife die in the wilderness, had become a stranger to his children, and had forfeited a large estate in the Mohawk valley in an effort to hold the province of New York for the king, but had been unable to maintain a critical alliance without the expenditure of sums of money that the taxpayers of Great Britain were no longer willing to pay.

Haldimand was in no position to sympathize. He knew who Guy Johnson's successor should be. On March 15, 1782, Lord Germain responded to Haldimand: "I have likewise the Satisfaction to acquaint You that Your Proposition of a Superintendent General of Indian Affairs is adopted, and Sir John Johnson has Received His Majesty's Warrant appointing him to that office."[21]

As a young man, Sir John had had no interest in dealing with the Indians. He had told his disappointed father to groom his cousin Guy for the position instead. Guy was charming, while Sir John was shy. Guy was fluent in Mohawk, while Sir John was not. But the war had forced Sir John

13. Winners and Losers

to do many things he had never thought he would have to do. After a rocky start at Oriskany, he had proved to be an effective militia commander. The war was coming to an end, and Sir John needed to remain relevant to the king and the king's ministers. Sir John's large estate had been confiscated by the Patriots. The salary he could earn as superintendent, together with his officer's pension, would allow him to support his growing family while he pursued a claim for his losses with the government commission established to assist Loyalists who had suffered economic harm because of their support for the king. It was understood that large landowners would not be made whole by the commission. The aggregate losses suffered were simply too great. It certainly occurred to Sir John that men who continued to offer important services to the Crown as the commissioners did their work might be looked upon more kindly than those who did not.

Sir John's intention was to keep Guy on as a kind of deputy. They had been more brothers than cousins since their teen years. Sir John would not let Guy be totally cast off, but there was no denying that the demotion was a dishonor, and Guy never recovered from it.[22]

* * *

Molly took another trip to Montreal in the summer of 1781, probably not realizing that Great Britain was about to throw in the towel and concede its 13 rebellious American colonies to the Patriots. From her perspective, Joseph, Sir John, and the Butlers were making life impossible for the rebels of upper New York. Surely her family and her people would soon be able to return to the Mohawk valley.

As usual, Molly visited Daniel and Anne Claus. They probably concealed their pessimism. The Six Nations' determination to get their land back was an asset to Great Britain's flagging war prospects. The Clauses were unlikely to say anything to Molly that would cause defeatist rumors to circulate.

Daniel again used the visit as an opportunity to keep Governor Haldimand updated on Molly and her family. Molly was bringing Susanna and Mary home to Carleton Island: "The Schoolmaster tells me the girls sufficiently read & write English." George was coming home for a vacation but would return with little Anne for another year of schooling: "The Boy to my knowledge has greatly improved in that respect, and is so far advanced in cyphering that with a little care and study he may easily acquire more of that Science than he will have Occasion for."[23]

Daniel must have gulped as he wrote those last words about young George. No fencing or French lessons for him such as his elder brother Peter had enjoyed at the same age. George's wealthy father was dead, and his estate was confiscated. George would live with his mother's people, and his life would be very different from what Sir William had planned. Still, Daniel's respect and affection for the memory of Sir William wouldn't allow him to give up completely on George's prospects in the wider world. The boy must keep studying: "I have supplied him with necessary Books & Stationary, he is a promising Lad abt. 14 years old."[24]

Molly, as always, attuned to the need to remain in the good graces of her benefactor, "entreated me [Daniel] to offer her most Sincere and hearty Respects and Thanks." Daniel concluded with his own appraisal of her mood: "She seemed to be happy in her children's improved State and left this with Satisfaction & Contentment."[25]

Haldimand's aide, Captain Mathews, responded with Haldimand's satisfaction that Molly was happy: "It being his Excellency's Wish, as well as on account of the Regard he bore the late Sir William Johnson as to reward the Services of her Family, to Shew her every Freindly Attention in His Power."[26]

* * *

After his victory over Lochry's detachment in late August, Joseph made his way back to Detroit. An accidental injury to his leg made it impossible for him to go farther. His wife, Catharine, devotedly made the long trip from Niagara to nurse him. They spent the winter of 1781–1782 at Detroit. By the time they returned to Niagara in the spring, the future of the American colonies and the fate of the Six Nations had been all but decided. Financially drained by a war now six years old that some had thought Britain would easily win, both Parliament and the British public had had enough. Peace negotiations were soon to begin in Paris.[27]

Nevertheless, days after Cornwallis's surrender at Yorktown, Virginia, some hostilities continued elsewhere, resulting in the death of Walter Butler in a skirmish near Johnstown.[28] At Carleton Island when messengers brought the news, Molly grieved for her old friend John Butler and saw Walter Butler's death as yet another sacrifice in the struggle to wrest back their homeland from the traitors who had seized it.

It is not clear whether Molly heard about the disaster at Yorktown before the St. Lawrence iced over for the winter. Joseph heard the news about both Yorktown and the Johnstown raid at Detroit in late April 1782, and he rushed eastward in response. Making a brief stop at Niagara to rally his men, he arrived at Oswego on June 18 with 300 Native American and 10 European American volunteers. He conducted one more raid on Fort Herkimer before being ordered to cease hostilities while peace negotiations went forward in Paris.[29]

* * *

Haldimand, an intelligent and honorable man, comprehended the loss the Six Nations had sustained as a result of their loyalty to the king. He also realized that he faced a Native American uprising if some reasonable solution to their plight was not worked out. Haldimand did not yet know the terms of the peace settlement, but he had already decided that the Mohawks in particular but also the other allied tribes must be given Canadian land by the British government as compensation for their lost territory. When Joseph met with Sir John at Montreal, Sir John told Joseph in general terms that he had assurances from Haldimand that the Six Nations would be looked after by the Crown. Sir John also asked Joseph to accompany him and a British officer, Lieutenant Colonel Henry Hope, on an inspection of the upper posts.[30]

Molly was in Montreal at about the same time for her annual trip to pick up her school-attending children. This time she was bringing Anne and George home for a vacation.[31] It was probably during this trip that Molly found out from Joseph and Sir John that there was a good chance that Canada would be their permanent home. They probably also discussed how much she could say to people at Carleton Island when she returned there. Nothing had been decided yet, so it is likely that Sir John encouraged her to emphasize the temporary nature of the truce and her certitude that the king would look out for the interests of the Six Nations. Although personally believing this last talking point to be true, Molly must have worried on her way back to Carleton Island about what to say to the sachems and senior matrons there that would not later be seen as misleading.

As for Joseph, he set out westward on August 21 with Sir John and Lieutenant Colonel Hope. For Sir John, this was reminiscent of the trip to Detroit he had made with his father two decades before. On this second trip, Sir John, Joseph, and Hope traveled even farther, reaching the western shore of Lake Huron on September 21. It was a strenuous journey, involving 34 portages, and probably reminded Sir John of why he had never wanted to be Indian affairs superintendent. Nevertheless, he took it in good spirit, and it was an important bonding experience for him and Joseph. It certainly occurred to Sir John during their month together that no matter how much his teenaged self had resented his father and Molly's relationship in the wake of his mother's illness and death, Joseph and Molly's sense of him as family would be very important in helping Sir John execute his challenging office in the difficult times ahead.

* * *

Meanwhile, Haldimand was urging the new government in London to consider the consequences if the peace settlement failed to take account of the interests of Britain's Native American allies. He also indicated that the financial aid they were accustomed to receiving from the British government could not suddenly be taken away.[32]

Lord Townshend's response to Haldimand's concerns was not encouraging. Haldimand was to take what steps he thought necessary to protect the Indian affairs superintendents and their officers as well as fur traders and the property of fur traders, but "the Measures hereafter to be pursued with the Indians, and Presents … require great Consideration and must be referred to my next Dispatch." Haldimand was to be under no illusion that things would continue as they had in the past: "In the Mean Time you will Continue in the Exertion of Your best Endeavours & Circumscribe the Expenses of Presents; and indeed to reduce, in every Department that enormous and lavish Expenditure of Public Money, which has almost exhausted the Revenue and Resources of this Country."[33]

In late April, Haldimand received a copy of the preliminary peace treaty and the king's proclamation of the cessation of hostilities. The boundary between Great Britain's Canadian colonies and the United States of America would run through the middle of the Great Lakes. The treaty failed to mention any claims of the Native Americans.[34] Joseph was stunned. He told General Allan Maclean, the new commander at Niagara, that "England has sold the Indians to Congress."[35]

Despite his shock at the terms of the peace treaty, Joseph knew he could not give up on the British. He immediately set out for Montreal to consult with Sir John and Daniel Claus. On the way there, Joseph stopped at Carleton Island and talked with Molly. She was in a very awkward position because news of the treaty had reached Carleton Island. She and Joseph agreed that she must continue to urge the Native Americans in the vicinity to have faith that the king would look out for his Six Nations allies and to remind them that they must have patience while things were worked out. Molly must repress the deep anxiety she now actually felt and project confidence that justice would be done.

On May 21, Joseph met with Haldimand in Quebec. In a formal speech, Joseph expressed his shock at the terms of the peace treaty. In response, Haldimand, acting on his own initiative without prior authorization from London, asked Joseph if he would be willing to accompany Major Samuel Holland, the British Army's surveyor general, to Cataraqui to look for a suitable settlement site for his people. Cataraqui, present-day Kingston, Ontario, was located on the north shore of Lake Ontario at the mouth of the St. Lawrence and Cataraqui Rivers. It was about 10 miles from Carleton Island. A relieved Joseph responded in the affirmative to Haldimand's proposal.[36]

13. Winners and Losers

While Joseph was in Quebec, Haldimand couldn't do enough for him. Haldimand presented Joseph with a letter of recommendation noting his "entire Approbation of his laudable and disinterested Services to the Royal Cause" and "the Personal Esteem I shall always bear him on that account." Joseph was also Haldimand's guest at an official dinner attended by Baron Friedrich Adolf Riedesel and his wife, Baroness Charlotte Riedesel. The baroness, who had helped nurse the wounded at Saratoga and who lived alongside her husband during his internment as a prisoner of war, was impressed with Joseph: "He conversed well" and "had a manly countenance. His character was gentle."[37]

Nor did Haldimand forget Molly. On May 27, he informed Sir John that "in Consideration of the early and uniform fidelity, attachment, and Zealous Services to the King's Government by Mrs. Mary Brant and her Family, I have thought it fit to Settle upon her a Yearly pension of one Hundred pounds currency, which you are hereby authorized and directed to pay her Quarterly."[38] The pension, though paid in currency rather than pounds sterling, was similar to the pension settled on widows of exiled colonial officers.

Molly's heart was bursting with relief when Joseph stopped at Carleton Island on the way to Cataraqui and announced all the good news. The war had brought so many horrible losses. Nothing Haldimand could do would ever bring back Molly's son Peter or her stepson William of Canajoharie. But her instinct that Sir William's king would keep better faith with her and her people than the Americans was proving correct.

The spot that Joseph and Major Holland selected for the Six Nations' new home had long ago been the site of a Wyandot settlement. One of Molly and Joseph's ancestors had been a woman captured from that village by the Mohawks. Now in a twist of fate, Molly and Joseph would make a home there with the dispossessed Mohawk nation.[39]

Meanwhile at Quebec, Haldimand also heaved a sigh of relief. His gamble that the British government would support a gift of land to its Native American allies had paid off. By the beginning of autumn, Haldimand was informed by Lord North (now back in power once again) that the king approved of his idea "to prevail upon the Mohawks to Settle to the Northward of that Lake provided the Country should be found Suited for their Convenience." The king felt a moral obligation: "These People are justly entitled to our Peculiar Attention, and it would be far from either generous or just in Us after our Session of their Territories and Hunting Grounds to forsake them." Lord North was not insensible to the benefits of this arrangement for the Crown. He noted that allowing these Native Americans to settle in Canada would prevent disruption of the fur trade.[40]

Haldimand was also authorized to distribute land to Sir John's officers and enlisted men for their "Loyalty and Services."[41] Fearful of American designs on Canada, North instructed Haldimand that "you will without Doubt think it prudent and Consistent with Sound Policy to Establish a principal part of those People in Such a Situation as May be most likely to Serve as a Barrier to the Province against any Incursions from the Inhabitants of those Colonies that have revolted from their allegiance."[42]

14

A Home in Canada

There was a fort at Cataraqui that Haldimand visualized as the center of a new town. Near the fort, on the west side of the harbor, he authorized the construction of two houses, one for Molly and the other for Joseph. The houses were 40 feet wide, 30 feet in depth, and one and one half stories tall.[1]

As Molly prepared to make the short move from Carleton Island to Cataraqui, she had in her household all six of her daughters; three enslaved people, Abraham, Juba, and Jenny; and William Lamb, now 13 years old.[2] Her son George, about age 14, was still at school in Montreal but would soon join the rest of the family at Cataraqui. The three enslaved people—listed as Abraham Johnston, a negro age 45; Juba Fundy, a Negro woman age 23; and Jane [Jenny] Fundy, a Negro Woman age 20—had been with Molly since the period when she was mistress of Johnson Hall. They helped her and her children escape Canajoharie in 1777 and had been with her through all of the tragedies and hardships since then. A fourth slave, December, who was with her at Canajoharie, had by then disappeared from the historical record. He either died in the intervening years, or took some opportunity during the chaos of the war to make his break for freedom.[3]

William Lamb, the other member of Molly's household, had been taken prisoner by Joseph at Harpersfield, New York, in 1780. Then only 10 years old, William was with his father and some other men on what Joseph deemed to be a scouting mission, although the party was also collecting maple sugar. The father was imprisoned at Chambly for the remainder of the war. The child was thought too young to share this captivity, so Molly agreed to take him into her home. William was not released with the other American prisoners at the end of the war, in part because the logistics of sending him back to New York alone would have been complicated. Molly may also have considered him to be her adoptive son. It was Mohawk tradition to adopt child captives in place of dead relatives. Since Peter had died in the war, Molly may have thought it very appropriate to keep the

Molly Brant's house in Cataraqui was adjacent to her brother Joseph's house. *A View of Cataraqui from Captain Brant's House*, by James Peachey, July 16, 1784. Library and Archives of Canada, Accession no. 1989-221-4.

boy with her. If William's mother was dead, Molly would have had few qualms about doing so, since Mohawks viewed children as belonging to the mother's clan. As a young adult, William eventually made his way back to New York State and was reunited with his father and an aunt.[4]

No sooner had Molly settled in at Cataraqui than the Senecas began making the argument that it would be safer for the Six Nations if all the tribes lived in closer proximity to each other. The Senecas went so far as to offer some of their land as a settlement site for the other tribes of the confederacy. Joseph was not comfortable with that proposal, but he began discussing with Haldimand the idea that the Six Nations should be granted land in the Grand River valley. The Grand River flows into Lake Erie from the north side of the lake. Its bottomlands are very fertile, and the proposed grant was near the Seneca's remaining territory.[5]

Before a final decision was made, Joseph and some other Mohawk sachems explored the idea of getting their land in the Mohawk valley back from the Americans. They attended a council at Fort Stanwix in September 1784. New York state governor Clinton and Peter Schuyler both attended the meeting. It soon became clear to Joseph that the Americans had no intention of allowing the Mohawks to reoccupy their lands, despite the risk of continuing Mohawk raids if a deal was not done. Although he did not have much confidence in the New Yorkers' good faith, Joseph took the opportunity of the council to assert the rights of Molly's children to the lands bequeathed them by Sir William.[6]

Sir William and Molly's children were minors at the time the family had been forced to flee the Mohawk valley. Under the terms of the peace treaty, they should have been entitled to the return of their property. Although Clinton and Schuyler made vague promises of assistance in this matter, the reality was that Congress could only recommend to the states that they return property, and Molly's children's lands were already occupied by voting New York citizens. Moreover, not only had the children's mother given intelligence to the British that resulted in the deaths of many Patriot militiamen at Oriskany, but their uncle Joseph and their half brother, Sir John, had burned many Patriot farms during the course of the war. No one in New York felt the slightest moral obligation to any member of the Johnson family.[7]

When Joseph left Fort Stanwix, he collected his wife Catharine, their baby, and his daughter Christina at Niagara and brought them to their new house at Cataraqui. He had decided two things. He should pursue the Grand River proposal with Haldimand and must go to London to seek compensation from the Loyalty Commission for the homes, furniture, livestock, and other personal property the Mohawks had left behind at Canajoharie and Fort Hunter.[8]

Molly was very glad that Joseph was willing to go to England to pursue their claims with the Loyalty Commission. She was well aware that it would be much easier to ignore the Mohawks' losses if their claims were made long distance. She would happily look after Catharine and the children while Joseph was away. Molly understood too the need to consolidate the Six Nations geographically by making the move to Grand River, but it is probably at this time that she told Joseph she would not be going.

The Grand River valley, though good land, was a remote wilderness location far from Europeans. That was its appeal for the Six Nations. It would be a long time before European American settlers hemmed them in again. But Molly had six daughters who had spent most or at least part of their childhoods at Johnson Hall, and had all received European American educations. The eldest, Elizabeth, had recently married Dr. Robert Kerr, a British officer and medical doctor stationed at Niagara. Margaret, the third eldest, may already have been courting with Captain George Farley, who was stationed at Cataraqui. She would soon marry him. Molly had no desire to move far from these daughters or to deprive her other daughters of marriage opportunities. In the end, the five daughters of Molly and Sir William who married would all wed British officers.[9]

Molly had spent the last seven years as a major diplomatic liaison between her people and the British government. The British government was now prepared to give the Six Nations a substantial tract of land. If Joseph succeeded in London, there would also be cash payments to compensate for their other losses. Haldimand had given her a generous pension and a comfortable house. She was ready to retire from the years of struggle and to live a quiet life. She wanted to enjoy her children and the grandchildren who would soon be coming.

* * *

Continuing eastward, Joseph arrived at Quebec on October 23. Governor Haldimand was leaving office in three weeks and returning to England. After meeting with Joseph, Haldimand wasted no time in finalizing the Grand River grant: "I do hereby authorize and permit the said Mohawk Nation, and such other of the Six Nations Indians as wish to settle in that Quarter to[,] ... settle upon the Banks of the River commonly called ... Grand River running into Lake Erie; allotting to them ... six miles deep from each side beginning at Lake Erie, and Extending in that proportion to the Head of the said River, which them and their posterity are to enjoy forever."[10]

Joseph's plan to travel to London changed abruptly when he learned at Quebec that six Mohawk sachems were being held hostage at Fort Stanwix. Joseph had left the council there just in time. Those Mohawk leaders who had lingered were being detained until remaining American prisoners at Niagara were released. Joseph made the arduous journey to Niagara only to find that the American prisoners had subsequently been allowed to return home. He immediately returned to Cataraqui to organize the move to Grand River.[11]

At some point in 1785, Molly received correspondence from officials in New York state suggesting that if she would come back to New York and use her influence to assist the State of New York in dealing with the Senecas (1,700 of whom still lived in western New York), these officials might be willing to be helpful with her children's land claims. She rejected the overture.[12] The treatment of the Mohawk sachems at Fort Stanwix was proof enough of how she would be treated if she returned to American territory. Ultimately her faith must be in the king of Great Britain and his Loyalty Commission for redress of her family's losses. She would not offend them or risk her own freedom by negotiating with the Americans.[13]

Joseph and Catharine and most of the Canajoharie Mohawks made the move to Grand River in the spring and summer of 1785. A census of Six Nations people living at Grand River later that year listed 448 Mohawks, 381 Cayugas, 245 Onondagas, 162 Loyalist Oneidas (the Oquagas), 129 Tuscaroras, and 78 Senecas. There were also some western Indians living there, for a total of 1,843 Native Americans.[14]

14. A Home in Canada

Despite this exodus, Molly was not left alone at Cataraqui, soon to be renamed Kingston. Most of the Fort Hunter Mohawks, under the leadership of John Deserontyn, decided to remain at nearby Quinte Bay, where they had settled the year before. The lands granted to the men of Sir John's regiment were also near Kingston, and Molly knew many of those men and their families.[15]

As soon as the Canajoharie Mohawks were settled at Grand River, Joseph retraced his path, stopping briefly at Kingston, and arrived at Quebec by midautumn. The Loyalty Commission had not yet acted on the Mohawks' claims, and Joseph knew that his personal advocacy was required. He sailed aboard a packet ship on November 6, 1785. By December 7, he was in London. He stayed there as the guest of Daniel and Anne Claus at their home at 18 College Street, Westminster. With the war ended, Daniel Claus, Guy Johnson, and John Butler were all in London to pursue their claims with the Loyalty Commission.[16]

* * *

Joseph was again treated well by official London on this his second trip to the British Empire's capital city. On January 4, 1786, he was granted an interview with Lord Sidney, secretary for the American colonies. Although Joseph spoke good English, it was a sufficiently important event that John Butler accompanied him as interpreter. Joseph was also received at court by King George for a second time and dined with the Prince of Wales. Joseph's old friend Lord Percy entertained him at his London mansion. During his stay, Joseph was introduced to the archbishop of Canterbury and the bishop of London, both of whom were interested in his prewar work of translating the Anglican catechism into the Mohawk language with John Stuart. Joseph also managed to take a short trip to Paris while he waited for an answer to the Mohawks' petitions. He was the first Mohawk Indian to visit that city.[17]

During this second visit to England Joseph sat for a portrait by Gilbert Stuart, who would later paint the most renowned portrait of George Washington. The Gilbert Stuart painting shows a mature, battle-hardened man of 43 whose eyes brim with intelligence, determination, and a certain sadness. Since no portrait of Molly was ever painted, this portrait of her only surviving sibling, an earlier portrait of Joseph painted by George Romney during Joseph's 1776 visit to England, and later portraits of Joseph painted by John Francis Rigaud, Charles Willson Peale, William de Berczy, and Ezra Ames constitute the only physical evidence we have of what Molly might have looked like.[18]

By spring, Joseph received good news. The Mohawks' tribal claim in the amount of 15,000 pounds was granted in full. This was better treatment than the enabling statute called for. The statute provided that claims were to be paid in full up to 10,000 pounds but that amounts over that figure were to be paid on a sliding scale. In addition to the tribe's compensation, Molly and Joseph received a joint grant of compensation for their personal losses in the amount of 1,449 pounds. Molly had claimed 1,206 pounds in losses, and Joseph had claimed 1,112 pounds in losses, so Molly received about 60 percent of her claim, and Joseph received about 65 percent of his claim. It may be that the commissioners decided to give Molly and Joseph less than 100 percent of their claims in order to grant the total tribal claim.[19] The commissioners were probably also aware that in addition to the compensation payment, the British government was providing Molly and her children with a house, and Molly was receiving a pension of 100 pounds per annum. In addition to his compensation payment, Joseph was soon granted two military pensions, which amounted to a total of approximately 91 pounds per year.[20]

Portrait of Molly Brant's brother, Joseph, painted during Joseph's second visit to London in 1786 when he was about age 43. *Joseph Brandt* [sic], *1786*, Gilbert Stuart, oil on canvas. Fenimore Art Museum, Cooperstown, New York. Gift of Stephen C. Clark. No 199.1961. Photograph by Richard Walker.

While in London, Joseph also asked Joseph Chew to file another petition on behalf of Molly's children for their losses. Chew did so, this time asserting that portions of the children's land had already been sold off and that he believed "no Part thereof will Ever be Restored to the said children." He was correct. In 1781 and 1782, the State of New York had confiscated the three oldest girls' property, despite the fact that they were all under the age of 21, "for adhering to the late Enemies of the people of the said state."[21]

Chew took the opportunity to remind the commissioners of Molly's services to the Crown and the price she and her children had paid for it:

"That Mrs. Brant for her connection with the Family of the Late Sir William Johnson, her Zeal and Endeavours in Persuading the Indian Nations, with whom she had great interest to continue firm to the Royal Cause, became such an Object of the Jealousie of the Leaders of the Rebellion ... [that she was] oblidged ... to quit her habbitation and Property at Canojiharie ... and Retire with her Infant Children to his Majesty's Fort and Garrison at Niagara." Joseph Brant filed a supporting affidavit stating that "his Sister from the first Moment took part with the British—She sent ammunition to the Loyalists and fed and assisted such as had taken Refuge in the woods."[22]

This petition was deferred, allegedly because of the difficulty in determining the value of the various properties Sir William had bequeathed to each of the children. Chew was told to come up with better documentation of value. It may also have been thought politically infeasible at the time to grant substantial amounts of compensation to so many illegitimate children of Sir William, when his legitimate heirs stood to be granted large compensation amounts. Sir John Johnson eventually received compensation of 38,995 pounds on a claim of 103,182 pounds in losses, or about 38 percent of his claim. When the Loyalty Commission concluded its work, it allowed a total of 3,292,455 pounds (with deductions of 180,000 pounds) on total claims of 8,026,045 pounds from all petitioners, or on average about 39 percent per claim.[23]

* * *

When Joseph departed London, he said goodbye to Daniel Claus and Guy Johnson for what would be the last time. Daniel died in Cardiff in late 1787, and Guy died in London a few months later. Anne Claus returned to Montreal after her husband's death in order to be near her only surviving child, William Johnson Claus, and her brother, Sir John.[24]

Molly heard the compensation news personally from Joseph on his way home to Grand River in June 1786. Although it was not everything she had asked for, the package meant security for her and her children, and there was hope that her children's claims would be granted if the family could provide evidence of land value. The compensation award to the Mohawks, together with the land grant at Grand River, was confirmation that Molly had not been wrong to urge her people to remain loyal to the king. The Oneidas, who had cast their lot with the Americans, continued to suffer encroachments on their territory, sometimes accompanied by violence. After a series of land sales in which the buyers had a strong advantage, by the 1830s most of the Oneidas would move to a reservation west of present-day Green Bay, Wisconsin. The fertile farmlands of central New York were simply too valuable to allow Native Americans, even

Christian Native Americans who had supported the American Revolution, to continue to occupy them.[25]

* * *

For the most part, Molly now turned her attention to her family and to local philanthropy, leaving Joseph to assume the role of the confederacy's leading diplomat, although she remained a respected elder stateswoman. Reverend John Stuart, Fort Hunter's former Anglican minister, arrived in Kingston in 1785. Having served as the chaplain for Sir John's regiment since 1781, it was natural that Stuart would now establish a congregation in the town where so many of Sir John's militiamen had settled. For the first few years, he conducted services at the fort. In 1792, the leading citizens of Kingston built St. George's Church. Of the 19 founding members, Molly was the only woman. Her son George, then about 23, and two sons-in-law were also founding members. By the time the church was erected, Kingston had become the largest town between Montreal and Detroit, consisting of about 50 houses and a population of several hundred. It also served as the market town for dozens of farming families in the vicinity.[26]

Like her brother Joseph, Molly was a committed Christian. A visitor to Kingston who observed her not long after the church was built and identified her as Sir William Johnson's relict, noted that "we saw an Indian woman, who sat in an honourable place among the English. She appeared very devout during divine service, and very attentive to the sermon."[27]

Molly made at least one more trip to Montreal in 1787. Her three youngest daughters were again attending school there, but in addition to visiting them, she had another mission.[28] Molly brought Elizabeth and Elizabeth's small children to visit Sir John, Lady Mary, and their family. They needed Sir John to help them provide the commissioners with additional evidence of land value that the commissioners were demanding before acting on Molly's children's claims. As executor of Sir William's will, Sir John's estimates of value were important; as a baronet and a war hero, so was his public embrace of his half siblings' cause.

Molly and Elizabeth were asking Sir John to take on a substantial project, but he agreed to do it. His love for his father, his respect for Molly's work on behalf of the British war effort, his understanding of how well these children of his father's second family had turned out under adverse circumstances, and his continuing need for Joseph and Molly's goodwill in his role as Indian Affairs superintendent all impelled him to take up the task. It probably took him days or weeks to assemble the information, but the following spring he filed a detailed affidavit as to the value of the various properties Sir William had bequeathed Molly's children.[29]

14. A Home in Canada

The effort was worth it. Molly's seven surviving children were awarded a total of 7,856 pounds, or about 43 percent of the original claim of 18,484 pounds made by Joseph Chew on their behalf.[30]

* * *

With this burden lifted from her mind, Molly now enjoyed a peaceful period. She became a frequent visitor to Niagara, where Elizabeth and her husband and children, resided. It was a two-day trip by ship across Lake Ontario from Kingston to Niagara, and Molly made the journey almost every summer. In addition to the joy of visiting Elizabeth's growing family, it was also an opportunity to see Joseph, who came from Grand River to consult with confederacy sachems and British officials at the annual summer conferences there.

It was at Niagara that Molly performed her last known diplomatic service. On July 20, 1791, she took part in a meeting between Joseph and some western sachems and an emissary sent by the American government, Captain Hendrick Aupaumut, a Stockbridge Indian who was an ally of the Oneidas. American settlers, backed by the American army, had continued their incursions into the Ohio Territory and were being fiercely resisted by the Shawnees, Miamis, and other tribes. Joseph was then engaged in an effort to build a confederacy among the Six Nations and the western tribes that could more effectively resist the Americans' encroachments. In the meeting, Joseph cast doubt on the sincerity of the Americans' peace overture. Molly supported him by pointing out that there were no women accompanying Hendrick's delegation. Traditionally, peace delegations brought their families with them. If the group was entirely male, it might turn into a raiding party. Hendrick's mission did not meet with success.[31]

Later that fall, the defeat of General Arthur St. Clair's army by 1,000 Shawnee and Miami warriors on a branch of the Wabash River caused a major rethinking of Indian policy by George Washington and Secretary of War Henry Knox.[32] Tired of the military casualties and the expense of defending settlers who encroached beyond agreed treaty lines, they also recognized that the tactic of making small payments to random groups of Native Americans to sign deeds for land that was often another tribe's territory wasn't working. Like most sophisticated Americans, Washington and Knox believed that in another generation or two, the growth of population along the border would push good hunting westward and that the tribes in the Ohio Territory would naturally move westward too. Meanwhile, Washington and Knox were willing to negotiate a real border with the Native Americans in exchange for peace.[33]

Although Joseph had not participated in the defeat of General St. Clair's army, he was regarded by Henry Knox as the foremost Native

American soldier and diplomat of his generation. The American secretary of war believed that with Joseph's assistance, he could make a deal with the western tribes. In February 1792, Knox invited Joseph to meet with him in Philadelphia: "The business of peace is the main business we wish to take up with you."[34]

Upon receipt of the secretary of war's letter, Joseph consulted with the Shawnees and the Miamis. They agreed that he should go hear what Knox had to say.[35] Joseph knew that he was on sensitive ground with the British in accepting this mission. They had treated the Six Nations honorably and were not unhappy to see the Americans consumed in frontier warfare with the western tribes. Yet in his heart, Joseph knew that the continued strength of the western tribes was the Six Nations' insurance policy that the British government would continue to view the Six Nations as a significant ally rather than a permanently weakened client.

Joseph conveyed the unwelcome news of his trip to Philadelphia to the British commander at Detroit, Alexander McKee: "There is now a field open for accommodation with the Americans, and which, as far as we consistently can, ought for our own Interest, and the happiness of our Women & Children endeavor to accomplish."[36]

Joseph was taking a chance with his personal safety by accepting Knox's invitation. Joseph would have to pass through New York state in order to get to Philadelphia. Less than 10 years after the war's end, there were still many people in upper New York who wished to see him dead.

Joseph was a brave man, and Henry Knox made every effort to ensure his safety. General Israel Chapin, one of the most eminent early settlers of western New York, was sent to escort Joseph, accompanied by three other military officers. On the first leg of the journey through New York, Joseph was brought to Chapin's home at Canandaigua. When the party passed through the Mohawk valley, they stayed at the home of a relative of General Schuyler. At Albany they took a boat down the Hudson River to New York City, counting on Joseph's European American attire to conceal his identity. The party arrived in Philadelphia without incident on June 20, 1792.[37]

Over the next few days, Joseph and Henry Knox held several negotiating sessions. Joseph favored a boundary at the Muskingum River. This was a moderate position, since some hard-liners among the western tribes insisted on the pre–Revolution boundary of the Ohio River.[38]

Knox was in a difficult position. The American government could not completely abandon the settlers who had moved farther west to the vicinity of Fort Harmer. Knox asked Joseph to return to the western tribes with an offer of additional compensation for the disputed territory, and he reminded Joseph that in a long war the western tribes would be "utterly ruined." He brought Joseph to meet George Washington so the president could personally assure Joseph of the American government's desire to make a deal.[39]

Joseph and Henry Knox came away from the meetings with respect for one another. Joseph acknowledged to Israel Chapin that he had been treated well by the secretary of war, and Knox described Joseph to Governor Clinton of New York as "a judicious and sensible man." Knox ordered General Anthony Wayne, who was at Pittsburgh, to take no military action until the western tribes could respond to the American proposals, but he knew it was not only unintended military action that could scuttle the deal. Knox wrote his wife Lucy that he feared that the settlers could destroy any chance for peace by some new outrage against the Indians.[40]

Joseph was disappointed in the deal the Americans were offering and feared that it had the potential to divide opinion among the western tribes. He personally did not want to give up the land between the Muskingum and Fort Harmer line, and believed that his negotiating position was a real concession, but he felt duty bound to present Knox's proposal.[41]

The trip home was more dangerous than the trip to Philadelphia, since news of Joseph's visit was now public knowledge. In New York City, Joseph looked out a window of the hotel where he was staying and saw a member of the Dygert family standing on the sidewalk below. It was the Dygerts, a German Flatts family active on the Tryon County Committee of Safety, who had plundered Molly's home when she fled Canajoharie in 1777. Joseph had responded by burning their farm later in the war. One of Joseph's escorts, Colonel Marinus Willett, went down to the street and warned Dygert that he would hang if he harmed Joseph. The disgruntled man departed and was not seen again, but surely Joseph did not feel safe until he passed back into Canada.[42]

* * *

By the time Joseph made it to Fort Erie, he was ill or at least he claimed to be. It was an arduous and stressful journey, and Joseph was now almost 50 years old, so he may have actually been sick, but it is also true that he did not favor the American proposal, and he may have not wanted to be strongly associated with it. He sent his son Isaac and six other Mohawks to deliver the American proposal to a council of western tribes.[43]

In any event, hard-liners got control of the meeting and sent an answer that the price of peace was a return to the pre–Revolution boundary of the Ohio River. By the time Joseph finally arrived, the council had disbanded, and war parties were heading for some of the settlements.[44]

The western tribes' hard-line position effectively called the Americans' bluff. Over the winter of 1792–1793, Washington and Knox decided that perhaps the Fort Harmer line wasn't so important after all. They decided to send three commissioners to a council at the Sandusky River to be held in the summer of 1793. The commissioners had real authority to give back territory in exchange for peace. Knox once again ordered General Wayne to hold in place at Pittsburgh.[45]

None of this made the British happy. They made it clear to the western tribes that they thought that the British government should be involved in mediating the boundary dispute. The Americans were adamantly opposed to any British involvement. The problem, however, was that in order to get to Sandusky, the American peace commissioners would have to travel through British held Niagara and Detroit.[46]

Although Molly was not involved in the 1793 negotiations, she had the opportunity to see some of the drama surrounding it play out at Niagara. Molly's girls were getting married. In 1791 Magdalene had married John Ferguson, an officer of the Indian Department, at Kingston. In 1793 two daughters got married, the youngest, Anne, to Captain Hugh Earl of the Royal Navy and Susanna to Lieutenant Henry LeMoine of the 24th Regiment. Susanna's wedding occurred on June 5, 1793, at Niagara.[47] The night before the wedding, Molly and all of her daughters attended a ball given by Upper Canada's lieutenant governor, John Graves Simcoe, in honor of the king's birthday.[48]

Molly must have been fascinated to see at the ball the three American commissioners who were then cooling their heels at Niagara, waiting for a boat that the British might or might not supply. The commissioners were undoubtedly also interested in observing Molly, because unlike her daughters, who attended the ball wearing English gowns, Molly chose to attend in full Native American dress.[49]

Interacting with Molly Brant and her daughters at this ball would also be the beginning of an education in diversity for the new governor's young wife, Elizabeth Simcoe. According to Mrs. Simcoe's journal, there were about 80 people present that evening, only 20 of them women. There was dancing beginning at 7 p.m., and at 11 p.m. supper was served. Despite the rustic setting, "the music and dancing were good, and everything was conducted with propriety." Brought up in England, Mrs. Simcoe was genuinely surprised at how polished Molly's daughters were and how easily they fit in at the event. "What excited the best feelings of my heart was the ease and affection with which the ladies met each other, although there were a number present whose mothers sprang from the aborigines of the country." To Mrs. Simcoe's amazement, "They appeared as well dressed as the company in general, and intermingled with them in a measure which evinced at once the dignity of their own minds, and the good sense of the others."[50]

Although Mrs. Simcoe was impressed with Molly's daughters, she was not yet ready to give Molly any credit for her daughters' social intelligence or their fine apparel: "These ladies possessed great ingenuity and industry, and have great merit; for the education they have acquired is owing principally to their own industry; as their father, Sir William Johnson, was dead." How could Molly have anything to do with the intelligent and vivacious young women her daughters had become, "for she retained the manners and dress of her tribe." Little did Elizabeth Simcoe understand the sacrifices Molly had made to bring her daughters to this moment in time. Mrs. Simcoe saw Molly in native dress and overheard her speak Mohawk to old friends of the Indian Department. She knew nothing of the sacrifice Molly had made to allow the girls to attend boarding school when she would have preferred to have them with her. Mrs. Simcoe also knew nothing of the years of struggle that culminated in a pension and compensation awards that allowed Molly to provide those elegant ball gowns that were so important to how a young lady was viewed by potential marriage partners. No, Mrs. Simcoe had no idea, but as time passed she would come to change her opinion of Molly's abilities.[51]

Molly was probably still at Niagara when the matter of the American commissioners came to a head. Simcoe realized that Joseph intended to put his people's interests ahead of those of his British allies. If the Americans would agree to the Muskingum River as the boundary, Joseph would put his considerable prestige behind the proposal. If the western tribes made peace with the United States, underpopulated British Canada was at much greater risk of invasion by the Americans.[52]

Simcoe alerted Alexander McKee, commander at Detroit, that he must stir up the hard-liners to insist on the pre–Revolution Ohio River boundary. McKee did his work well. When Joseph arrived at a precouncil meeting of the western tribes to deliver the good news that the Americans were willing to negotiate boundaries, he found that insistence on the Ohio River boundary had taken hold among the participants.[53]

Joseph refused to deliver a letter stating that the tribes would only meet with the commissioners at Sandusky if the Ohio River boundary was agreed to in advance. The letter was instead delivered by a delegation led by one of the hard-liners, Buckongehala.[54]

The desperate commissioners responded that they were willing to give up everything along the Ohio except tracts that were already settled and that the American government would pay additional compensation for the settled tracts. The commissioners had finally been allowed to proceed to the Detroit River. They had a schooner waiting to take them to Sandusky if the tribes would only agree to meet them there.[55]

Joseph made an impassioned plea that the tribes go to Sandusky and hear what the commissioners had to say. He told his listeners bluntly that the Americans were now the dominant power on the continent and that the British had refused any military assistance to resist them. This was a brave stance for a man whose own tribe was now settled on British Canadian land. Joseph's words had some initial effect, but strong private lobbying of the foremost sachems by McKee again turned the tide in favor of the hard-liners.[56]

Joseph withdrew from the council, and 16 tribes signed a letter virtually dictated by McKee stating that the Ohio River line was nonnegotiable. The commissioners, who had waited at the Detroit River for the tribes' reply for 12 days, gave up and went home.[57]

The British were ecstatic. McKee wrote to Simcoe that the warring tribes "will form an extensive Barrier between the British & American Territory."[58]

The Americans reverted to force. By the late summer of 1794, Anthony Wayne's forces destroyed all Native American settlements along the Auglaize and Maumee Rivers. At the Battle of Fallen Timbers in November 1794, Wayne scored a decisive victory. The tribes who had rejected Joseph's advice were forced to sign a stringent treaty that put them under the protection of the American government and ceded to the Americans all of eastern and southern Ohio and part of present-day Indiana.[59]

* * *

While Molly was undoubtedly sad to hear of the failure of her brother's efforts and of the tragic fate of the Ohio Territory tribes, her focus by then was on tragedies of a more private nature. On January 28, 1794, her eldest daughter, Elizabeth, died at the age of 32.[60] For almost two decades, Elizabeth had been Molly's major partner in getting their family through the hardships of war and exile. How could Elizabeth possibly be gone? Molly spent the summer at Niagara helping Elizabeth's stricken husband care for the couple's five small children. But now grief, stress, and the accumulating years began to have their effect on Molly's health.

In mid–September, the governor's wife planned to travel to Kingston for the winter. A ship had been reserved for her private use, but Molly needed to return to Kingston too, and she was still a person important enough to be shown some consideration by the people who mattered in colonial Canada. Mrs. Simcoe reported in her journal that "I relented in favour of Brant's sister, who was ill and very desirous to go." Mrs. Simcoe was now willing to drop the snap judgment she had made the year before at the governor's ball, when she saw Molly in her native dress and overheard her speaking Mohawk: "She speaks English well, and is a civil and very sensible old woman."[61]

14. A Home in Canada

Shortly after Molly arrived at Kingston, she relinquished the house she had been given by Governor Haldimand a decade before and, together with her only unmarried daughter, Mary, she moved into the home of her daughter Magdalene and Magdalene's husband, John Ferguson.[62]

The move did not end Molly's sorrows. In October, her daughter Susanna's baby son, Edward William LeMoine, died. As winter enveloped Kingston, many became ill, including Governor Simcoe, who had joined his wife there. Mrs. Simcoe was beside herself with worry: "He has had such a cough that some nights he could not lie down, but sat in a chair, total loss of appetite, and such headaches that he could not bear any person but me to walk across the room or speak loud."[63]

Molly soldiered on throughout the harsh winter, and Elizabeth Simcoe soon had cause to be grateful for her friendship: "Captain Brant's sister prescribed a root, it is I believe calamus ... which really relieved his cough in a very short time."[64]

So many years, so many challenges, so many accomplishments, In 1795, Molly Brant entered her 60th year. There was one more tragedy yet to endure.

Molly had come to regret her daughter Susanna's choice of Henry LeMoine as a husband. He was erratic, demanding, and perhaps abusive. Weakened by grief over the loss of her baby and by the disappointment of an unhappy marriage, Susanna sickened and died in December 1795 at only 23 years old. For Molly, it was the second wrenching loss of a daughter in less than two years, and it came on the heels of news that Isaac, Joseph's son, was dead at Grand River of an infected wound received when Joseph had to defend himself from his son's alcoholic rage.[65]

Not long after Susanna's death, Henry LeMoine appeared at Magdalene's home and asked to speak to Molly. He wanted, he informed her, to ask for Mary's hand in marriage. LeMoine knew that Six Nations men often married a sister of a deceased wife, and there was precedent in Molly's own family. Molly's brother, Joseph, had married as his second wife Peggie's sister, Susanna's namesake. But this was very different. There were no surviving children to consider, and LeMoine was making this request within weeks of Susanna's death, not at the end of a yearlong mourning period. Molly wanted nothing to do with the idea. She refused to let LeMoine ask Mary directly. Magdalene backed her up.

LeMoine took a pistol out of his jacket. There may have been a horrible instant when Molly thought Magdalene's life was in danger. Instead, LeMoine put the pistol to his own head and blew his brains out in the Fergusons' parlor.[66]

This is the last event we know about in Molly's final days. She died a few months later. Her funeral service was conducted on April 16, 1796, at St. George's Church by Reverend John Stuart, who had known her since the happy days with Sir William and their children at Johnson Hall. Molly was 60 years old, the same age as her beloved Sir William when he died.[67]

Epilogue

After his mother's death, Molly's only surviving son, George, moved to Grand River near his uncle, Joseph, and married a Native American woman. Molly's daughters, Magdalene, Mary, and Anne, all lived the remainder of their lives in Kingston. Her daughter Margaret lived most of her life there, but after her husband's death she went to live with three of her four children in England. On her way to board the ship departing from New York City, Margaret stopped in Johnstown and visited Johnson Hall. She is the only one of Molly's children ever known to have returned to the Mohawk valley after the family's flight from Canajoharie in 1777.[1]

Molly's brother Joseph died in 1807 at age 64. He was disappointed that he never succeeded in establishing a confederacy between the Six Nations and the western tribes that he saw as his people's surest protection. One of Joseph's daughters, Elizabeth, married Molly's grandson, William Johnson Kerr.[2]

Today there are approximately 29,000 members of the Six Nations of the Grand River, about 13,000 of whom live on the Six Nations of the Grand River reserve, with most of the remainder living in the vicinity of nearby Brantford, Ontario.[3]

Molly was buried in St. George's churchyard in Kingston. If a marker was placed at her grave, it has long since disappeared. The church, now known as St. Paul's, instead has a stone that was placed in the graveyard many years later and marks "The Burying Place of the Children and Grandchildren of Sir William Johnson."[4]

Two centuries after Molly's death, the Canadian government corrected this oversight by erecting a plaque in Kingston that refers to Molly as Sir William's wife and reads in part: "Molly Brant wielded great influence among the Iroquois and was responsible for much of Johnson's success in dealing with them. Following the outbreak of the American Revolution she and her younger brother Joseph played a leading role in persuading the Confederacy to support Britain. In 1777 she fled to Canada and after the war in recognition of her services was granted a pension by the government." As further acknowledgment of her role in the birth of Canada, the Canadian government issued a commemorative stamp in Molly's honor in 1986.[5]

Born at a time when her people were struggling to maintain their economic and cultural identity in the face of European encroachments, Molly Brant fell in love with a man who envisioned a more humane détente between her people and his than did most Europeans of his time. For 15 years she worked with him to make that détente a reality while raising a family that was a harbinger of a more diverse world to come. After Sir William's death, a century and a half before American women could vote, Molly refused to accept the consequences of war and exile in silence and submission. She spoke at Six Nations council meetings and dared to negotiate with American and British officers, raising her voice and making demands when it was necessary to carry her point. In a time when European American tradition forbade women's participation in politics and diplomacy, Molly Brant, relying on the very different traditions of the Six Nations, used her intelligence, courage, and determination to rise from the crushing circumstances of her exile from her people's ancestral lands in America's Mohawk valley, and forged a new home for her family and her people in the cultural mosaic of Canada.

Chapter Notes

Abbreviations Used

DRCHSNYD *Documents Relative to the Colonial History of the State of New York*, digital format, hathitrust.org.
IAP—Maryly Penrose, *Indian Affairs Papers: American Revolution* (Franklin Park, NJ: Liberty Bell Associates, 1978).
Loyalist Claims, Series I—*American Loyalist Claims, Exchequer and Audit Dept., Series I, 1776-1831, Public Records of Great Britain* (Kraus—Thomson Organization Limited: 1972).
Loyalist Claims, Series II—*American Loyalist Claims, Exchequer and Audit Dept., Series II, 1776-1831, Public Records of Great Britain* (Kraus—Thomson Organization Limited: 1973).
SFHUPC—Sir Frederick Haldimand, *Unpublished Papers and Correspondence, 1758-1784*(London: World Microfilms Publications, The British Library, 1977).
SWJP—William Johnson, *The Papers of Sir William Johnson* (Albany: University of the State of New York, 1921-1965).
SWJPD—Sir William Johnson, *The Papers of Sir William Johnson*, HathiTrust, digital format, https://catalog.hathitrust.org/Record/000622241.
Tryon County Committee of Safety Minutes—Maryly B. Penrose, *Mohawk Valley in the Revolution: Committee of Public Safety Papers & Genealogical Compendium Tryon County Committee of Public Safety.*

Introduction

1. Daniel K. Richter, *The Ordeal of the Longhouse: The Peoples of the Iroquois League in the Era of European Colonization* (Chapel Hill: University of North Carolina Press, 1992), 1, 3, 11, 15, 17. See also Ned Blackhawk, *The Rediscovery of America* (New Haven: Yale University Press, 2023), 80.
2. Richter, *The Ordeal of the Longhouse*, 2, 11–13.
3. Richter, 58–59.
4. Richter, 57–58, 86, 148. See also Blackhawk, *The Rediscovery of America*, 92.
5. Richter, *The Ordeal of the Longhouse*, 104.
6. Richter, 102, 108. See also Blackhawk, *The Rediscovery of America*, 83, 87, 94.
7. Richter, 109–10.
8. Richter, 120.
9. Richter, 173–74, 188.

Chapter 1

1. "Return of the Loyalists Male and Female on Carleton Island Specifying Their Age & Number of Rations Drawn Out of the Kings Stores/per diem," dated November 26, 1783, SFHUPC, reel 58, p. 344.
2. Barbara Graymont, "Konwatsitsiaienni," in *Dictionary of Canadian Biography*, Vol. 4, gen. ed. David M. Hayne (Toronto: University of Toronto Press, 1966), 416.

3. Barbara J. Sivertsen, *Turtles, Wolves and Bears: A Mohawk Family History* (Westminster, MD: Heritage Books, 2006), 69–70.
4. Sivertsen, *Turtles, Wolves and Bears*, 165.
5. Isabel Thompson Kelsay, *Joseph Brant, 1743–1807: Man of Two Worlds* (Syracuse: Syracuse University Press, 1984), 39–40.
6. Sivertsen, *Turtles, Wolves and Bears*, 165.
7. Kelsay, *Joseph Brant, 1743–1807*, 42–43. Kelsay favors 1742 as the date of the trip, with Joseph born in the Ohio River valley in 1743. Joseph told family members that he was born in Canajoharie, so it is possible that the family did not set out on its journey until after his birth in 1743. See also Ned Blackhawk, *The Rediscovery of America* (New Haven: Yale University Press, 2023), 110, 125.
8. Kelsay, *Joseph Brant, 1743–1807*, 43.
9. Kelsay, 41.
10. Kelsay, 41–44.
11. Kelsay, 44.
12. Daniel K. Richter, *The Ordeal of the Longhouse: The Peoples of the Iroquois League in the Era of European Colonization* (Chapel Hill: University of North Carolina, 1992), 276.
13. Kelsay, *Joseph Brant, 1743–1807*, 45.
14. Sivertsen, *Turtles, Wolves and Bears*, 127–32.
15. Sivertsen, 164.
16. Kelsay, *Joseph Brant, 1743–1807*, 52.
17. Kelsay, 53.
18. Christian Daniel Claus and Conrad Weiser, "A Journey to Onondaga, 1750," translated and edited by Helga Doblin and William A. Starna, in *In Mohawk Country*, ed. Dean R. Snow, Charles T. Gehring, and William A. Starna (Syracuse: Syracuse University Press, 1996), 238. See also Kelsay, *Joseph Brant, 1743–1807*, 53.
19. Kelsay, *Joseph Brant, 1743–1807*, 54.
20. Sivertsen, *Turtles, Wolves and Bears*, 166.
21. Sivertsen, 181. See also Daniel Claus, "Annecodotes of the Mohawk Chief Captn. Joseph Brant," IAP, Appendix A, 316–17.
22. Kelsay, *Joseph Brant, 1743–1807*, 62.
23. Kelsay, 89.
24. Peter Johnson to Sir William Johnson, November 18, 1773, SWJP, 12: 1042–43; and Peter Johnson to Sir William Johnson, April 30, 1774, SWJP, 8:1139–40.
25. A copy of a translation of an extract from a letter from Mary Brant to Daniel Claus, April 12, 1781, SFHUPC, Add. MSS 21774, reel 51, p. 180.
26. Lois M. Huey and Bonnie Pulis, *Molly Brant: A Legacy of Her Own* (Youngstown, NY: Old Fort Niagara Association, 1997), 34. See also Sivertsen, *Turtles, Wolves and Bears*, chap. 12, 312n31, which quotes a letter from Taylor and Duffin to Daniel Claus mentioning Molly's sadness over the deaths of her son Peter Johnson and her stepson William of Canajoharie, both of whom could write fluent English, and her frustration that she currently had no one to help her with this task.
27. Sivertsen, *Turtles, Wolves and Bears*, 120.
28. Sivertsen, 166.
29. Qtd. in Sivertsen, 166.
30. Barbara Alice Mann, *Iroquoian Women: The Gantowisas* (New York: Peter Lang, 2000), 253–54, 279.
31. Sivertsen, *Turtles, Wolves and Bears*, 167.
32. Sivertsen, 167.

Chapter 2

1. Fintan O'Toole, *White Savage: William Johnson and the Invention of America* (New York: Farrar, Straus and Giroux, 2005), 19–20.
2. O'Toole, *White Savage*, 21–24. See also James Thomas Flexner, *Lord of the Mohawks: A Biography of Sir William Johnson* (Boston: Little, Brown, 1979), 8.
3. O'Toole, *White Savage*, 25.
4. O'Toole, 36–37. See also Flexner, *Lord of the Mohawks*, 11.
5. O'Toole, *White Savage*, 38.
6. Qtd. in Flexner, *Lord of the Mohawks*, 10.
7. O'Toole, *White Savage*, 35–37.
8. Flexner, *Lord of the Mohawks*, 15–17.
9. Barbara J. Sivertsen, *Turtles, Wolves and Bears: A Mohawk Family History* (Westminster, MD: Heritage Books, 2006),, 80. See also Flexner, *Lord of the Mohawks*, 16; and O'Toole, *White Savage*, 65.
10. O'Toole, *White Savage*, 43. See also Flexner, *Lord of the Mohawks*, 19.

11. Flexner, *Lord of the Mohawks*, 17-18.
12. O'Toole, *White Savage*, 43-44.
13. Flexner, *Lord of the Mohawks*, 22. See also O'Toole, *White Savage*, 43.
14. Flexner, *Lord of the Mohawks*, 62.
15. O'Toole, *White Savage*, 45.
16. Qtd. in O'Toole, 45.
17. O'Toole, 45.
18. O'Toole, 45-46.
19. O'Toole, 46.
20. Lt. Michael Tyrell to William Johnson, May 28, 1741, SWJP, 1:14.
21. O'Toole, *White Savage*, 64.
22. Sivertsen, *Turtles, Wolves and Bears*, 133.
23. Sivertsen, 131-33.
24. Qtd. in Sivertsen, 133.
25. Sivertsen, 133-135.
26. Barbara Alice Mann, *Iroquoian Women: The Gantowisas* (New York: Peter Lang, 2000), 241.
27. Flexner, *Lord of the Mohawks*, 45.
28. Flexner, 49.
29. Flexner, 98, 82, 85.
30. Flexner, 49. See also O'Toole, *White Savage*, 71-72.
31. O'Toole, *White Savage*, 73.
32. Flexner, *Lord of the Mohawks*, 52.
33. Flexner, 53-55.
34. Flexner, 45-46.
35. Flexner, 58.
36. Flexner, 62-63. See also O'Toole, *White Savage*, 73.
37. O'Toole, *White Savage*, 83.
38. Flexner, *Lord of the Mohawks*, 64-65. See also O'Toole, *White Savage*, 86.
39. O'Toole, *White Savage*, 108.
40. O'Toole, 85.
41. Flexner, *Lord of the Mohawks*, 98, 137.
42. Flexner, 99.
43. Lois M. Huey and Bonnie Pulis, *Molly Brant: A Legacy of Her Own* (Youngstown, NY: Old Fort Niagara Association, 1997), 55.
44. Flexner, *Lord of the Mohawks*, 97-98.
45. David Kobrin, *The Black Minority in Early New York* (Albany: University of the State of New York, State Education Department, Office of State History, 1971), 8-9.
46. "Account against Estate of Sir Peter Warren," SWJPD,13:29.
47. "Memorandum of such things as I would have done Untill I come Home again" by Sir William Johnson, dated January 2, 1754, SWJP, 9:120-21; Francis Wade to Sir William Johnson, April 20, 1766, SWJP, 5:192; and "An Inventory" and "Articles in the Negroe Room West Storehouse," SWJPD, 13:651-52.
48. Kobrin, *The Black Minority in Early New York*, 10.
49. Flexner, *Lord of the Mohawks*, 113.

Chapter 3

1. James Thomas Flexner, *Lord of the Mohawks: A Biography of Sir William Johnson* (Boston: Little, Brown, 1979), 121.
2. Flexner, *Lord of the Mohawks*, 121.
3. Fintan O'Toole, *White Savage: William Johnson and the Invention of America* (New York: Farrar, Straus and Giroux, 2005), 112. See also Flexner, *Lord of the Mohawks*, 125.
4. Flexner, *Lord of the Mohawks*, 140-41. See also O'Toole, *White Savage*, 113.
5. O'Toole, *White Savage*, 132-33.
6. Qtd. in Flexner, *Lord of the Mohawks*, 136.
7. O'Toole, *White Savage*, 114.
8. Qtd. in O'Toole, 119.
9. Flexner, *Lord of the Mohawks*, 139-41.
10. Flexner, 137, 141-42.
11. Flexner, 143-44.
12. Flexner, 144-48. See also O'Toole, *White Savage*, 142.
13. Flexner, *Lord of the Mohawks*, 148-50.
14. Flexner, 151-53. See also O'Toole, *White Savage*, 143.
15. Flexner, *Lord of the Mohawks*, 151.
16. O'Toole, *White Savage*, 153-54.
17. Flexner, *Lord of the Mohawks*, 184.
18. Flexner, 173. See also David L. Preston, *The Texture of Contact: European and Indian Settler Communities and the Frontiers of Iroquoia, 1667-1783* (Lincoln: University of Nebraska Press, 2009), 185.
19. Flexner, *Lord of the Mohawks*, 181.
20. Sir William Johnson to Lord Loudon, December 10, 1757, SWJP, 2:761.
21. Flexner, *Lord of the Mohawks*, 182.
22. Qtd. in Flexner, 184.
23. Flexner, 137.
24. O'Toole, *White Savage*, 171.
25. Qtd. in Flexner, *Lord of the Mohawks*, 232.

26. Qtd. in Flexner, 230.
27. Qtd. in Flexner, 232.
28. O'Toole, *White Savage*, 171–72.
29. Barbara J. Sivertsen, *Turtles, Wolves and Bears: A Mohawk Family History* (Westminster, MD: Heritage Books, 2006), 24.
30. Flexner, *Lord of the Mohawks*, 232.
31. Flexner, 345.
32. Goldsbrow Banyar to Sir William Johnson, December 12, 1760, SWJP, 3:287.
33. Preston, *The Texture of Contact*, 191.
34. Flexner, *Lord of the Mohawks*, 192–94.
35. Flexner, 195–96.
36. Flexner, 198.
37. Flexner, 199.
38. Flexner, 200.
39. Flexner, 200.
40. Flexner, 201.
41. Flexner, 201.
42. Flexner, 201.
43. Flexner, 202. See also O'Toole, *White Savage*, 204.
44. Flexner, *Lord of the Mohawks*, 204.
45. O'Toole, *White Savage*, 204–8.
46. Flexner: *Lord of the Mohawks*, 205–7.
47. O'Toole, *White Savage*, 206. See also Warren Johnson, "Journal of Warren Johnson, 1760–61," in *Mohawk Country*, ed. Dean R. Snow, Charles T. Gehring, and William A. Starna (Syracuse: Syracuse University Press, 1996), 259.
48. Flexner, *Lord of the Mohawks*, 208.
49. O'Toole, *White Savage*, 207–8.
50. Qtd. in Flexner, *Lord of the Mohawks*, 210.

Chapter 4

1. James Thomas Flexner, *Lord of the Mohawks: A Biography of Sir William Johnson* (Boston: Little, Brown, 1979),, 212.
2. Flexner, *Lord of the Mohawks*, 212–23.
3. Sir William Johnson, *Journal of Niagara Campaign, July 26–October 14 1759*, SWJPD, 13:125.
4. Johnson, *Journal of Niagara Campaign, July 26–October 14 1759*, 13:139.
5. Qtd. in Flexner, *Lord of the Mohawks*, 215.
6. Flexner, 173 and qtd in Flexner, 174.
7. Warren Johnson, "Journal of Warren Johnson, 1760–61," in *Mohawk Country*, ed. Dean R. Snow, Charles T. Gehring, and William A. Starna (Syracuse: Syracuse University Press, 1996), 255, 257, 264, 269.
8. Flexner, *Lord of the Mohawks*, 137.
9. For a sample of items purchased by Molly Brant, see "Items from Day Book of Robert Adems June 10, 1768–July 14, 1773," SWJPD, 13:603, 608. See also "Extracts from Account Book of John Butler," SWJPD, 13:508.
10. "Extracts from Account Book of John Butler," 13:508–9.
11. Sir Adam Gordon to Sir William Johnson, October 5, 1763, SWJPD, 13:376).
12. "Items from Day Book of Robert Adems Johnstown June 10, 1768–July 14, 1773," SWJPD, 13:532, 538, 543, 550, 556, 575, 580.
13. Lois M. Huey and Bonnie Pulis, *Molly Brant: A Legacy of Her Own* (Youngstown, NY: Old Fort Niagara Association, 1997), 31, 33.
14. Sir William Johnson to either Thomas Flood or Robert Adems, March 31, 1766, SWJP, 5:138. The name of the recipient of the letter is unknown. It is addressed "Sir." Some have thought the recipient was Thomas Flood, Sir William's overseer, but a letter from Francis Wade (the Philadelphia merchant who bought and sold slaves for Sir William) to Sir William dated April 16, 1766, apologizes to Sir William for not being able to sell "your Negro boy" because "Mr. Adams" was in town with him for such a short period. SWJP, 5:176.
15. Will of Sir William Johnson, SWJP, 12:1070. See also "Return of the Loyalists Male and Female on Carleton Island Specifying Their Age & Number of Rations Drawn Out of the Kings Stores/per diem," dated November 26, 1783" SFHUPC, reel 58, p. 344..
16. Flexner, *Lord of the Mohawks*, 218.
17. Fintan O'Toole, *White Savage: William Johnson and the Invention of America* (New York: Farrar, Straus and Giroux, 2005), 211.
18. Flexner, *Lord of the Mohawks*, 216.
19. Flexner, 216. See also Johnson, "Journal of Warren Johnson, 1760–61," 256.
20. O'Toole, *White Savage*, 230.
21. Flexner, *Lord of the Mohawks*, 218.
22. Flexner, 219.
23. Flexner, 219–20.
24. Qtd. in Flexner, 220.

25. Johnson, "Journal of Warren Johnson, 1760-61," 256-57.
26. Johnson, 250-53.
27. Johnson, 255, 60.
28. Johnson, 260-62.
29. Johnson, 254.
30. Johnson, 263.
31. Johnson, 265.
32. Johnson, 258.
33. Johnson, 258.
34. Johnson, 258.
35. Johnson, 258.
36. Flexner, *Lord of the Mohawks*, 225-26. Flexner says that Joseph received $50 rather than 50 pounds. This may be a typographical error.
37. Sir William Johnson to Alexander Colden, January 28, 1761, SWJP, 3:312.
38. Sir William Johnson to Alexander Colden, January 28, 1761, SWJP, 3:312.
39. Johnson, "Journal of Warren Johnson, 1760-61," 254, 257.
40. Johnson, 259.
41. Johnson, 258.
42. Johnson, 266-67.
43. Johnson, 266-67, 258.
44. O'Toole, *White Savage*, 220. See also Flexner, *Lord of the Mohawks*, 223.
45. O'Toole, *White Savage*, 221.
46. O'Toole, 222.
47. O'Toole, 221, 232.
48. O'Toole, 221.
49. O'Toole, 221-25.
50. O'Toole, 227.
51. Flexner, *Lord of the Mohawks*, 241-46.
52. Qtd. in O'Toole, *White Savage*, 225.
53. Sir William Johnson, "Detroit Journal," SWJPD, 13:271.

Chapter 5

1. Qtd. in James Thomas Flexner, *Lord of the Mohawks: A Biography of Sir William Johnson* (Boston: Little, Brown, 1979), 246.
2. Flexner, *Lord of the Mohawks*, 255.
3. Isabel Thompson Kelsay, *Joseph Brant, 1743-1807: Man of Two Worlds* (Syracuse: Syracuse University Press, 1984), 71-72.
4. Kelsay, *Joseph Brant, 1743-1807*, 76.
5. Kelsay, 72.
6. Reverend Eleazar Wheelock to Sir William Johnson, November 2, 1761, SWJP, 3:556.
7. Kelsay, *Joseph Brant, 1743-1807*, 72.
8. Sir William Johnson to Reverend Eleazar Wheelock, July 21, 1762, SWJP, 3:832.
9. Flexner, *Lord of the Mohawks*, 228-30.
10. Flexner, 230-31.
11. Flexner, 231.
12. Sir William Johnson to Witham Marsh, February 4, 1763, SWJP, 4:40.
13. Qtd. in Flexner, *Lord of the Mohawks*, 230.
14. The only sources for birthdates of Molly's daughters and younger son are "Return of the Loyalists Male and Female on Carleton Island Specifying Their Age & Number of Rations Drawn Out of the Kings Stores/per diem," dated November, 26, 1783, SFHUPC, reel 58, p. 344, and one reference in Sir William Johnson, "Detroit Journal," SWJPD, 5:271, stating that Captain Etherington informed him that Molly had given birth to a girl. This child was Elizabeth unless the baby born in the fall of 1761 subsequently died. Molly, however, listed her two oldest daughters, Elizabeth and Magdalene, as ages 20 and 18, respectively, in the 1783 document, which would place their birthdates in 1763 and 1765. It was Mohawk custom to perform a condolence ceremony before conducting business with anyone who had lost a relative. Sir William notes in his journal that condolence ceremonies were performed for him on two occasions by the Mohawks when a grandchild died. No such reference is ever made to a condolence ceremony for a child of his. While it is possible that no mention was made of the child's condolence ceremony because the records of Indian conferences were official documents and the child was illegitimate, it is more likely that Molly shaved two years off the ages of her two oldest daughters in the 1783 document. On several occasions during the Revolution, she expressed concern that her daughters were being rendered unmarriageable because of the seizure of their dowries by the Patriots. She may have feared that they would be too old for marriage before she could obtain restitution from the Crown. Molly had smallpox in the year 1765. She may have miscarried during that year as a result of the illness. That would account for the gap between Magdalene's probable birth in

1763 and Margaret's birth in 1767. It is very unlikely that Molly gave birth to a healthy child in 1765 who survived the smallpox epidemic that swept Johnson Hall.
15. Flexner, *Lord of the Mohawks*, 238.
16. Flexner, 238.
17. Flexner, 260, 252.
18. Kelsay, *Joseph Brant, 1743–1807*, 89, 93.
19. Kelsay, 95. See also Robert G. Parkinson, *Heart of American Darkness: Bewilderment and Horror on the Early Frontier* (New York: Norton, 2024), 62–84.
20. Kelsay, *Joseph Brant, 1743–1807*, 94.
21. Kelsay, 94.
22. Flexner, *Lord of the Mohawks*, 257 and qtd in 258.
23. Kelsay, *Joseph Brant, 1743–1807*, 96.
24. Flexner, *Lord of the Mohawks*, 260–61.
25. Flexner, 260–62.
26. Flexner, 261.
27. Kelsay, *Joseph Brant, 1743–1807*, 96. See also Parkinson, *Heart of American Darkness*, 94.
28. Sir William Johnson, "A Meeting with the Canajoharies" at Canajoharie, March 3, 1763, SWJP, 4:60.
29. Kelsay, *Joseph Brant, 1743–1807*, 104.
30. Sir William Johnson to Reverend Henry Barclay, November 24, 1763, SWJP, 10:935.
31. Kelsay, *Joseph Brant, 1743–1807*, 98–99.
32. Kelsay, 99–100.
33. Kelsay, 99, 110.
34. John Macomb to Sir William Johnson, September 25, 1763, SWJP, 4:207.
35. Witham Marsh to Sir William Johnson, May 28, 1764, SWJP, 4:432n.
36. "An Inscription for a Monument," SWJP, 4:897–98.
37. Sir William Johnson to George Croghan, January 17, 1765, SWJP, 11:537.
38. "Journal of Indian Affairs," January 20, 1765, SWJP, 11:553.
39. "Journal of Indian Affairs," February 7, 1765, SWJP, 11:596.
40. Qtd. in Lois M. Huey and Bonnie Pulis, *Molly Brant: A Legacy of Her Own* (Youngstown, NY: Old Fort Niagara Association, 1997), 21.
41. Sir William Johnson to William Gamble, June 12, 1769, SWJP, 7:14.
42. "Account against the Crown," October 7, 1769, 12:763.
43. "Account against the Crown," July 1, 1772, SWJPD, 12:1000.
44. "Account against the Crown," SWJPD, 12:1019.
45. Charles Lee to Sir William Johnson, July 25, 1764, SWJPD, 13:328.
46. Sir William Johnson to Cadwallader Colden, June 20, 1765, SWJP, 4:773.
47. Sir William Johnson to Cadwallader Colden, June 20, 1765.
48. Lord Adam Gordon to Sir William Johnson, October 5, 1765, SWJPD, 13:376.
49. SWJP, 4:853n.
50. Qtd. in Earle Thomas, *The Three Faces of Molly Brant* (Kingston, Ontario: Quarry, 1996), 62.
51. Lord Adam Gordon to Sir William Johnson, October 5, 1765, SWJPD, 13:375.
52. Lord Adam Gordon to Sir William Johnson, October 5, 1765, SWJPD, p. 13:376.
53. Kelsay, *Joseph Brant, 1743–1807*, 109–10. See also Barbara J. Sivertsen, *Turtles, Wolves and Bears: A Mohawk Family History* (Westminster, MD: Heritage Books, 2006), 135.
54. Kelsay, *Joseph Brant, 1743–1807*, 110.
55. Thomas Jones, *History of New York during the Revolutionary War: And of the Leading Events in the Other Colonies at That Period*, Vol. 2, ed. Edward Floyd De Lancey (New York: New York Historical Society, 1879), 374.
56. Jones, *History of New York during the Revolutionary War*, 2:374.
57. Kelsay, *Joseph Brant, 1743–1807*, 110.
58. Thomas, *The Three Faces of Molly Brant*, 142.
59. Qtd. in "Preface," SWJP, 3:xii.
60. "Will of Sir William Johnson," January 27, 1774, SWJP, 12:1066.

Chapter 6

1. John Duncan to Sir William Johnson, September 13, 1765 SWJP, 4:844n.
2. James Thomas Flexner, *Lord of the Mohawks: A Biography of Sir William Johnson* (Boston: Little, Brown, 1979),, 312.
3. Flexner, *Lord of the Mohawks*, 313.
4. Qtd. in Flexner, 312.
5. Flexner, 313.

6. "Indian Proceedings Johnson Hall September 5–19, 1766" SWJP, 12:185.
7. Sir William Johnson to General Thomas Gage, October 4, 1766, SWJP, 12:204.
8. "Journal of Indian Affairs," December 18–30, 1766, SWJP, 12:244.
9. John Tabor Kempe to Sir William Johnson, March 17, 1767, SWJPD, 12:282.
10. Lord Adam Gordon to Sir William Johnson, May 17, 1767, SWJP, 12:318. See also James Rivington to Sir William Johnson, October 2, 1770, SWJP, 7:924.
11. Isabel Thompson Kelsay, *Joseph Brant, 1743–1807: Man of Two Worlds* (Syracuse: Syracuse University Press, 1984), 113.
12. Reverend Thomas Brown to Sir William Johnson, September 13, 1766, SWJP, 5:375n.
13. Reverend Thomas Brown to Sir William Johnson, January 30, 1767, SWJP, v. V, p.488n.
14. Ro. Picken to Sir William Johnson, February 27, 1767, SWJP, 5:504n.
15. Qtd. in Flexner, *Lord of the Mohawks*, 320.
16. Sir William Johnson to Reverend Eleazar Wheelock, August 8, 1766, SWJP, 5:343.
17. Reverend Thomas Barton to Sir William Johnson, July 22, 1767, SWJP, 5:604.
18. Reverend Thomas Barton to Sir William Johnson, July 22, 1767.
19. Sir William Johnson to Reverend Thomas Barton, January 5, 1768, SWJP, 6:66.
20. Reverend Thomas Barton to Sir William Johnson, March 25, 1768, SWJP, 6:170–71. See also Ned Blackhawk, *The Rediscovery of America* (New Haven: Yale University Press, 2023), 167; and Robert G. Parkinson, *Heart of American Darkness: Bewilderment and Horror on the Early Frontier* (New York: Norton, 2024), 79.
21. Sir William Johnson to General Thomas Gage, April 17, 1766, SWJP, 12:76.
22. Sir William Johnson to Major Jelles Fonda, June 29, 1770, SWJP, 7:777.
23. "Will of Sir William Johnson," January 27, 1774, SWJP, 12:1064.
24. George Johnson was at boarding school when Molly Brant was asked to list the names and ages of her dependents who were receiving rations from the king's stores in 1783. This is the only source of birth dates for the six younger children. (Peter and Elizabeth's birth dates are mentioned in other sources.) George's birth date is an estimate based on the ages listed by Molly for his next elder sibling, Margaret, and his next younger sibling, Mary, both of whom were on Carleton Island with their mother. See Lois M. Huey and Bonnie Pulis, *Molly Brant: A Legacy of Her Own* (Youngstown, NY: Old Fort Niagara Association, 1997), 96.
25. Huey and Pulis, *Molly Brant*, 85–86. Frederick Haldimand to Daniel Claus, September 9, 1779, SFHUPC, Add. MSS 21774, reel 51, p. 65; Daniel Claus to Frederick Haldimand, September 13, 1779, SFHUPC, Add. MSS 21774, reel 51, p. 68; and Daniel Claus to Frederick Haldimand, August 30, 1779, SFHUPC, Add. MSS 21774, reel 51, pp. 57–58.
26. Qtd. in Flexner, *Lord of the Mohawks*, 273.
27. Sir William Johnson to Reverend Charles Inglis, April 4, 1770, SWJP, 7:597–99.
28. Sir William Johnson to Reverend Charles Inglis, April 4, 1770.
29. Sir William Johnson to Reverend Charles Inglis, April 4, 1770.
30. Sir William Johnson to Reverend Charles Inglis, April 4, 1770.
31. Kelsay, *Joseph Brant, 1743–1807*, 114, 117–18.
32. Kelsay, 115–16.
33. Kelsay, 116–17, 121.
34. "Return of the Loyalists Male and Female on Carleton Island Specifying Their Age & Number of Rations Drawn Out of the Kings Stores/per diem," dated November, 26, 1783, in *Sir Frederic Haldimand: Unpublished Papers and Correspondence, 1758–84* (London: World Microfilms Publications, copyright The British Library, 1977), reel 58, p. 344.
35. Qtd. in Thomas Jones, *History of New York during the Revolutionary War: And of the Leading Events in the Other Colonies at That Period*, Vol. 2, ed. Edward Floyd De Lancey (New York: New York Historical Society, 1879), 374.
36. Huey and Pulis, *Molly Brant*, 59.
37. Sir William Johnson to General Thomas Gage, April 17, 1766, SWJP, 12:76. For the trip to New Lebanon Springs, see Flexner, *Lord of the Mohawks*, 314–15.

38. Qtd. in Flexner, *Lord of the Mohawks*, 314.
39. Sir William Johnson to Samuel Johnson, December 1, 1767, SWJP, 5:840–41.
40. Guy Johnson to John Tabor Kempe, October 1, 1767, SWJP, 12:365.
41. Sir William Johnson to John Penn, February 29, 1768, SWJP, 12:453. See also Sir William Johnson to Thomas Gage, March 5, 1768, SWJP, 12:460.
42. Fintan O'Toole, *White Savage: William Johnson and the Invention of America* (New York: Farrar, Straus and Giroux, 2005), 272.
43. Flexner, *Lord of the Mohawks*, 302.
44. Qtd. in Flexner, 320.
45. O'Toole, *White Savage*, 273.
46. O'Toole, 274–75.
47. "Congress at Fort Stanwix [September 15—October 30, 1768]," SWJP, 12:628. See also O'Toole, *White Savage*, 273.
48. Sir William Johnson to Thomas Gage, October 13, 1768, SWJP, 12:605–6. See also SWJP, 12:617n3.
49. Daniel Claus to Sir William Johnson, September 30, 1768, SWJP, 6:422.
50. "Congress at Fort Stanwix [September 15–October 30, 1768]," SWJP, 12:619.
51. O'Toole, *White Savage*, 276. See also Flexner, *Lord of the Mohawks*, 330.
52. O'Toole, *White Savage*, 276–77. See also Parkinson, *Heart of American Darkness*, 112–14.
53. Flexner, *Lord of the Mohawks*, 326–27.
54. Sir William Johnson to Thomas Gage, December 21, 1768, SWJP, 12:674–75.
55. Flexner, *Lord of the Mohawks*, 299–301.
56. Qtd. in Flexner, 301. See also John Wetherhead to Sir William Johnson, November 17, 1768, SWJP, 6:463.
57. Qtd. in Flexner, *Lord of the Mohawks*, 301.
58. Flexner, 296.
59. "Journal of Indian Affairs," November 20, 1768, SWJP, 12:656. See also Sir William Johnson to Thomas Gage, April 14, 1769, SWJP, 12:416.
60. Jones, *History of New York during the Revolutionary War*, 2:373–74.
61. Sir William Johnson to Henry Van Shaack, March 3, 1770, SWJP, 12:448.
62. O'Toole, *White Savage*, 287.
63. Rachel Wetherhead to Sir William Johnson, November 8, 1786, SWJP, 6:451.
64. Bill of sale from Peter Remsen to Sir William Johnson, October 28, 1769, SWJP, 7:231. See also "Return of the Loyalists Male and Female on Carleton Island Specifying Their Age & Number of Rations Drawn Out of the Kings Stores/per diem."

Chapter 7

1. "Return of the Loyalists Male and Female on Carleton Island Specifying Their Age & Number of Rations Drawn Out of the Kings Stores/per diem," dated November 26, 1783, in *Sir Frederic Haldimand: Unpublished Papers and Correspondence, 1758-84* (London: World Microfilms Publications, copyright The British Library, 1977), reel 58, p. 344.
2. Norman Macleod to Sir William Johnson, March 12, 1770, SWJP, 7:483.
3. James Rivington to Sir William Johnson, May 3, 1770, SWJP, 7:629.
4. James Rivington to Sir William Johnson, June 18, 1770, SWJP, 7:752.
5. Sir William Johnson to Reverends Peters, Smith, and Barton, April 16, 1770, SWJP, 7:566.
6. Reverend Charles Inglis to Sir William Johnson, March 28, 1770, SWJP, 7:504–5.
7. Reverend Charles Inglis to Reverend Daniel Burton, June 15, 1770, SWJP, 7:746.
8. Reverend Charles Inglis to Reverend Daniel Burton, June 15, 1770, SWJP, 7:748.
9. Reverend Charles Inglis to Reverend Daniel Burton, June 15, 1770, SWJP, 7:749.
10. Reverend Charles Inglis to Sir William Johnson, June 21, 1770, SWJP, 7:762.
11. Reverend Charles Inglis to Sir William Johnson, June 21, 1770, SWJP, 7:766.
12. Sir William Johnson to Goldsbrow Banyar, March 10, 1770, SWJP, 12:792.
13. Sir William Johnson to Thomas Gage, April 6, 1770, SWJP, 12:814.
14. Sir William Johnson to Thomas Penn, July 4, 1770, SWJP, 7:785.
15. Sir William Johnson to Thomas Gage, August 22, 1770, SWJP, 12:849–50.
16. "An Indian Conference," SWJP, 12:844.
17. Isabel Thompson Kelsay, *Joseph Brant, 1743-1807: Man of Two Worlds*

(Syracuse: Syracuse University Press, 1984), 129, 133.
18. Kelsay, *Joseph Brant, 1743-1807*, 134.
19. Kelsay, 134; and Barbara J. Sivertsen, *Turtles, Wolves and Bears: A Mohawk Family History* (Westminster, MD: Heritage Books, 2006), 12-13, 16. See also Barbara Alice Mann, *Iroquoian Women: The Gantowisas* (New York: Peter Lang, 2000), 266; and Daniel K. Richter, *The Ordeal of the Longhouse: The Peoples of the Iroquois League in the Era of European Colonization* (Chapel Hill: University of North Carolina, 1992), 20-21.
20. Sivertsen, *Turtles, Wolves and Bears*, 152.
21. Sir William Johnson to General Thomas Gage, August 9, 1771, SWJP, 8:219.
22. Earl of Dunmore to Sir William Johnson, August 24, 1771, SWJP, 8:234.
23. Sir William to General Thomas Gage, September 9, 1771, SWJP, 8:258.
24. Hugh Wallace to Sir William Johnson, October 25, 1771, SWJP, 8:300.
25. Sir William to General Thomas Gage, November 16, 1771, SWJP, 8:317.
26. James De Lancey to Sir William Johnson, January 19, 1772, SWJP, 12:933.
27. Hugh Wallace to Sir William Johnson, May 10, 1772, SWJP, 8:477.
28. Sir William Johnson to Hugh Wallace , May 21, 1772, 8:492.
29. Sir William Johnson to Henry Glen, December 28, 1772, 8:678.
30. John Cottgrave to Thomas Flood, November 21, 1771, SWJP, 8:320.
31. Sir William Johnson to Augustine Prevost, SWJP, May 22, 1772, 12:961.
32. Sir William Johnson to Daniel Claus, June 11, 1772, SWJP, 12:966. See also Daniel Claus to Sir William Johnson, July 3, 1772, SWJP, 8:526.
33. Sir William Johnson to Arthur Lee, March 28, 1772, SWJP, 12:953.
34. Sir William Johnson to General Thomas Gage, August 6, 1772, SWJP, 8:562.
35. Kelsay, *Joseph Brant, 1743-1807*, 123. See also SWJP, 8:556n; and Sir William to Charles Inglis, August 27, 1772, SWJP, 8:584.
36. Court statement, SWJP, 8:687.
37. Sir William Johnson to Thomas Gage, November 18, 1772, SWJP, 8:639.
38. James Thomas Flexner, *Lord of the Mohawks: A Biography of Sir William Johnson* (Boston: Little, Brown, 1979),, 337-38.
39. Dr. R. Huntley to Sir William Johnson, January 2, 1773, SWJP, 12:1010.
40. Dr. R. Huntley to Sir William Johnson, March 6, 1773, SWJP, 12:1013.
41. Sir William Johnson to Thomas Gage, November 18, 1772, SWJP, 8:639.
42. Hugh Wallace to Sir William Johnson, December 3, 1772, SWJP, 8:651-52.
43. Hugh and Alexander Wallace to Sir William Johnson, December 9, 1772, SWJP, 8:657.
44. Flexner, *Lord of the Mohawks*, 345.
45. Mayor Thomas Moncrieffe to Sir William Johnson, March 4, 1773, SWJP, 8:729.

Chapter 8

1. John Baptist Van Eps to Sir Wiliam Johnson, February 20, 1773, SWJP, 8:719
2. Sir William Johnson to Thomas Gage, April 6, 1773, SWJP, 8:753.
3. Guy Johnson to Sir William Johnson, February 10, 1773, SWJP, 8:711; Guy Johnson to Sir William Johnson, February 16, 1773, SWJP, 8:715; and Hugh Wallace to Sir William Johnson, January 12, 1773, SWJP, 8:691.
4. Mayor Thomas Moncrieffe to Sir William Johnson, March 4, 1773, SWJP, 8:729.
5. Peter Silvester to Sir William Johnson, March 22, 1773, SWJP, 8:740.
6. Sir William Johnson to Thomas Gage, May 15, 1773, SWJP, 8:798.
7. Sir William Johnson to Thomas Gage, June 2, 1773, SWJP, 8:814.
8. Daniel Claus to Sir William Johnson, August 20, 1773, SWJP, 8:867.
9. Guy Johnson to Sir William Johnson, August 26, 1773, SWJP, 8:877.
10. Sir William Johnson to Frederick Haldimand, October 7, 1773, SWJP, 8:901.
11. Hugh Wallace to Sir William Johnson, September 22, 1773, 8:892.
12. Robert Adems to Sir William Johnson, October 25, 1773, SWJP, 8:909.
13. Peter Johnson to Sir William Johnson, November 18, 1773, SWJP, 12:1043.
14. Will of Sir William Johnson, SWJP, 12:1063.
15. Sir William Johnson to Frederick

Haldimand, December 8, 1773, SWJP, 8:938.
16. Captain James Stevenson to Sir William Johnson, March 13, 1771, SWJP, 8:16.
17. Captain James Stevenson to Sir William Johnson, April 1, 1774, SWJP, 8:1108.
18. Captain James Stevenson to Sir William Johnson, March 31, 1774, SWJP, 8:1103.
19. Francis Wade to Sir William Johnson, February 2, 1774, SWJP, 8:1019–20.
20. Francis Wade to Sir William Johnson, February 2, 1774..
21. Francis Wade to Sir William Johnson, February 2, 1774.
22. Peter Johnson to Sir William Johnson, April 30, 1774, SWJP, 8:1139.
23. Francis Wade to Sir William Johnson, March 6, 1774, SWJP, 8:1063.
24. Peter Johnson to Sir William Johnson, April 30, 1774, SWJP, 8:1139.
25. Peter Johnson to Sir William Johnson, May 31, 1774, SWJP, 8:1163.
26. Peter Johnson to Sir William Johnson, May 31, 1774.
27. John Blackburn to Sir William Johnson, March 5, 1774, SWJP, 8:1060.
28. Sir William Johnson to John Blackburn, May 27, 1774, SWJP, 8:1160–61.
29. Hugh Wallace to Sir William Johnson, June 27, 1774, SWJP, 8:1179.
30. Sir William Johnson to Thomas Gage, July 4, 1774, SWJP, 12:1115. For a more complete description of the atrocity, see Robert G. Parkinson, *Heart of American Darkness: Bewilderment and Horror on the Early Frontier* (New York: Norton, 2024), xvii–xix, 176–83. Michael Cresap was not present at the Yellow Creek Massacre, but he had engaged in violence against Ohio valley Native Americans previously and was the commander of the militia forces that attacked Ohio valley Native Americans after some Native Americans retaliated for the Yellow Creek murders.
31. Sir William Johnson to Daniel Claus, July 3, 1774, SWJP, 12:1112.
32. Isabel Thompson Kelsay, *Joseph Brant, 1743-1807: Man of Two Worlds* (Syracuse: Syracuse University Press, 1984), 136–37.
33. Sir William Johnson to Thomas Gage, July 4, 1774, SWJP, 12:1116.
34. Sir William Johnson to Capt. John Donnell, June 28, 1774, 12:1111.
35. Hugh Wallace to Sir William Johnson, June 27, 1774, SWJP, 8:1179.
36. Qtd. in James Thomas Flexner, *Lord of the Mohawks: A Biography of Sir William Johnson* (Boston: Little, Brown, 1979), 347.
37. Flexner, 347.
38. Qtd. in Fintan O'Toole, *White Savage: William Johnson and the Invention of America* (New York: Farrar, Straus and Giroux, 2005), 323.
39. Flexner, *Lord of the Mohawks*, 347.
40. Guy Johnson to Thomas Gage, July 12, 1774, SWJP, 12:1121; and Guy Johnson to John Penn, July 22, 1774, SWJP, 8:1186. See also Flexner, *Lord of the Mohawks*, 347.
41. Flexner, *Lord of the Mohawks*, 348; and O'Toole, *White Savage* 323–34. The obituary of Sir William Johnson that appeared in the *New York Gazette & Weekly Mercury*, August 1, 1774, is reprinted in Parkinson, *Heart of American Darkness*, 195.
42. Will of Sir William Johnson, January 27, 1774, SWJP, 12:1063.
43. Sir William Johnson to Catherine Corry, April 29, 1763, SWJP, 4:105.
44. Will of Sir William Johnson, January 27, 1774, SWJP, 12:1075.
45. Will of Sir William Johnson, January 27, 1774, SWJP, 12:1075.
46. Will of Sir William Johnson, January 27, 1774, SWJP, 12:1064, 1071.
47. Will of Sir William Johnson, January, 27, 1774, SWJP, 12:1064.
48. Will of Sir William Johnson, January, 27, 1774, SWJP, 12:1064.
49. Will of Sir William Johnson, January 27, 1774, SWJP, 12:1070.
50. Will of Sir William Johnson, January 27, 1774, SWJP, 12:1068–70.
51. Will of Sir William Johnson, January 27, 1774, SWJP, 12:1065.
52. Will of Sir William Johnson, January 27, 1774, SWJP, 12:1065.

Chapter 9

1. Thomas Gage to the Earl of Dartmouth, July 18, 1774, SWJP, 8:1185.
2. Isabel Thompson Kelsay, *Joseph Brant, 1743-1807: Man of Two Worlds* (Syracuse: Syracuse University Press, 1984), 140.
3. Sometimes also referred to as the Committee of Public Safety. Both

Notes—Chapter 10

"Committee of Public Safety" and "Committee of Safety" are used depending on the document under discussion.

4. "Minutes" in the Minute Book of the Committee of Safety of Tryon County, the "Old New York Frontier" by Samuel Ludlow Frey, and "Minutes and Proceedings of the Tryon County Committee of Safety" with documents from the New York Historical Society Collections (Tryon County MSS, box 1), compiled in Mohawk Valley in the Revolution, ed. Maryly Penrose (Franklin Park, NJ): Liberty Bell Associates, 1978, Document 1, pp. 1-2.

5. Tryon County Committee of Safety Minutes, undated, Document 2, p. 3.

6. Kelsay, *Joseph Brant, 1743-1807*, 139-40.

7. Guy Johnson to John Blackburn, September 12, 1774, SWJP, 8:1199-2000.

8. Guy Johnson to Thomas Gage, November 10, 1774, SWJPD, 13:691. See also Kelsay, *Joseph Brant, 1743-1807*, 146.

9. Guy Johnson to Thomas Gage, December 14, 1774, SWJPD, 13:700.

10. Thomas Gage to Guy Johnson, December 28, 1774, SWJPD, 13:703. See also Kelsay, *Joseph Brant, 1743-1807*, 146.

11. Alexander Flick, "Chronology of Guy Johnson," SWJPD, 4:xii; and "The Papers of Sir William Johnson," HathiTrust, https://babel.hathitrust.org/cgi/pt?id=mdp.39015071343563;view=1up;seq=15.

12. Tryon County Committee of Safety Minutes, May 19, 1775, Document 3, p. 4.

13. Tryon County Committee of Safety Minutes, May 19, 1775, Document 3, p. 5.

14. Tryon County Committee of Safety Minutes, May 21, 1775, Document 4, p. 6.

15. Kelsay, *Joseph Brant, 1743-1807*, 147.

16. Tryon County Committee of Safety Minutes, May 21, 1775, Document 4, p. 6, and May 24, 1775, Document 5, p. 8.

17. Tryon County Committee of Safety Minutes, May 29, 1775, Document 6, pp. 9-10.

18. Letter from the Tryon County Committee of Public Safety to Guy Johnson, June 2, 1775, Tryon County Committee of Safety Minutes, Document 7, pp. 12-13.

19. Tryon County Committee of Safety Minutes, June 4, 1775, Document 8, p. 15.

20. Kelsay, *Joseph Brant, 1743-1807*, 149.

21. Kelsay, 149.

22. Kelsay, 151-52.

23. Kelsay, 152-54.

24. Tryon County Committee of Safety Minutes, June 11, 1775, Document 9, p. 16.

25. Tryon County Committee of Safety Minutes, July 10, 1775, Document 15, pp. 22-23.

26. Letter from the Tryon Committee of Safety to the Albany and Schenectady Committees of Safety, July 13, 1775, Tryon County Committee of Safety Minutes, Document 16, p. 24.

27. Tench Tilghman, *Memoir of Lieut. Col. Tench Tilghman: Secretary and Aide to Washington*, ed. S.A. Harrison (Albany, NY: J. Munsell, 1876), 87.

28. Tilghman, *Memoir of Lieut. Col. Tench Tilghman*, 87.

29. Tilghman, 87.

30. Tilghman, 88.

31. Tilghman, 87.

32. Ethan Allen, *The Narrative of Colonel Ethan Allen* (New York: Corinth Books, 1961), 15-18. See also Guy Johnson to the Earl of Dartmouth, October 12, 1775, DRCHSNYD, et seq. 8:655 (8:637).

33. Allen, *The Narrative of Colonel Ethan Allen*, 20.

34. Allen, 20-22.

35. Guy Johnson to the Earl of Dartmouth, October 12, 1775, DRCHSNYD, et seq. 8:665 (8:637).

36. Kelsay, *Joseph Brant, 1743-1807*, 158.

37. Kelsay, 158.

38. Kelsay, 159-61.

Chapter 10

1. "Minutes" in the Minute Book of the Committee of Safety of Tryon County, the "Old New York Frontier" by Samuel Ludlow Frey, and "Minutes and Proceedings of the Tryon County Committee of Safety" with documents from the New York Historical Society Collections, compiled in Mohawk Valley in the Revolution ed. Maryly Penrose (Franklin Park, NJ): Liberty Bell Associates, 1978, October 27, 1775, Document 28, p. 50.

2. Tryon County Committee of Safety Minutes, October 27, 1775, Document 28, p. 51.

3. Tryon County Committee of Safety Minutes, October 27, 1775, Document 28, p. 50.

4. Tryon County Committee of Safety

Minutes, November 7, 1775, Document 30, p. 57.

5. Tryon County Committee of Safety Minutes, November 6, 1775, Document 29, p. 56.

6. Tryon County Committee of Safety Minutes, October 27, 1775, Document 28, p. 52.

7. Tryon County Committee of Safety, November 7, 1775, Document 30, p. 57.

8. Nathaniel Woodhull to Colonel Nicholas Herkimer, December 9, 1775, SWJP, 8:1214, notes.

9. Tryon County Committee of Safety Minutes, December 30, 1775, Document 35.

10. Guy Johnson to Lord George Germain, January 26, 1776, DRCHSNYD, et seq. 8:685 (8:657).

11. Isabel Thompson Kelsay, *Joseph Brant, 1743-1807: Man of Two Worlds* (Syracuse: Syracuse University Press, 1984), 163-65.

12. "Speech of Captain Brant to Lord Germain" as dictated to Joseph Chew, secy., March 14, 1776, DRCHSNYD et seq. 8:699 (8:671).

13. Kelsay, *Joseph Brant, 1743-1807*, 165-67.

14. Qtd. in Kelsay, 171.

15. Kelsay, 170, 534-35.

16. Lois M. Huey and Bonnie Pulis, *Molly Brant: A Legacy of Her Own* (Youngstown, NY: Old Fort Niagara Association, 1997), 55n113. See also Lieutenant Peter Johnson, Return of Officers Recommended for Promotion, Comm. in 1775/76, Carleton Papers—Loyalists and British Soldiers, 1772-1784, United Empire Loyalists Association of Canada, Sir Guy Carleton Branch, stored at Library and Archives of Canada, Item No. 29604, Indian Affairs Document, p. 10209, Microfilm M-368, Reference MG23B1, Date 1776-10-04.

17. Guy Johnson to Lord George Germain, August 9, 1776, DRCHSNYD et seq. 8:709-10 (8:681-82).

18. Guy Johnson to Lord George Germain, August 9, 1776, DRCHSNYD.

19. Guy Johnson to Lord George Germain, August 9, 1776, DRCHSNYD.

20. Janice Potter-MacKinnon, *While the Women Only Wept* (Montreal: McGill-Queen's University Press, 1993), 56-57.

21. Potter-MacKinnon, *While the Women Only Wept*, 50.

22. Governor William Tryon to the Earl of Dartmouth, February 8, 1776, DRCHSNYD, et seq. 8:692 (8:664).

23. Tryon County Committee of Safety Minutes, May 14, 1776, Document 39.

24. Joseph Bloomfield, "The Revolutionary War Journal of Joseph Bloomfield," in *Citizen Soldier: The Revolutionary War Journal of Joseph Bloomfield*, ed. Mark E. Lender and James Kirby Martin (Newark: New Jersey Historical Society, 1982), 47-48.

25. Bloomfield, "The Revolutionary War Journal of Joseph Bloomfield," 47-48.

26. Bloomfield, 48-49.

27. Bloomfield, 48-49.

28. Bloomfield, 48-49.

29. Bloomfield, 48-49.

30. Bloomfield, 48-49.

31. Bloomfield, 50.

32. Bloomfield, 50.

33. Bloomfield, 59. See also "Declaration of Mr. Thomas Gumersall, Deputy Assistant to the Commissary General of Stores and Provisions, born at Leeds, in Yorkshire," August 6, 1776, DRCHSNYD, et seq. 8:710 (8:683).

34. Bloomfield, "The Revolutionary War Journal of Joseph Bloomfield," 59.

35. Bloomfield, 55.

36. Bloomfield, 56.

37. Tryon County Committee of Safety Minutes, Documents 41 and 42, pp. 79-82.

38. Bloomfield, "The Revolutionary War Journal of Joseph Bloomfield," 59.

39. Bloomfield, 61.

40. Bloomfield, 61.

41. Barbara Graymont, *The Iroquois in the American Revolution* (Syracuse: Syracuse University Press, 1972), 101.

42. Bloomfield, "The Revolutionary War Journal of Joseph Bloomfield," 63.

43. Bloomfield, 72-73.

44. Bloomfield, 72-73.

45. Bloomfield, 63.

46. Tryon Committee of Safety Minutes, July 13, 1776, Document 46, p. 85.

47. Bloomfield, "The Revolutionary War Journal of Joseph Bloomfield," 84.

48. Bloomfield, 91.

49. Bloomfield, 98.

50. Catherine S. Crary, *The Price of Loyalty: Tory Writings from the Tory Era* (New York: McGraw-Hill, 1973), 80, 203.

51. Tryon County Committee of Safety Minutes, July 14, 1776, Document 49, p. 87.

52. Kelsay, *Joseph Brant, 1743-1807*, 184.
53. Kelsay, 184.
54. Kelsay, 186.
55. Crary, *The Price of Loyalty*, 80.
56. Crary, 80.
57. Kelsay, *Joseph Brant, 1743-1807*, 188-92.

Chapter 11

1. "Minutes" in the Minute Book of the Committee of Safety of Tryon County, the "Old New York Frontier" by Samuel Ludlow Frey, and "Minutes and Proceedings of the Tryon County Committee of Safety" with documents from the New York Historical Society Collections (Tryon County MSS, box 1), compiled in Mohawk Valley in the Revolution, ed. Maryly Penrose (Franklin Park, NJ): Liberty Bell Associates, 1978, October 20, 1776, Document 52, p. 91.
2. Tryon County Committee of Safety Minutes, April 3, 1777, Document 65, p. 109.
3. Isabel Thompson Kelsay, *Joseph Brant, 1743-1807: Man of Two Worlds* (Syracuse: Syracuse University Press, 1984), 193.
4. Kelsay, *Joseph Brant, 1743-1807*, 195. See also Allan W. Eckert, *The Wilderness War* (Boston: Little, Brown, 1978), 109-10.
5. Kelsay, *Joseph Brant, 1743-1807*, 195.
6. Kelsay, 195.
7. Daniel Claus to William Knox, October 16, 1777, DRCHSNYD, et seq. 8:746 (8:718).
8. Kelsay, *Joseph Brant, 1743-1807*, 195.
9. Ethan Allen, *The Narrative of Colonel Ethan Allen* (New York: Corinth Books, 1961), 218. See also Andrew Jackson O'Shaughnessy, *The Men Who Lost North America* (New Haven: Yale University Press, 2013), 143-44.
10. Kelsay, *Joseph Brant, 1743-1807*, 196.
11. Daniel Claus to William Knox, October 16, 1776, DRCHSNYD, et seq. 8:746 (8:718). See also Allen, *The Narrative of Colonel Ethan Allen*, 217.
12. Kelsay, *Joseph Brant, 1743-1807*, 196.
13. Tilar J. Mazzeo, *Eliza Hamilton: The Extraordinary Life and Times of the Wife of Alexander Hamilton* (New York: Gallery Books, 2018), 50-52.
14. Allen, *The Narrative of Colonel Ethan Allen*, 221-23.
15. Kelsay, *Joseph Brant, 1743-1807*, 199-200.
16. Kelsay, 201.
17. Allen, *The Narrative of Colonel Ethan Allen*, 225, 228.
18. Daniel Claus to William Knox, October 16, 1777, DRCHSNYD, et seq. 8:749 (8:721); and Allen, *The Narrative of Colonel Ethan Allen*, 226. Daniel Claus says that Molly estimated a force of 900 men. See Daniel Claus, "Annecodotes [sic] of the Mohawk Chief Captn. Joseph Brant," IAP, Appendix A, p. 321.
19. Allen, *The Narrative of Colonel Ethan Allen*, 226.
20. Daniel Claus to William Knox, November, 6, 1777, DRCHSNYD, et seq. 8:752 (8:724).
21. Allen, *The Narrative of Colonel Ethan Allen*, 227.
22. Allen, 227.
23. Daniel Claus to William Knox, November 6, 1777, DRCHSNYD, et seq. 8:753 (8:725).
24. Tryon County Committee of Safety Minutes, note, p. 127, and p. 253.
25. Allen, *The Narrative of Colonel Ethan Allen*, 228; and Daniel Claus to William Knox, October 16, 1777, DRCHSNYD, et seq. 8:749 (8:721).
26. Tryon County Committee of Safety Minutes, August 12, 1777, Document 75, p. 126.
27. Margaret Johnson Farley, "Testimony of a Child of Molly Brant," in Lois M. Huey and Bonnie Pulis, *Molly Brant: A Legacy of Her Own* (Youngstown, NY: Old Fort Niagara Association, 1997), Appendix D, p. 115.
28. Tryon County Committee of Safety Minutes, August 25, 1777, Document 76, p. 127.
29. Farley, "Testimony of a Child of Molly Brant," 115.
30. Daniel Claus to Sir Frederick Haldimand, 8/30/79, SFHUPC, reel 51, p. 58.
31. Farley, "Testimony of a Child of Molly Brant," 115.
32. Daniel Claus to Sir Frederick Haldimand 8/30/ 1779, SFHUPC, reel 51, p. 58.
33. Farley, "Testimony of a Child of Molly Brant," 116. See also Daniel Claus

to William Knox, November 6, 1777, DRCHSNYD, et seq. 8:752 (8:724).

34. Affidavit of Hendrick S. Moyer, dated April 20, 1778, IAP, p. 127; and Letter from Jelles Fonda to Commissioners of Indian Affairs, April 21, 1778, IAP, p. 134. See also Barbara Graymont, *The Iroquois in the American Revolution* (Syracuse: Syracuse University Press (1972), 146–47; and Declaration of Peter Doxtator, December 22, 1852, IAP, 350–1.

35. Qtd. in Tryon County Committee of Safety Minutes, September 17, 1777, Document 79, p. 133. Although some historians have been puzzled about William of Canajoharie's fate, suggesting that he may have died at the Battle of Oriskany in August 1777, William of Canajoharie was sometimes described as William Johnson by European Americans during the pre-revolutionary period and is likely to have been called by that name in what the Committee of Safety viewed as a legal document ordering his arrest. William was also the father of a male child who used the surname Johnson throughout his life.

36. Tryon County Committee of Safety Minutes, September 17, 1777, Document 79, p. 133.

37. *A Schedule of Real Estate of the Children of Mrs. Mary Brant as Exhibited by Joseph Chew Their Guardian, the Same Being in Tryon County and Province of New York*, attached to Memorial of Joseph Chew Guardian ... , dated 23 March 1784, Loyalty Commission Claims, Series II, A.O. 13, Bundle 11, p. 334, describes Peter as "an officer in his Majesty's 26th Reg who dyed at Philadelphia in 1777." See also Thomas Jones, *History of New York during the Revolutionary War: And of the Leading Events in the Other Colonies at That Period*, Vol. 2, ed. Edward Floyd De Lancey (New York: New York Historical Society, 1879), 375. Twenty years later and after Molly had died, a son-in-law, John Ferguson, Magdalene's husband, stated in a request for a land grant that Peter had died during the Battle of Long Island that took place in August 1776. His statement was not correct. Joseph Chew was responsible for preparing the compensation claims for Molly's children during the mid-1780s and was in regular consultation with Joseph Brant and Daniel Claus, family members who had contemporaneous knowledge of the circumstances of Peter's death. Justice Jones, who also places Peter's death at Philadelphia in 1777, was a friend of Sir William, resided on an estate on Long Island where he was in regular contact with British officers and New York Loyalists during the British occupation of New York City, and was contemporaneously writing a history of the Revolutionary War. Also, Joseph Brant took part in the Battle of Long Island. It is extremely unlikely that he would have failed to inform Molly of Peter's death when he made his way to upper New York soon after the battle, but there is no evidence that Molly learned of her son's death until sometime after her arrival at Fort Niagara in the late fall or early winter of 1777. See also Huey and Pulis, *Molly Brant*, p. 55nn113, 114.

Chapter 12

1. Daniel Claus to William Knox, November 6, 1777, DRCHSNYD, et seq. 8:753 (8:725).

2. Daniel Claus to William Knox, November 6, 1777.

3. Daniel Claus to Sir Frederick Haldimand, August 30, 1779, SFHUPC, reel 51, p. 58.

4. Daniel Claus to Sir Frederick Haldimand, August 30, 1779. Daniel Claus translates Sayengaraghta's name as "Cayenwraghton" in this letter.

5. Daniel Claus to Sir Frederick Haldimand, August 30, 1779.

6. Daniel Claus to Sir Frederick Haldimand, August 30, 1779.

7. Joseph Brant to Daniel Claus, January 23, 1778, Eighteenth Century Selection of Documents Relating to Indian Affairs, reel C-11773, Images 20 and 21, http://heritage.canadiana.ca/view/oocihm.lac_mikan_102179.

8. Isabel Thompson Kelsay, *Joseph Brant, 1743–1807: Man of Two Worlds* (Syracuse: Syracuse University Press, 1984), 212.

9. Qtd.. in Kelsay, *Joseph Brant, 1743–1807*, 213.

10. Lois M. Huey and Bonnie Pulis, *Molly Brant: A Legacy of Her Own* (Youngstown, NY: Old Fort Niagara Association, 1997), 53.

Notes—Chapter 12

11. Mary Brandt [sic] to Daniel Claus, June 23, 1778, Eighteenth Century Selections of Documents Relating to Indian Affairs, reel C-11773, Image 30, http://heritage.canadiana.ca/view/oocihm.lac_mikan_102179.
12. Kelsay, *Joseph Brant, 1743-1807*, 215-16.
13. Kelsay, 216.
14. Kelsay, 224.
15. Kelsay, 218-20.
16. Kelsay, 225.
17. Mary Brandt [sic] to Daniel Claus, June 23, 1778..
18. Mary Brandt [sic] to Daniel Claus, June 23, 1778.
19. Taylor and Duffin to Daniel Claus, October 26, 1778, SFHUPC, reel 51, pp. 9-10.
20. Taylor and Duffin to Daniel Claus, October 26, 1778..
21. Taylor and Duffin to Daniel Claus, October 26, 1778
22. Taylor and Duffin to Daniel Claus, October 26, 1778
23. Daniel Claus to Sir Frederick Haldimand, November 5, 1778, SFHUPC, reel 51, p. 11.
24. Kelsay, *Joseph Brant, 1743-1807*, 231-34.
25. Barbara J. Sivertsen, *Turtles, Wolves and Bears: A Mohawk Family History* (Westminster, MD: Heritage Books, 2006), 312n31.
26. Huey and Pulis, *Molly Brant*, 55-57. William Lamb, the young Patriot boy, lived with Molly and her family at Carleton Island and did not return to New York state until he was a young man. See "Return of the Loyalists Male and Female on Carleton Island Specifying Their Age & Number of Rations Drawn Out of the Kings Stores/per diem," dated November 26, 1783, SFHUPC, reel 58, p. 344. See also Huey and Pulis, *Molly Brant*, 67-69.
27. Daniel Claus to Sir Frederick Haldimand, August 30, 1779, SFHUPC, Add. MSS 21774, reel 51, pp. 57-58.
28. Sir Frederick Haldimand to Lieutenant Colonel Bolton, June 7, 1779, SFHUPC, Add. MSS 21764, reel 45, pp. 18-19.
29. Sir Frederick Haldimand to Lord George Germain, October 24, 1778, SFHUPC, Add. MSS 21714, reel 20, pp. 17-18.
30. Huey and Pulis, *Molly Brant*, 57.
31. Daniel Claus to Sir Frederick Haldimand, August 30, 1779, SFHUPC, Add. MSS 21774, reel 51, pp. 57-58.
32. Kelsay, *Joseph Brant, 1743-1807*, 246-47, 255.
33. Kelsay, 258.
34. Daniel Claus to Sir Frederick Haldimand, August 30, 1779, SFHUPC, Add. MSS 21774, reel 51, p. 57.
35. Qtd. in Huey and Pulis, *Molly Brant*, 59.
36. Sir Frederick Haldimand to Guy Johnson, September 9, 1779, SFHUPC, Add. MSS 21767, reel 47, p. 29.
37. Sir Frederick Haldimand to Guy Johnson, September 9, 1779.
38. Guy Johnson to Sir Frederick Haldimand, September 9, 1779, SFHUPC, Add. MSS 21767, reel 47, p. 31.
39. In his letter to Governor Haldimand describing the arrangement, Claus said that Molly was leaving her two youngest girls, ages 10 and 8, with him to attend school. Based on the ages, this was Mary and Susanna, not Susanna and Anne. Either Claus thought it best not to inform Haldimand that one of Molly's school-age children was not remaining in Montreal or he himself was confused about the birth order. Daniel Claus to Sir Frederick Haldimand, September 13, 1779, SFHUPC, Add. MSS 21774, reel 51, pp. 67-68.
40. Daniel Claus to Sir Frederick Haldimand, September 13, 1779.
41. Guy Johnson to Lord George Germain, November 11, 1779, DRCHSNYD, et seq. 8:807 (8:779).
42. Sir Frederick Haldimand to Lord George Germain, September 13, 1779, SFHUPC, Add. MSS 21714, reel 20, pp. 46-47 (no. 32).
43. Sir Frederick Haldimand to Lord George Germain, September 13, 1779.
44. Sir Frederick Haldimand to Lord George Germain, September 13, 1779.
45. Sir Frederick Haldimand to Lord George Germain, September 13, 1779.
46. Kelsay, *Joseph Brant, 1743-1807*, 261.
47. Kelsay, 264-65.
48. Guy Johnson to Lord George Germain, November 11, 1779, DRCHSNYD, et seq. 8:807-8 (8:779-80).
49. Mary Brant to Daniel Claus, October 5, 1779, Claus Family Papers, The Loyalist Collection (1755-1886), Library and Archives of Canada, NAC Archival Ref.

No. NAC MG 19, F 1), copy also available at the University of New Brunswick.

50. Mary Brant to Daniel Claus, October 5, 1779.

51. Mary Brant to Daniel Claus, October 5, 1779.

52. Kelsay, *Joseph Brant, 1743-1807*, 270.

53. Captain Alexander Fraser to General Frederick Haldimand, March 21, 1780, SFHUPC, Add. MSS 21787, reel 58, pp. 116-17

54. Captain Alexander Fraser to General Frederick Haldimand, March 21, 1780.

55. Captain Alexander Fraser to General Frederick Haldimand, March 21, 1780.

56. Captain Alexander Fraser to General Frederick Haldimand, March 21, 1780.

57. Captain Alexander Fraser to General Frederick Haldimand, March 21, 1780.

58. Sivertsen, *Turtles, Wolves and Bears*, 22, 174; and Kelsay, *Joseph Brant, 1743-1807*, 277.

59. Captain Alexander Fraser to General Frederick Haldimand, June 21, 1780, SFHUPC, Add. MSS 21787, reel 58, pp. 150-51.

60. Captain Alexander Fraser to General Frederick Haldimand, June 21, 1780.

61. Captain Alexander Fraser to General Frederick Haldimand, June 21, 1780.

62. Captain Alexander Fraser to General Frederick Haldimand, June 21, 1780.

63. Lord George Germain to Sir Frederick Haldimand, March 17, 1780, SFHUPC, Add. MSS 21714, reel 20, pp. 30-31.

64. Captain Robert Mathews to Captain Alexander Fraser, July 17, 1780, SFHUPC, Add. MSS 21788, reel 59, p. 94.

65. Captain Robert Mathews to Captain Alexander Fraser, July 17, 1780.

Chapter 13

1. Isabel Thompson Kelsay, *Joseph Brant, 1743-1807: Man of Two Worlds* (Syracuse: Syracuse University Press, 1984), 290.

2. Kelsay, *Joseph Brant, 1743-1807*, 292-94.

3. Kelsay 295-98, 301.

4. Qtd. in Kelsay, 297.

5. Kelsay, 290.

6. Daniel Claus to Captain Robert Mathews, July 26, 1781, SFHUPC, Add. MSS 21774, reel 51, p. 208.

7. Captain Alexander Fraser to Sir Frederick Haldimand, December 13, 1780, SFHUPC, Add. MSS 21787, reel 58, pp. 201-2.

8. Qtd. in Lois M. Huey and Bonnie Pulis, *Molly Brant: A Legacy of Her Own* (Youngstown, NY: Old Fort Niagara Association, 1997), 63.

9. Lord George Germain to Sir Frederick Haldimand, August 8, 1780, SFHUPC, Add. MSS 21710, reel 20, pp. 52-53.

10. Guy Johnson to Lord George Germain, November 11, 1779, DRCHSNYD, et seq. 8:808 (8:780).

11. Kelsay, *Joseph Brant, 1743-1807*, 280.

12. Qtd. in Huey and Pulis, *Molly Brant*, 71.

13. John Deserontyn to Daniel Claus, April 12, 1781, IAP, 271.

14. Kelsay, *Joseph Brant, 1743-1807*, 307-8.

15. Mary Brant to Daniel Claus, April 12, 1781 (as translated from Mohawk to English by Daniel Claus), SFHUPC, Add. MSS 21774, reel 51, pp. 180-81.

16. John Deserontyn to Daniel Claus, April 12, 1781, IAP, p. 271.

17. John Deserontyn to Daniel Claus, April 12, 1781, IAP, p. 271.

18. Kelsay, *Joseph Brant, 1743-1807*, 308.

19. Kelsay, 310.

20. Memorial of Guy Johnson to Sir Frederick Haldimand, undated, SFHUPC, Add. MSS 21766, reel 47, pp. 28-29.

21. Lord George Germain to Sir Frederick Haldimand, March 15, 1782, SFHUPC, Add. MSS 21710, reel 20, pp. 61-62.

22. "List of Officers belonging to the Indian Department at Niagara," dated December 4, 1783, signed by John Johnson as Superintendt. Genl. and Inspectr. Genl. Indn. Affairs and listing Guy Johnson as "Superintendent," IAP, 303-5.

23. Daniel Claus to Captain Robert Mathews, July 26, 1781, SFHUPC, Add. MSS 21774, reel 51, p. 208.

24. Daniel Claus to Captain Robert Mathews, July 26, 1781, SFHUPC, Add. MSS 21774, reel 51, p. 208. George may have been tall for his age. He was actually 12 years old. Margaret was 14.

25. Daniel Claus to Captain Robert Mathews, July 26, 1781, SFHUPC, Add. MSS 21774, reel 51, p. 208.

26. Captain Robert Mathews to Daniel Claus, July 30, 1781, SFHUPC, Add. MSS 21774, reel 51, p. 210.
27. Kelsay, *Joseph Brant, 1743-1807*, 312, 322.
28. Kelsay, 323.
29. Kelsay, 323, 327-28.
30. Kelsay, 323, 327-28.
31. Daniel Claus to Captain Robert Mathews, July 25, 1782, SFHUPC, Add. MSS 21774, reel 51, p. 279.
32. Daniel Claus to Captain Robert Mathews, July 25, 1782, SFHUPC, Add. MSS 21774, reel 51, p. 279.
33. Lord Townshend to Sir Frederick Haldimand, October 19, 1782, SFHUPC, Add. MSS 21710, reel 20, pp. 73-74.
34. Kelsay, *Joseph Brant, 1743-1807*, 339.
35. Qtd. in Kelsay, 340.
36. Kelsay, 342.
37. Qtd. in Kelsay, 342.
38. Sir Frederick Haldimand to Sir John Johnson, May 27, 1783, SFHUPC, Add. MSS 21775, reel 52, p. 124.
39. Kelsay, *Joseph Brant, 1743-1807*, 343.
40. Lord North to Sir Frederick Haldimand, August 8, 1783, SFHUPC, Add. MSS 21710, reel 20, pp. 89-90.
41. Lord North to Sir Frederick Haldimand, August 7, 1783, SFHUPC, Add. MSS 21710, reel 20, p. 85.
42. Lord North to Sir Frederick Haldimand, August 8, 1783, SFHUPC, Add. MSS 21710, reel 20, p. 88.

Chapter 14

1. Isabel Thompson Kelsay, *Joseph Brant, 1743-1807: Man of Two Worlds* (Syracuse: Syracuse University Press, 1984), 350, 365.
2. "Return of the Loyalists Male and Female on Carleton Island Specifying Their Age & Number of Rations Drawn Out of the Kings Stores/per diem," dated November 26, 1783, SFHUPC, reel 58, p. 344. Molly listed her two eldest daughters, Elizabeth and Magdalene, as ages 20 and 18 in this official list of persons receiving rations from the king's stores at Carleton Island in November 1783. If Elizabeth is the daughter whose birth is recorded in Sir William's journal in the fall of 1761, she was actually 22 in 1783, and Magdalene was 20. It is known that Molly was anxious about the marriageability of her daughters, given the loss of their dowries. She may have decided to strike two years off both of the two eldest girls' ages so as not to exacerbate the problem. She may have been particularly uncomfortable declaring their real ages in a document that officers at Carleton Island would see, because these men were a major source of acceptable husbands for the girls. It is also possible that the daughter mentioned in Sir William's 1761 journal entry died, but other evidence indicates that the child was Elizabeth. In 1776, Captain Bloomfield described Elizabeth as being very beautiful. It is much more likely that the 22-year-old Bloomfield would say this about a 15-year-old than a 13-year-old. Also, in his letters from Philadelphia in early 1774, 14-year-old Peter Johnson refers to Elizabeth as a peer, telling their father to have her write to him so they can both improve their English writing skills. It is more likely Elizabeth was 12 at the time rather than 10.
3. "Return of the Loyalists Male and Female on Carleton Island" lists Molly's slaves as Abraham Johnston, a Negro, age 45; Juba Fundy, a Negro woman, age 23; and Jane Fundy, a Negro woman, age 20.
4. Lois M. Huey and Bonnie Pulis, *Molly Brant: A Legacy of Her Own* (Youngstown, NY: Old Fort Niagara Association, 1997), 67-69.
5. Kelsay, *Joseph Brant, 1743-1807*, 350-51.
6. Kelsay, 360.
7. Lorenzo Sabine, *The American Loyalists or Biographical Sketches of Adherents to the British Crown in the War of the Revolution* (Boston: Little and Brown, 1847), 99n, . 103. See also Kelsay, *Joseph Brant, 1743-1807*, 360.
8. Kelsay, *Joseph Brant, 1743-1807*, 362-63.
9. Huey and Pulis, *Molly Brant*, 85-89.
10. Kelsay, *Joseph Brant, 1743-1807*, 363.
11. Kelsay, 364, 366, 369.
12. Huey and Pulis, *Molly Brant*, 77. After Molly's death, her daughter Magdalene's husband, John Ferguson, in a petition seeking additional compensation for his wife from the government of Canada,

made the assertion that Molly traveled to Schenectady in 1785 to reject the overture. Such a trip is highly unlikely. By this time, Molly knew that the Mohawk sachems had been taken hostage at Fort Stanwix, and she could expect a similar or worse fate, especially since many people in the Mohawk valley hated her because she was known to have given intelligence to the British prior to the Battle of Oriskany. In the same petition, Ferguson also made the assertion that Peter Johnson was killed at the Battle of Brooklyn. Contemporaneous sources Joseph Chew, Peter's guardian, and Thomas Jones, Sir William's friend, state that Peter died of camp fever outside Philadelphia in the late summer of 1777. See Loyalty Claims, Series II, A.O.13, Bundle 11, p. 334; and Thomas Jones, *History of New York during the Revolutionary War: And of the Leading Events in the Other Colonies at That Period*, Vol. 2, ed. Edward Floyd De Lancey (New York: New York Historical Society, 1879), 375.

13. Kelsay, *Joseph Brant, 1743-1807*, 366.

14. Kelsay, 369-70.

15. Catherine S. Crary, *The Price of Loyalty: Tory Writings from the Tory Era* (New York: McGraw-Hill, 1973), 425-26; and Janice Potter-MacKinnon, *While the Women Only Wept* (Montreal: McGill-Queen's University Press, 1993), 17.

16. Kelsay, *Joseph Brant, 1743-1807*, 380.

17. Kelsay, 380, 385, 387-88.

18. Kelsay, 169, 386-88, 571, 577, 644.

19. Barbara Graymont, *The Iroquois in the American Revolution* (Syracuse: Syracuse University Press, 1972), 28. For a description of the terms of the enabling statute, see Hugh Edward Egerton, ed., "Preface" in *The Royal Commission of the Losses and Services of American Loyalists, Being the Notes of Mr. Daniel Parker Coke, M.P., One of the Commissioners during That Period*, xxxix (New York: Arno Press and the *New York Times*, 1969).

20. Kelsay, *Joseph Brant, 1743-1807*, 390.

21. *Memorial of Joseph Chew*, 15 March 1786, Loyalist Claims, Series II, A. O. 13, Bundle 11, pp. 336-37. For three separate certificates relating to the confiscation and sale of the property of Magdalin [sic] Johnson, Elizabeth Johnson, and Margaret Johnson, see Loyalist Claims, Series II, A.O. 13, Bundle 13, pp. 458-60.

22. Memorial of Joseph Chew, March 15, 1786, Loyalist Claims, II, A.O.13, Bundle 11, p. 337; and Affidavit of Joseph Brant, April 5, 1786, Loyalist Claims, Series I, A.O. 12, v. 22, p. 55.

23. Loyalist Claims, Series I, Vol. 109, p. 176, claim, 351; and Sabine, *The American Loyalists or Biographical Sketches of Adherents to the British Crown in the War of the Revolution*, 111-12.

24. Kelsay, *Joseph Brant, 1743-1807*, 391.

25. Kelsay, 367.

26. Earle Thomas, *The Three Faces of Molly Brant* (Kingston, Ontario: Quarry 1996), 142. See also Huey and Pulis, *Molly Brant*, 104.

27. Qtd. in Huey and Pulis, *Molly Brant*, 77-79.

28. "Evidence of the Claims of the Children of Mary Brant" by Dr. Robert Kerr, July 2, 1787, Loyalist Claims, Series I, A.O. 12, v. 27, p. 259.

29. Huey and Pulis, *Molly Brant*, 104; sworn statement of Sir John Johnson, March 3, 1788, Loyalist Claims, Series I, v. 27, p. 262.

30. Loyalist Claims, Series I, Memorial of Joseph Chew, 15 March 1786, A.O 12, v.22, p. 48 and Loyalist Claims, Series I, Claims 2137- 2141, v. 109, p. 120 (to their guardian Joseph Chew for the unmarried children) and p. 140 (George Farley in right of his wife Margaret), and p. 188 (Robert Kerr in right of his wife Elizabeth). The claims granted use the surname Brant rather than Johnson since the children were always described as the children of Mary Brant in Joseph Chew's petitions.

31. Kelsay, *Joseph Brant, 1743-1807*, 450.

32. Kelsay, 456.

33. Kelsay, 468-9.

34. Qtd. in Kelsay, 462.

35. Kelsay, 464-5.

36. Qtd. in Kelsay, 465.

37. Kelsay, 466-68.

38. Kelsay, 470-71.

39. *Ibid.* and Qtd. in Kelsay, 471.

40. Kelsay, 473-74 and Qtd. in Kelsay, 473.

41. Kelsay, 471.

42. Kelsay, 474.

43. Kelsay, 476–78.
44. Kelsay, 480–81.
45. Kelsay, 489–90.
46. Kelsay, 487–88.
47. Thomas, *The Three Faces of Molly Brant*, 145.
48. *The Diary of Mrs. John Graves Simcoe*, ed. J. Ross Robertson, Toronto: Coles Publishing Company, 1973, 166.
49. *Ibid.* Molly may have dressed in Native American attire as a matter of ethnic pride. She had, however, sometimes worn British gowns at Johnson Hall when entertaining distinguished British and European American guests with Sir William. In addition to probably finding a British ball gown less comfortable than Native American dress, the material for such gowns was expensive. She may have felt that such dresses were necessary for her daughters' social success among the British, but may have found them an unnecessary affectation for a middle-aged widow.
50. *Ibid.*
51. *Ibid.*
52. Kelsay, *Joseph Brant, 1743–1807*, 498.
53. *Ibid.*
54. Kelsay, 500.
55. Kelsay, 500, 503.
56. Kelsay, 502.
57. Kelsay, 503–4.
58. Qtd. in Kelsay, 504.
59. Kelsay, 510, 518.
60. Thomas, *The Three Faces of Molly Brant*, 152. See also Huey and Pulis, *Molly Brant*, 105.
61. Simcoe (ed. Robertson), 247.
62. Thomas, *The Three Faces of Molly Brant*, 152.
63. *Ibid.*; Simcoe (ed. Robertson), 274.
64. Simcoe (ed. Robertson), 274–5.
65. Thomas, *The Three Faces of Molly Brant*, 152; Kelsay, *Joseph Brant, 1743–1807*, 563–65.
66. Thomas, *The Three Faces of Molly Brant*, 152.
67. Thomas, 153.

Epilogue

1. Lois M. Huey and Bonnie Pulis, *Molly Brant: A Legacy of Her Own* (Youngstown, NY: Old Fort Niagara Association, 1997), 86–89.
2. Huey and Pulis, 85–86.
3. "Six Nations of the Grand River: Population Statistic, August 2023," Six Nations of the Grand River, sixnations.ca/app/uploads/2023/10/LMMemStatsAugust2023.pdf.
4. For a photo of the gravestone, see Earle Thomas, *The Three Faces of Molly Brant* (Kingston, Ontario: Quarry, 1996), 153.
5. For a photo of the plaque, see Thomas, *The Three Faces of Molly Brant*, 153. For the commemorative stamp, see Huey and Pulis, *Molly Brant*, 81.

Bibliography

Manuscript Collections

Library and Archives of Canada. The Loyalist Collection, Claus Family Papers.

United Empire Loyalists' Association of Canada, Guy Carleton Branch (stored at the Library and Archives of Canada). Carleton Papers—Loyalists and British Soldiers, 1772–1784.

Books

Allen, Thomas B. *Tories*. New York: Harper, 2010.

Archer, Richard. *As If an Enemy's Country: The British Occupation of Boston and the Origins of the American Revolution*. Oxford: Oxford University Press, 2010.

Blackhawk, Ned. *The Rediscovery of America*. New Haven: Yale University Press, 2023.

Crary, Catherine S. *The Price of Loyalty: Tory Writings from the Revolutionary Era*. New York: McGraw-Hill, 1973.

Crompton, Samuel Willard. *The Mohawk*. New York: Chelsea House Publishers, 2010.

Eckert, Allan W. *The Wilderness War*. Boston: Little, Brown, 1978.

Fenn, Elizabeth. *Pox Americana*. New York: Hill and Wang, 2001.

Flexner, James Thomas. *Lord of the Mohawks: A Biography of Sir William Johnson*. Boston: Little, Brown, 1979.

Graymont, Barbara. *The Iroquois in the American Revolution*. Syracuse: Syracuse University Press, 1972.

Haldimand, Sir Frederick. *Unpublished Papers and Correspondence, 1758–84*. London: World Microfilms Publications, The British Library, 1977.

Hibbert, Christopher. *Redcoats and Rebels: The American Revolution through British Eyes*. New York: Norton, 1990.

Huey, Lois M., and Bonnie Pulis. *Molly Brant: A Legacy of Her Own*. Youngstown, NY: Old Fort Niagara Association, 1997.

Jasanoff, Maya. *Liberty's Exiles*. New York: Vintage Books, 2011.

Kelsay, Isabel Thompson. *Joseph Brant, 1743–1807: Man of Two Worlds*. Syracuse: Syracuse University Press, 1984.

Logusz, Michael O. *With Musket & Tomahawk*. Havertown, PA: Casemate Publishers, 2012.

Mann, Charles C. *1491*. New York: Vintage Books, 2011.

Mann, Mary Alice. *Iroquoian Women: The Gantowisas*. New York: Peter Lang, 2000.

Mazzeo, Tilar J. *Eliza Hamilton: The Extraordinary Life and Times of the Wife of Alexander Hamilton*. New York: Gallery Books, 2018.

McCullough, David. *1776*. New York: Simon & Schuster Paperbacks, 2005.

Norton, Mary Beth. *The British-Americans: The Loyalist Exiles in England, 1774–1789*. Boston: Little, Brown, 1972.

Norton, Mary Beth. *Liberty's Daughters: The Revolutionary Experience of American Women, 1750–1800*. Boston: Little, Brown, 1980.

O'Shaughnessy, Andrew Jackson. *The Men Who Lost America*. New Haven: Yale University Press, 2013

O'Toole, Fintan. *White Savage: William Johnson and the Invention of America*. New York: Farrar, Straus and Giroux, 2005.

Parkinson, Robert G. *Heart of American*

Darkness: Bewilderment and Horror on the Early Frontier. New York: Norton, 2024.

Potter-MacKinnon, Janice. While the Women Only Wept. Montreal: McGill-Queen's University Press, 1993.

Preston, David L. The Texture of Contact: European and Indian Settler Communities and the Frontiers of Iroquoia, 1667–1783. Lincoln: University of Nebraska Press, 2009.

Richter, Daniel K. The Ordeal of the Longhouse: The Peoples of the Iroquois League in the Era of European Colonization. Chapel Hill: University of North Carolina Press, 1992.

Sellers, Stephanie A. Native American Autobiography Redefined: A Handbook. New York: Peter Lang, 2007.

Sivertsen, Barbara J. Turtles, Wolves and Bears: A Mohawk Family History. Westminster, MD: Heritage Books, 2006.

Thomas, Earle. The Three Faces of Molly Brant. Kingston, Ontario: Quarry, 1996.

Wilbur, Keith C. Revolutionary Medicine, 1700–1800. 2nd Old Saybrook, CT: Globe Pequot, 1997 (2nd Edition).

Wood, Gordon S. The American Revolution: A History. New York: Modern Library, 2003.

Reference Works

American Loyalist Claims, Exchequer and Audit Dept., Series I, 1776–1831: Public Records of Great Britain. Kraus-Thomson Organization, 1972.

American Loyalist Claims, Exchequer and Audit Dept., Series II, 1776–1831: Public Records of Great Britain. Kraus-Thomson Organization, 1973.

Coke, Daniel Parker, M.P. The Royal Commission on the Losses and Services of American Loyalists 1783 to 1785 Being the Notes of Mr. Daniel Parker Coke, M.P., One of the Commissioners during That Period. Edited by Hugh Edward Egerton. New York: Arno Press and the New York Times, 1969.

"John Butler." Dictionary of Canadian Biography. 1966.

"Konwatsitsiaienni." Dictionary of Canadian Biography. 1966.

Penrose, Maryly. Indian Affairs Papers: American Revolution. Franklin Park, NJ: Liberty Bell Associates, 1978.

Penrose, Maryly. Mohawk Valley in the Revolution: Committee of Public Safety Papers & Genealogical Compendium, Tryon County Committee of Safety. Franklin Park, NJ: Liberty Bell Associates, 1978.

Sabine, Lorenzo. The American Loyalists or Biographical Sketches of Adherents to the British Crown in the War of the Revolution. Boston: Little, Brown, 1847.

Diaries, Journals, and Memoirs

Allen, Ethan. The Narrative of Colonel Ethan Allen. New York: Corinth Books, 1961. Originally published 1779.

Andreani, Paolo. "Travels of a Gentlemen from Milan" (1790). In Mohawk Country, ed. Dean R. Snow, Charles T. Gehring, and William A. Starna, 318–33. Syracuse: Syracuse University Press, 1996.

Anonymous. "Description of the Country between Oswego and Albany 1757." In Mohawk Country, ed. Dean R. Snow, Charles T. Gehring, and William Starna, 242–49. Syracuse: Syracuse University Press, 1996.

Bloomfield, Joseph. The Revolutionary War Journal of Joseph Bloomfield. Edited by Mark E. Lender and James Kirby Martin. Newark: New Jersey Historical Society, 1982.

Claus, Christian Daniel, and Conrad Weiser. "A Journey to Onondaga, 1750." In Mohawk Country, ed. Dean R. Snow, Charles T. Gehring, and William A. Starna, 238–41. Syracuse: Syracuse University Press, 1996.

Grant, Anne. Memoirs of an American Lady. New York: D. Appleton, 1846.

Johnson, Warren. "Journal of Warren Johnson, 1760–1761." In Mohawk Country, ed. Dean R. Snow, Charles T. Gehring, and William A. Starna, 250–23. Syracuse: Syracuse University Press, 1996.

Johnson, William. The Papers of Sir William Johnson. Albany: University of the State of New York, 1921–1965.

Jones, Thomas. History of New York during the Revolutionary War: And of the

Leading Events in the Other Colonies at That Period, Vol. 2. Edited by Edward Floyd De Lancey. New York: New York Historical Society, 1879. Reprinted by ULAN Press, 2015.

Marbois, François. "Journey to the Oneidas." In *Mohawk Country*, ed. Dean R. Snow, Charles T. Gehring, and William A. Starna, 300–317. Syracuse: Syracuse University Press, 1996.

Simcoe, Elizabeth. *The Diary of Mrs. John Graves Simcoe*. Edited by J. Ross Robertson. Toronto: Coles Publishing, 1973. Originally published in 1911 by William Briggs.

Tilghman, Tench. *Memoir of Lieut. Col. Tench Tilghman, Secretary and Aide to Washington*. Edited by Samuel Alexander Harrison. Albany, NY: J. Munsell, 1876.

Van den Bogaert, Harmen Meyndertsz. "A Journey to Mohawk and Oneida Country, 1634–1635." In *Mohawk Country*, ed. Dean R. Snow, Charles T. Gehring, and William A. Starna, 1–8. Syracuse: Syracuse University Press, 1996.

Articles and Book Chapters

Allen, Robert S. "Loyalist Military Settlement in Quebec." In *The Loyal Americans*, ed. Robert S. Allen, 92. Ottawa: National Museums of Canada, 1983.

Allen, Robert S. "The Loyalist Provincial Corps." In *The Loyal Americans*, ed. Robert S. Allen, 11. Ottawa: National Museums of Canada, 1983.

Condon, Ann Gorman. "The Foundations of Loyalism." In *The Loyal Americans*, ed. Robert S. Allen, 2. Ottawa: National Museums of Canada, 1983.

Danvers, Gail D. "Gendered Encounters: Warriors, Women, and William Johnson." *Journal of American Studies* 35, no. 2 (August 2001): 187–202.

Feister, Lois M., and Bonnie Pulis. "Molly Brant: Her Domestic and Political Roles in Eighteenth Century New York." In *Northeastern Indian Lives, 1632–1816*, ed. Robert S. Grumet, 295–320. Amherst: University of Massachusetts Press, 1996.

Green, Gretchen L. "Gender and the Longhouse: Iroquois Women in a Changing Culture." In *Women & Freedom in Early America*, ed. Larry D. Eldridge, 7–25. New York: New York University Press, 1997.

Johnston, Jean. "Ancestry and Descendants of Molly Brant." *Ontario History* 63 (1971): 86–95.

Rawlyk, George A. "Loyalist Military Settlement in Upper Canada." In *The Loyal Americans*, ed. Robert S. Allen, 100–107. Ottawa: National Museums of Canada, 1983.

Snow, Dean R., et al. "Introduction." In *Mohawk Country*, ed. Dean R. Snow, Charles T. Gehring, and William Starna, xvii–xxiv. Syracuse: Syracuse University Press, 1996.

Electronic Sources

Daniel Claus Papers. Eighteenth Century Selection of Documents Relating to Indian Affairs. https://heritage.canadiana.ca/view/oocihm.lac_mikan_102179.

Flick, Alexander C. "Chronology of Daniel Claus." In *The Papers of Sir William Johnson*, Vol. 4, xi–xiii. https://babel.hathitrust.org/cgi/pt?id=mdp.39015071343563;view=1up;seq=15.

Johnson, Sir William. *The Papers of Sir William Johnson*. HathiTrust, digital format. https://catalog.hathitrust.org/Record/000622241.

O'Callaghan, E. B., ed. *Documents Relative to the Colonial History of the State of New York*. http://babel.hathitrust.org/cgi/pt?id=umn.31951002213920k;view=1up;seq=5.

Six Nations of the Grand River. "Six Nations of the Grand River: Population Statistic, August 2023." sixnations.ca/app/uploads/2023/10/LMMemStatsAugust2023.pdf.

Index

Abanakis 82
Abraham, an enslaved man 40, 77, 83, 140, 169; *see also* Johnston, Abraham
Abraham, chief sachem of Tionoderoge 124, 125, 129
the Adamant 117, 120
Adams, Samuel 79
Adems, Robert 40, 93
adultery 11
Albany, NY 13, 17, 20, 22, 25, 29, 31, 33, 42, 41, 54, 55, 65, 66, 92, 94, 96, 103, 109, 113, 126, 127, 128, 135, 136, 139
Albany Committee of Public Safety 106, 107, 126
Albany conference of 1746 20, 21
Albany County, NY 81, 84
Allegheny Mountains 33, 56
Allen, Ethan 114–116
allies 22, 27, 28, 34, 41, 42 46, 54–56, 61, 106, 110, 113, 114, 119, 120, 127, 128, 133, 135, 136, 143, 144, 146, 154, 165–167, 177, 181
American army 177
American Revolution 7, 12, 23, 32, 49, 87, 88, 94, 158, 175, 179, 181
Ames, Ezra 173
Amherst, Gen. Jeffrey 33, 34, 37, 38, 40–42, 46, 53–55, 62
Amsterdam, NY 3, 52
Andrewstown, NY 145
Anglaize River 182
Anglican catechism 82
Anglican Church 62, 69, 82, 100, 148, 176; *see also* Church of England
Anne I, queen of Great Britain 1, 17
Antiroyalists 84
apprenticeship 97
Arnold, Benedict 138–139
arson 136
artillery 35
Asharego, Daniel 12
Assaregoa, General 161; *see also* Haldimand, Gen. Frederick

assimilation 79
the Association (Loyalist) 129
the Association (Patriot) 109, 112, 118, 126
Atlantic Ocean 13
Aylmer, Mathew 15

Banyar, Goldsbrow 81
Barclay, the Rev. Henry 9, 11, 16, 18, 19, 30, 56
baronet 15, 28–30, 47, 59, 62, 65, 89, 90
Barrell, William 97
Barton, the Rev. Thomas 67
bateaux 25, 34
Battle of Fallen Timbers 182
Battle of Lake George 27, 28, 34, 36, 50, 59, 71, 108
Battle of Lexington and Concord 108
Battle of Niagara 34–**36,** 40, 46, 55, 59
Battle of Oriskany 137–138, 145, 163, 171
Battle of Saratoga 142
Battle of Trenton 154
Battle of Yorktown 164
Bayoux, Mme. Blanche
Bear Clan 9–10
Belle of the Province 91
Bennett, the Rev. Cornelius 57
Berczy, William de 173
Bermuda 121
Bible 82
Bird, Lt. Henry 136
Blackstone, Dr. 79
Bloody Scout 27
Bloomfield, Capt. Joseph 123–129
Bolton, Lt. Col. 148, 149, 154, 156
Boston, MA 63, 65, 78, 79, 81, 98, 105, 108, 110, 134
Boston Massacre 79
Boston Tea Party 98
Boswell, James 121
Braddock, Gen. Edward 25, 28
Bradstreet, Col. John 33
Brant, Catherine Croghan 155, 164, 171, 172

209

210 Index

Brant, Christina 82, 171
Brant, Joseph 9–11, 26, 32–34, 37, 43, 48–51, 54–57, 61, 66, 70, 71, 79, 82, 83, 87, 99, 101, 105–109, 111–113, 116, 117, 120–122, 128, 130–140, 142, 144–150, 152, 153, 155, 165, 158, 160–162, 164, 165, 167, 169–171, 173, **174,** 175–179, 181–184
Brant, Peter (Tehonwaghkwangeraghkwa) 7, 9, 10, 38
Brant, Susanna 82, 111, 140, 146, 149, 155
Brant Keghneghtaga 19, 30; see also Brant, Johnson
Brant Saquainguaragton 7–**8**
Brant's Volunteers 132, 135, 145, 147, 153, 164
British army 20, 51, 166
British Constitution 65
British Crown 28, 56, 59, 60, 72–74, 76, 78, 80, 81, 120, 128, 135, 144, 146, 163, 165, 167, 174
British Empire 59, 173
British fleet 121
British government 146, 166, 171, 173, 174
British navy 180
Brooklyn, NY 130
Brown, the Rev. Thomas 66
Buckongehala 181
Burgoyne, Gen. John 135, 136, 138–142
Burton, the Rev. Daniel 79
Burying Place of the Children and Grandchildren of Sir William Johnson 185
Butler, John 102, 111, 119, 122., 123, 125, 133, 135, 137, 143, 145–150, 153, 156, 158, 161, 164
Butler, Mrs. John 139
Butler, Walter 16
Butler, Walter, the younger 111, 117, 147, 160, 164
Butler's Rangers 145, 147, 148, 153

Calvinism 50
Campbell, Daniel 30
Campbell, Capt. Donald 47, 49
Campbell, Maj. John 115, 120
Canada 3–4, 20, 21, 30, 40, 42, 51, 54, 61, 93, 111–114, 117, 120–125, 131, 167, 168
Canadesagey 143, 179–182, 186
Canadian colonies 166
Canadian Native Americans 5, 20, 21, 28, 40, 41, 42, 51, 52, 54, 92, 93, 100, 113, 115, 116, 135, 150, 154
Canadian Patriots 114
Canajoharie 10, 16, 17, 20, 27, 28, 30, 33, 37, 38, 41 43–45, 50, 51, 54, 55, 57–59, 61, 64, 68, 70, 71, 75, 76, 79, 81, 85, 87, 90, 92, 95, 96, 99, 105, 107, 111, 112, 115–118, 126–128, 133, 134, 136, 138–140, 143, 144, 146, 169, 171, 173, 185; see also upper castle
Canajoharie, NY 3, 7
Canandaigua, NY 178
Canawaraghere 158
canoes 34, 111
captives 4
Cardiff, Wales 175
Carleton, Gen. Guy 110, 114, 161
Carleton Island 12, 77, 153, 154, 156, 157, 158, 160, 163–167, 169
casualties 28
Cataraqui 166, 167, 169, **170,** 171–173
Cataraqui River 165
Catherine of Aragon, queen of England 82
Catherine, senior matron Turtle Clan 155
Catholicism 4, 5, 15, 82, 96
Caughnawagas 5, 40, 41, 112
Cayugas 3, 7, 9, 55, 68, 98, 110, 128, 130, 142, 147, 150, 153, 172
Chamberlain, the Rev. Theophilus 57, 61, 62, 70
Chambly 169
Charlotte, queen of Great Britain 120
Cherokees 10
Cherry Valley, NY 44, 158
Cherry Valley Massacre 147
Chew, Joseph 94, 102, 117, 121, 174, 175, 177
China 10
Chippewas 46
Christian, son of Elizabeth of the Bear Clan and William Johnson 19
Christianity 4, 5, 13, 32, 50, 57, 62, 75, 79, 83, 96, 148, 175
Christina, daughter of Margaret 9
Christina, senior matron of the Bear Clan 10–12
Christmas 25, 120
Church of England 15, 16, 19, 26, 50, 56, 75, 79; see also Anglican Church
Clark, George Rogers 161
Claus, Anne, the younger 74, 78
Claus, Anne Johnson (Nancy) 18, 19, 30–32, 37, 38, 51, 52, 59, 61, 62, 74, 78, 80, 88, 91, 94, 97, 101, 103, 111, 112, 117, 121, 131, 144, 149, 151, 161, 163, 173, 175
Claus, Catherine 88, 90, 91, 93, 94
Claus, Daniel 11–13, 32, 51, 52, 58, 68, 74, 78, 80, 81, 84, 86, 92, 93, 94, 97, 100, 101, 103, 108, 110, 115, 116, 117, 121, 123, 126, 135, 136, 137, 138, 142, 143–146, 149, 150, 151, 154, 157, 159, 161, 163, 164, 166, 173, 175
Claus, William Johnson 63, 100, 117, 175
Clermont, Hance 37

Index

Clinton, Gov. George 20–21, 158, 170, 171, 179
Clinton, Gen. Henry 131, 145
Clinton, Gen. James 150, 153
Cobleskill, NY 145
Colden, Alexander 44
Colden, Cadwallader 59, 60, 63
Colden, Cadwallader III 130
Colden family 130
Coldenham 130, 131
Columbia University 65; *see also* King's College
colonel of the forces to be raised out of the Six Nations 21; *see also* Johnson, Sir William
colonel of the Indians 152; *see also* Brant, Joseph
colonel of the Six Nations 28, 35; *see also* Johnson, Sir William
colonies 56, 72, 79, 83, 101, 102, 105, 168
Common law of England 79
confederacy council 142, 143, 155, 186
Congregationalism 50, 66, 75, 79
Congress 166, 171
Connecticut 25, 50, 66, 130
Conoys 74
Continental Army 59, 121, 122, 139, 147, 158
Continental Congress 106, 108, 113125
Cooper, the Rev. Myles 79, 80
Cornwallis, Gen. 164
corporal punishment 70
Corry, Catherine 102
Corry, husband of Catherine Corry 37
Cosby, Gov. William 16
Cottgrave, John 85
County Meath, Ireland 15, 57
Cowes, Isle of Wight 42
Cresap, Michael 98
Croghan, George 30, 58, 74, 81, 86
Crown Point 25, 27, 40
Cuillerier, Angelique 47–49
Cuillerier, Antoine 47
Cushing, Thomas 79

Dartmouth, Earl of 105, 115, 116, 123
Dayton, Col. Elias 123–127, 131, 135
Dease, Dr. John 86, 95, 100, 102, 117, 121
December, an enslaved man 77, 140, 169
DeLancey, James 84, 91
DeLancey family 16, 39
Delawares 47, 57, 73, 74
Detroit 36, 46, 47, 49, 52, 53, 96, 123, 161, 162, 164, 178, 180, 181
Detroit River 181, 182
Deygert, (Dygert) Peter 141
Deygert (Dygert) family 179

Dieskau, Baron Ludwig 27, 28
Dillon, Mr. and Mrs. 18
diphtheria 94
Dissenters 80
Doxtater, Honyery 141
Dunmore, Lord (Earl) 83–84; *see also* Murray, John
Dutch Reformed Church 25

Earl, Anne Johnson 78, 91, 151, 158, 165, 180, 185
Earl, Capt. Hugh 180
elders 113
Elizabeth, niece of Christina, senior matron of the Bear Clan 19
Elmira, NY 153
England 60, 80, 89, 90, 95, 98, 99, 121, 123, 128, 130; *see also* Great Britain
English language 12, 16, 50, 51, 85, 163, 182
epidemics 4, 10; *see also* influenza; measles; smallpox
Etherington, Captain 48
Europe 3, 4, 5, 10, 25, 43, 55, 58, 62, 76, 131, 132, 143, 156, 186
European Americans 21, 31, 40, 43–46, 48, 53, 58, 61, 64–66, 68–70, 72, 83, 84, 90, 101, 111, 115, 128, 132, 136, 142, 147, 158, 160, 164, 178, 186
exile 104, 182, 186

Falmouth, England 117, 120, 121
Farley, Capt. George 171, 185
Farley, Margaret Johnson 71, 139, 144–146, 149, 151, 158, 171, 185
Farrell, Catherine Johnson 27–28
Farrell, Mathew 27
Ferguson, John 180, 183
Ferguson, Magdalene Johnson 52, 68, 76, 88–90, 94, 105, 109, 111, 129, 151, 158, 180, 183, 185
Finger Lakes 3
Five Nations 4, 5
Fort Chartre 55
Fort Dayton 138
Fort Edward 27, 29; *see also* Fort Lyman
Fort Erie 179
Fort Frontenac 33
Fort Harmer 178
Fort Herkimer 164
Fort Hunter 10, 11, 16, 17, 18, 48, 50, 56, 62, 75, 79, 82, 89, 111, 116, 123–125, 127, 129, 131, 135, 171, 173, 175, 177
Fort Johnson 22, 23, 26, 29–31, 38, 39, 40–43, 45–49, 51, 52, 62, 66, 89, 90, 96, 100, 101, 117
Fort Levis 41
Fort Lyman 27; *see also* Fort Edward

Fort Mifflin 141
Fort Necessity 25
Fort Niagara 33–35, **36**, 37, 46, 78, 96, 123, 131, 140, 143, 145, 146, 148–156, 159–162, 164, 166, 171, 172, 175, 180–182
Fort Ontario 110–112, 119
Fort Oswego 28, 34, 35
Fort Pitt 36, 46
Fort Stanwix 43, 73, 74, 112, 135, 137, 138, 143, 171, 172
Fort Stanwix conference 74–75, 78
Fort Ticonderoga 25
Fort William Henry 29
Fowler, David 50
France 3, 4, 5, 9, 19, 20, 25, 33, 35, 36, 40–42, 55, 63, 146
Franklin, Ben 74, 97
Franklin, Gov. William 74, 97
Fraser, Capt. Alexander 154–158
French and Indian War 25, 52, 101; *see also* Seven Years War
French Canadians 21, 28, 34, 35
French fleet 33
French language 86, 88, 93, 97, 163
Freud, Dr. Sigmund 5
Frey, Henry 85, 102, 106, 130, 138, 145
Frey, John 106, 138
Fundy, Jenny 169; *see also* Jenny, an enslaved woman
Fundy, Juba 169; *see also* Juba, an enslaved woman
fur trade 4, 17, 21, 33, 49, 68, 69, 84, 86, 167

Gage, Gen. Thomas 37, 55, 64, 74–76, 81, 87, 92
Gansevoort, Col. Peter 137–138
Gates, Gen. Horatio 139, 142
Genessee River 3
Genessee River Valley 143
George II, King of Great Britain 21, 28, 31, 34, 36, 42
George III, King of Great Britain 92, 94, 106, 107, 110, 116–120, 122, 123, 130, 132, 134, 136, 143, 144, 147, 149, 153, 157, 161, 163, 165, 167, 172, 173
Germain, Lord George 120, 123, 135, 149, 152, 157–159, 161, 162
German Flatts, NY 17, 29, 54, 63, 64, 71, 81, 85, 113, 118, 119, 126–129, 131, 134, 136–139, 145, 146, 158
God 4, 62, 80
Gonwatsijayenni 7
Gordon, Lord Adam 60–62, 65, 121
Gospel of St. Mark 82
grand jury 107
Grand River 170, 172
Grand River Valley 170–173, 175, 183, 184

Great Britain 3, 5, 14, 20, 21, 25, 33, 35, 40, 42, 46, 55, 64, 68, 101, 105, 108, 109, 114–117, 121, 125, 153, 163, 165, 171, 175, 180–182, 185; *see also* England
Great Carrying Place 25, 27
Great Lakes 4, 35, 166
Great League of Peace and Power 3
Green Bay, Wisconsin 175
Green Mountain Boys 114
Guy Park 52, 91, 93, 103, 107, 109, 110, 127

Haldimand, Gen. Frederick 34–36, 68, 95, 143, 144, 146, 149–152, 155–159, 161, 162, 164–170, 172, 183
Hancock, John 79
Hare, Capt. John 122
Hare, Mrs. John 122
Hare, William 57
Harpersfield, NY 169
Harry, an enslaved man 40
Hastings, Lieutenant 93
Haudenosaunee 3; *see also* People of the Longhouse
Hendrick Aupaumut, Capt. 177
Hendrick Theyanoguin 12, 27, 99
Henry, son of Catherine, senior matron of the Turtle Clan, Tekarihoga 155
Henry VIII, king of England 82
Herkimer, Nicholas 71, 109, 133–135, 137, 138
Highland Regiment 37
Highlanders 99, 124, 125
Holland, Maj. Samuel 166–167
Hope, Col. Henry 165
housekeeper 32, 51, 102, 104
Howe, Gen. William 121, 131, 133, 135, 141
Hudson River 3, 25, 42, 94, 121, 135, 136, 145, 178
Huntley, Dr. R. 86, 88, 93
Hurons 4, 47, 112
Hutchinson, Gov. Thomas 79

Illinois country 55
immigrant 11
indentured servant 23, 97
Indian conference 71–73, 81, 83, 91, 92, 98, 113, 128, 135, 144
Indian Department 30, 46, 54, 57, 63, 66, 70, 74, 81, 92, 93, 98, 102, 105, 107, 108, 111, 113, 115, 117, 122, 128, 134, 135, 143, 144, 151, 152, 154, 155, 158, 160, 180
Indian School 12
Indiana 182
Indigenous people 40
influenza 4
Inglis, the Rev. Charles 69, 79, 80, 83
inoculation 58–59

Index

Intolerable Acts 98
Ireland 16–18, 25, 45–47, 57, 73, 121
Iroquois 3; *see also* Six Nations
Isaac, sachem of the Oquagas 57, 130–131
Isaac Karaguantier 66, 70, 72, 107, 179, 183
Ithaca, NY 3

Jacob, the elder son of Margaret 9
Jacob, the younger, son of Margaret 11
Jacomine, daughter of Margaret 10
James II, King of England 15, 28
Japan 73
Jenny, an enslaved woman 40, 104; *see also* Fundy, Jenny
Johannes Dekarihokenh 30, 54
John, an enslaved man 83
John Deserontyn 160–162, 173
Johnson, Brant 19, 43, 57, 61, 99, 101–104, 125; *see also* Keghneghtaga, Brant
Johnson, Catharine 101; *see also* Weisenberg, Catherine
Johnson, Chistopher 15, 16, 24, 45, 57
Johnson, George 62, 78, 86, 103, 144, 145, 146, 148, 149, 151, 159, 163, 164, 165, 169, 185
Johnson, Guy 32, 46, 52, 57, 60, 65, 80–85, 87, 91–93, 97, 100 103, 105, 110, 112, 123, 130, 135, 146, 149–154, 158–163, 173
Johnson, the Rev. Jacob 74–75
Johnson, John, father of Guy 46
Johnson, Sir John 12, 27, 31, 32, 46, 48, 62, 64, 68, 80–84, 88–91, 95, 97, 100, 101, 103, 105–110, 118, 120, 122–126, 129, 131–133, 135, 137, 138, 149, 150, 152, 153, 158, 162, 163, 165–167, 173, 175, 176; *see also* Weisenberg, John
Johnson, Margaret Campbell 61
Johnson, Mary (Polly), wife of Guy Johnson 18, 31, 32, 52, 57, 59, 80, 81, 88, 91, 97, 100, 103, 111, 112, 119, 124 148
Johnson, Mary, daughter of Molly Brant 78, 151, 159, 163, 183, 185
Johnson, Mary, daughter of Guy and Mary Johnson 88, 90, 91, 93, 94
Johnson, Lady Mary Watts 91, 97, 101, 105, 119, 120, 124, 126, 127, 128, 130, 131, 149, 176
Johnson, Peter Warren 12, 30, 38, 41–43, 48, 66, 76, 85, 86, 88, 89, 92–99, 101, 102, 105, 107–109, 111, 114–117, 121, 123, 128, 141, 156, 167, 169
Johnson, Samuel 71
Johnson, Tagawirunta William 22, 30; *see also* William of Canajoharie
Johnson, Warren 20, 37, 42, 43, 45, 89
Johnson, Sir William 7, 9–11, 13–20, 22, 25, **26**, 27, 28, 30–32, 34–40, 43–47,
49–61, 63–67, 72–82, 84–91, 93–103, 105, 106, 108, 112, 115, 120, 121, 123–130, 133, 142–145, 149–155, 160, 162–164, 167, 171, 175, 176, 181, 184, 186; *see also* colonel of the Six Nations; superintendent of Indian Affairs; Warraghiyagey
Johnson family 14, 16, 52, 81, 83, 88, 95, 106, 108, 110, 116, 126, 151
Johnson Hall 23, 52, **53**, 54, 55, 57–66, 68, 71, 73, 75, 76, 78, 79, 83, 85, 87, 89–91, 93, 95, 98–100, 103, 105, 107, 110, 111, 115, 117–120, 122–128, 149, 169, 171, 184, 185
Johnston, Abraham, 169; *see also* Abraham, an enslaved man
Johnston, John 57
Johnstown, NY 23, 42, 52, 75, 76, 84, 85, 89, 93, 117, 119, 124, 126–128, 139, 141, 158, 164, 185
Johnstown courthouse 84, 118
Johnstown jail 141
Jones, Judge Thomas 61, 62, 76
Juba, an enslaved woman 40, 104; *see also* Fundy, Juba

Kanawha River 74
Keepers of the Council Fire 3, 141; *see also* Onondagas
Keepers of the Eastern Door 3; *see also* Mohawks
Keepers of the Western Door 3, 33, 46; *see also* Senecas
Kentucky 74
Kerr, Elizabeth Johnson 49, 68, 76, 88–90, 94, 98, 105, 109, 111, 129, 140, 151, 158, 171, 176, 177, 183, 185
Kerr, Dr. Robert 171, 177, 182
Kerr, William Johnson 185
King George's War 9, 19, 28, 31, 152; *see also* War of the Austrian Succession
King Hendrick 7
King of Great Britain 7
King William's War 5
King's College 56, 71, 79; *see also* Columbia University
King's Royal Regiment 137, 150, 158, 173, 176
Kingsborough 43, 44, 48
Kingsland patent 63, 64, 68, 70, 85, 87, 103
Kingston, Ontario 33, 62, 148, 166, 173, 177, 180, 182, 183, 185; *see also* Cataraqui
Kirkland, the Rev. Samuel 50, 51, 79, 106, 107, 109, 112, 113, 128
Klock, George (Ury) 44, 56, 64, 65, 87, 95, 98, 99, 106, 128, 134
Klock, Jacob 106, 119
Klock, Mrs. Jacob 119
Klock family 118

Index

Knox, Henry 177–180
Knox, Lucy 179
Konwatsitsiaienni 7

La Gallette 37, 41
Lake Champlain 25, 40, 135, 158
Lake Erie 54, 170, 172
Lake George 27; *see also* Lake St. Sacrement
Lake Huron 165
Lake Ontario 28, 33, 34, 40, 110, 112, 135, 153
Lake St. Sacrement 25, 27; *see also* Lake George
Lamb, William 148, 169, 170
Lancaster, PA 67
landowner 24
Langden, Richard 17–18
Latin language 16
Lea, daughter of Margaret 10
Lebanon, CT 12, 49
Lee, Dr. Arthur 86
Lee, Maj. Charles 59
LeMoine, Edward William 183
LeMoine, Lt. Henry 180, 183
Le Moine, Susanna Johnson 78, 151, 158, 163, 180
Linnall, Lieutenant 37
Little Abraham of the Mohawks 55
Livingston, Walter 126
Livingston family 39
Lochry, Col. Archibald 162, 164
Logan 98
London, England 7, 17, 28, 34, 46, 54, 63, 64, 79, 86, 95, 98, 99, 106, 115–117, 121, 166, 172–175
London Magazine 121
the Lord Hyde 121
Louisbourg 121
lower castle 10, 44, 45, 124, 127; *see also* Tiononderoge
Loyalists 114, 119, 122, 127, 129–132, 135, 136, 139, 140, 145–147, 158, 163, 172
Loyalty Commission 171–173, 175
Lykas 10–11
Lyman, Maj. Gen. Phineas 50

Maclean, Gen. Allen 78, 166
madeira 22, 38, 42, 66
magistrates 107
Manhattan, NY 122
Margaret, mother of Molly Brant 7, 9–13, 26, 30, 50, 54, 70, 71, 80–82, 85, 89, 111, 140, 144, 149, 160
Maria, daughter of Saquainguaragton 7
Mary II, queen of England 15
Massachusetts 25, 79, 98, 107

massacre 29, 79
Mathews, Capt. Robert 157, 164
Maumee River 182
McDonnell family 122
McGrah, Sgt. Christopher 22, 88, 102
McGrah, Mary, the elder 22, 28
McGrah, Mary, the younger 22, 87, 102
McKee, Alexander 178, 181, 182
Mcleod, Capt. Norman 78
merchants 10, 30, 77, 84, 94, 98, 107
Miamis 177, 178
militia 21, 25, 27–29, 34, 35, 41, 54, 94, 99, 101, 106, 107, 111, 112, 114, 115, 119, 131, 133, 138, 139
Mingos 10
missionaries 4, 5, 57, 79, 80, 113
Mississippi River 55
Mohawk bible 62
Mohawk District 108
Mohawk language 7, 11, 12, 26, 51, 82, 85, 97, 117, 160, 162, 173, 182
Mohawk River 16, 17, 37, 38, 42, 43, 64, 127, 136, 145, 147, 152
Mohawk River valley 3, 5, 7, 9, 10, 17, 19, 21, 24, 25, 29, 32, 33, 44, 45, 52, 54, 59, 65, 68, 72, 77, 79, 81, 84–86, 88, 90, 93, 97, 100–102, 105, 107, 108, 115–118, 120–124, 126, 130–132, 134, 135, 138–140, 153
Mohawks 3, 4, 5, 7, 9, 10, 17–21, 26, 27, 33, 37, 44–46, 48–51, 55–60, 64, 68, 70, 75, 76, 78, 79, 87, 89, 95, 98, 99, 101, 107–117, 119–129, 131, 132, 135, 138, 140–142, 148, 150, 152, 153, 159, 160, 165, 167, 169, 170–173, 175, 179
Mohicans 158
Moncrieffe, Mayor Thomas 90–91
Monongahela River valley 25, 28
Montcalm, Gen. Louis-Joseph de 29
Montgomery, Gen. Richard 114
Montour, Henry 57
Montreal, Canada 5, 34, 37, 40–42, 46, 52, 55, 59, 68, 86, 89, 92, 93, 112, 114, 131, 142, 144, 146, 149–151, 153, 156, 158, 163, 165, 166, 169, 175, 176
Moore, Gov. Henry 63
Moor's Indian Charity School 49, 50, 54, 55, 66; *see also* Indian school
Morris, Capt. Staats 13, 14, 25
Mount Johnson 17, 18, 20, 22, 30, 31, 52; *see also* Williamsburg
Munseys 74
Murray, John, Earl of Dunmore 83; *see also* Dunmore, Lord
Muskingum River 178, 179

Nanticokes 74
Native Americans 21, 22, 24, 26, 27, 29,

31, 3334, 40, 41, 43–46, 53–56, 58, 63, 64, 66–68, 70, 74–76, 81, 83, 89, 92, 96, 98, 102, 106, 110, 112, 114, 116, 119, 123, 125, 127, 129, 132, 135–138, 143, 144, 147, 152–154, 157–160, 162, 164–167, 172, 175–177, 180, 185
Neggen Aoghyatonghsera (Peggy) 57, 61, 66, 82, 155
Netherlands 3
New England 26, 146
New France 4
New Hampshire 25
New Jersey 74, 97, 123
New Lebanon Springs, NY 71
New Orleans, LA 55
New World 101
New York (city of) 16, 17, 20, 22, 23, 28, 29, 38, 39, 42, 56, 58, 63, 64, 68, 76, 78, 79, 81, 84, 86, 88–98, 105, 106, 118, 121, 123, 124, 130–132, 153, 141, 145–147, 149, 159, 178, 179
New York (province of) 3, 9, 14, 16, 17, 23, 25, 26, 44, 46, 60, 81, 84, 87, 99, 107, 124, 130, 135, 136, 143, 149, 155
New York (state of) 170–172, 174, 175, 178, 179
New York Assembly 21, 28, 59, 84, 85, 91, 102, 106
New York Council 85, 91
New York currency 103
New York Harbor 121
Newmarket 121
Niagara Carrying Place 54; *see also* Battle of Niagara; Fort Niagara
Nickus of the Wolf Clan 50–51
North, Lord 167, 168
North America 5, 16, 17, 33, 42, 47, 59, 65, 97, 120, 121, 147
North Carolina 3, 64
Northumberland, Duke of 131
Nova Scotia 20

O'Bryen, Lady Susan Strangway 59–62
O'Bryen (husband of Lady Susan) 59
Ogilvie, the Rev. John 11, 80
Ohio (state of) 182
Ohio River 9, 25, 74, 178, 179, 181, 182
Ohio River valley 3, 12, 25, 33, 36, 46, 54, 88, 98
Ohio Territory 177, 182
Old Testament 82
Old World 101
Onagsakearet 7
Oneida Creek 3
Oneida Lake 37
Oneidas 3, 9, 16, 17, 37, 51, 55, 57, 59, 63, 64, 68, 75, 79, 108, 109–114, 128, 130, 131,

137, 138, 140–142, 153, 158, 160, 161, 172, 175, 177
Onondagas 3, 37, 41, 55, 68, 72, 91, 107, 109, 110, 128, 129, 130, 141, 142, 158, 172
Oquaga 16, 17, 57, 70, 130, 131, 133, 172
Oriska 137, 138, 141
Oswegatchies 40, 41
Oswego 37, 40, 41, 55, 66, 70, 110, 135, 136, 138, 139, 153, 154, 158, 164
Oswego River 28, 37
Ottawas 54
Owasco Lake 3

Palatine 17
Palatine Germans 19, 29, 44, 71
Paris, France 164
Parliament 28, 36, 63, 105, 157, 159, 164
patent holders 24
patriarchy 45, 52, 89
Patriots 9, 51, 80, 81, 107–109, 111–114, 116, 119, 122, 123, 125–131, 133, 134, 136–139, 142, 143, 146, 150, 153, 158, 162, 163
Paulus Hook 131
peace commissioners 180–181
Peale, Charles Willson 173
peer 15
Penn family 33
Pennsylvania 9, 11, 13, 33, 64, 74, 75, 86, 130, 153
People of the Longhouse 3; *see also* Haudenosaunee
Pepperell, Sir William 20
Percy, Earl 131, 173
Peters, Paulus 12, 99
Philadelphia, PA 12, 13, 23, 42, 65, 78, 86, 93–99, 102, 105, 141, 178, 179
Philips, Alexander 18
Philips, Hamilton 18
pleurisy 29
Pontiac 54, 74
Pontiac's War 54, 55, 74
Port Bill 98
Port of Boston 105
Portsmouth, England 121
Powell, Gen. 162
premarital sex 13; *see also* sexual relations
Preston, Captain 79
Prevost, Maj. Augustine 86
Prideaux, Col. John 34–35
prisoners 22, 40
prize system 15, 59
Proclamation of 1763 72
Protestantism 4, 15, 16, 146
provincial congress 108
Puritans 26, 79
Putman, Clarissa 89–90, 120

216 Index

Putman, Margaret 89
Putman, William 90

Quebec 22, 34, 40, 117, 143, 166, 167, 172
Queen Anne's Chapel 75
Quinte Bay 173

Rawdon, Lord 131
regulars 27, 28, 34, 42, 114, 136
Remson, Peter 77
Rhode Island 25, 147
Riedesel, Baroness Charlotte 167
Riedesel, Baron Friedrich Adolph 167
Rigaud, John Francis 173
Rivington, James 65, 79
Rome, NY 74
Romney, George 173
Ross, Maj. John 159
Royal Navy 15, 18
rum 22

Sacandaga River 87
sachem 12, 27, 30, 34, 35, 44, 54, 58, 76, 80, 99, 101, 109, 112, 118, 124, 127, 129, 143, 147, 155, 160, 165, 170, 172, 182
St. Clair, Gen. Arthur 177
Saint Croix 77
St. George's Anglican Church (Kingston, Ontario) 176, 184
St. George's Anglican Church (Schenectady) 75
St. John's Episcopal Church 75, 100, 126
St. Lawrence River valley 5
St. Leger, Gen. Barry 135-139
St. Paul's Church, Kingston, Ontario 185
Sander of the Wolf Clan 50, 51
Sandusky River 54, 180, 181
Saratoga, NY 20, 136, 139, 140; see also Battle of Saratoga
Saratoga Springs 83
Sayengaraghta 143, 145, 147, 150, 152, 153
Scheifflin, Matilda 160
Schenectady, NY 16, 17, 30, 68, 75, 83, 89, 90, 103, 105, 123, 126, 150
Schoharie Creek 16, 145
Schoharie valley 158
Schuyler, Katherine 136
Schuyler, Gen. Philip 122, 127, 128, 133, 134, 136, 161, 170, 171
Scottish Highlands 73
Senecas 3-5, 33, 34, 46, 47, 54, 55, 68, 96, 128, 130, 131, 136, 142, 143, 145, 147, 148, 150, 152, 153, 170, 172
Senior matrons 45, 71, 74 109, 110, 129, 143, 150, 155, 165
settlers 9, 17, 20, 43, 54, 56, 57, 64, 67, 68, 71, 73, 101, 110, 115, 128, 129, 142, 158, 177

Seven Years' War 25, 55; see also French and Indian War
sexual relations 11-13, 30, 62, 87-88, 96; see also premarital sex
Shawnees 47, 57, 73, 98, 177, 178
Sidney, Lord 173
Silvester, Peter 92
Simcoe, Elizabeth 180-183
Simcoe, Lt. Gov. John Graves 180, 183
Six Nations confederacy 3, 9, 10, 13, 17, 20, 21, 26, 28, 32, 35, 41, 43, 45, 49, 51, 54, 57-59, 66, 71, 73, 74, 76, 80-84, 86, 87, 89, 91, 92, 94, 98-101, 105-112, 114, 120, 123, 127-131, 133-138, 142-144, 146-150, 152, 155, 159, 161, 162, 164- 167, 170 172, 177, 178, 185, 186
Six Nations languages 86
slaveholder 23, 24
slaves 23, 39, 55, 68, 77, 97, 103, 104, 128, 136, 140, 169
smallpox 4, 41, 55, 58, 59, 78, 121
Society for the Propagation of the Gospel 79
Society in Scotland for Propagating Christian Knowledge 49
Sons of Liberty 65
squaws 61
Stacey, Lt. Col. William 147-148
Stamp Act 63, 65
Staten Island, NY 121, 130
Sterling, James 49
Stevenson, Capt. James 96, 102
Stockbridge Indians 177
Stone Arabia, NY 17, 105
Stuart, Gilbert 173
HMS *Suffolk* 130
Sullivan, Gen. John 150, 153, 158
superintendent for Indian affairs 28, 48, 72, 106, 120, 162, 166, 176
Supreme Court of the province of New York 62
Susquehanna River 57, 152
Susquehanna River valley 3, 13, 16, 57, 82, 130
Syracuse, NY 3, 142

Taylor, Mr. 146
Taylor & Duffin 145, 146
Taylor & Forsyth 161
Tekarihoga 155
tenants 16, 44, 55, 62, 64, 65, 73, 75, 93, 99, 101, 106, 122, 131-133
3rd New Jersey Regiment 123
Thomas, son of Elizabeth of the Bear Clan and William Johnson 19
Three Rivers 48
Tice, Gilbert 117, 121, 131, 155

Index

Ticonderoga 108, 114, 121, 135, 136
Tilghman, Lt. Col. Tench 113
Tiononderoge 10–12, 16–18, 20, 27, 30, 42, 43, 45; *see also* lower castle
Tower of London 121
Townshend, Lord 166
traders 17, 21, 74, 128, 161
trenches 35
Trinity Church 79
Tryon, Gov. William 84, 87, 122, 123
Tryon, Mrs. William 87
Tryon County, NY 85, 102, 107, 108, 112, 114, 127, 130, 141, 158
Tryon County Committee of Public Safety 105–109, 112, 116, 118, 119, 123, 126, 127, 129, 133, 134, 138–141
Tryon County Loyalists 135
Tryon County militia 106, 133
tuberculosis 82
Turtle Clan 9, 30, 155
Tuscaroras 3, 55, 57, 68, 130, 172
26th Regiment 93
Tyrell, Michael 18

Unadilla, NY 133–135, 138, 145
United States of America 166, 170, 172, 175, 179, 181, 182, 186
upper castle 7, 28, 44; *see also* Canajoharie

Vandreiul de Cavagnial, Pierre de Rigaud 82
Van Schaack, Henry 77
Vermont 25
Virginia 25, 64, 74, 83, 164
Vitry, Angelique 22, 30
Vroman's Land, NY 158

Wabash River 177
Wade, Francis 94, 96, 97
Wade, Mrs. Francis 97
Waggoner, Joseph 134
Walker, George 129
Wall, Edward 76, 85, 109
Wallace, Hugh 37, 84, 88, 89, 93, 94, 98, 99
Wallace, Mrs. Hugh 88
War of the Austrian Succession 9; *see also* King George's War

Warraghiyagey 18, 20, 108; *see also* Johnson, Sir William
Warren, Michael 15
Warren, Oliver 57
Warren, Peter 15, 16, 20, 23, 24, 38, 57–59, 65
Warren family 58
Washington, George 25, 113, 131, 141, 147, 154, 173, 177–179
Watts, John 91, 131
Watts, Peggy 124
Wayne, Gen. Anthony 179–181
Weatherhead, Mr. 77
Webb, Gen. Daniel 29
weddings 61, 62
Weisenberg, Catherine (Weissenburg, WysenBurgh, Wysenburk, Wysenburg) 17–20, 22, 27, 29, 30, 31, 38, 43, 48, 76, 85, 95, 102, 165
Weisenburg, John 48; *see also* Johnson, Sir John
West Germany 73
West Virginia 74
Westminster 173
whaleboats 34
Wharton, Samuel 74
Wheelock, the Rev. Eleazar 12, 49, 50, 54, 66, 74, 75, 79
Wheelock, Ralph 66
Whigs 80
widows and widowers 11, 82, 113, 130, 143
Willett, Col. Marinus 179
William of Canajoharie 22, 38, 43, 66–68, 101–104, 111, 116, 118, 125, 141, 148, 167; *see also* Johnson, Tagawirunta William
William III, king of England 15
Williamsburg 52, 103, 110, 127; *see also* Mount Johnson
Windsor Castle 121
Wolfe, Gen. James 40
Wood Creek 37
World War II 73
Wormwood, Elizabeth 87–88
Wormwood, Susannah 87–88
Wraxall, Peter 30
Wyandots 47
Wyoming valley 75, 145, 147, 148

Yorktown 164

www.ingramcontent.com/pod-product-compliance
Lightning Source LLC
Chambersburg PA
CBHW032042300426
44117CB00009B/1155